IMAGES
of America

Lake Winnepesaukah Amusement Park

On the Cover: A merry-go-round has been a mainstay at Lake Winnepesaukah since 1935. Here, Adrienne White, granddaughter of Carl and Minette Dixon, is pictured with friends on an early model. Thirty years later, Evelyn White, Minette's daughter, invited her three young grandchildren (ages three to seven) to each paint a horse of their own. This is one of many examples of how the ethos of the family business has been handed down for generations. (Courtesy of the Lake Winnepesaukah Archives.)

IMAGES
of America

Lake Winnepesaukah Amusement Park

Tennyson Dickinson
Foreword by Tom Griscom

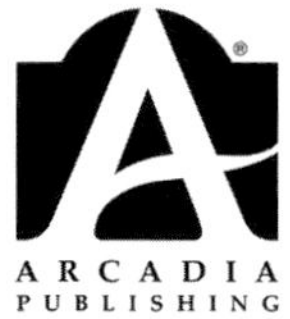

ISBN 978-1-4671-6255-5

Published by Arcadia Publishing
Charleston, South Carolina

Printed in the United States of America

Library of Congress Control Number: 2024951900

For all general information, please contact Arcadia Publishing:
Telephone 843-853-2070
Fax 843-853-0044
E-mail sales@arcadiapublishing.com

Visit us on the Internet at www.arcadiapublishing.com

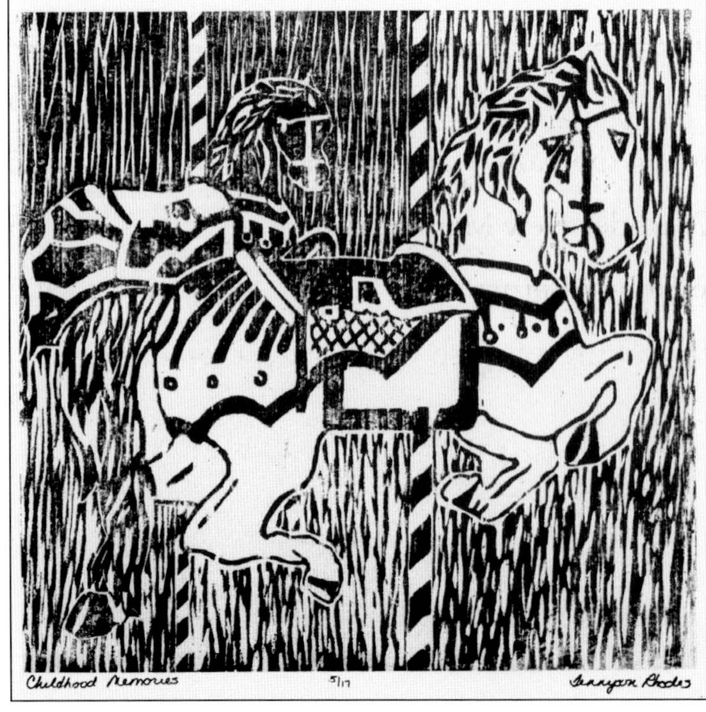

To all those who have made memories at Lake Winnepesaukah, may you treasure them as we do. (Courtesy of the Lake Winnepesaukah Archives.)

Contents

FOREWORD

If you grew up or live in north Georgia, a few miles south of Chattanooga, there is a family gem located off Lakeview Drive—Lake Winnepesaukah. "Lake Winnie" has been a special place for 100 years—a safe, clean, family venue where, even for a brief time, cares are left behind. Opened June 1, 1925, Carl and Minette Dixon used the Native American word Winnepesaukah, meaning "beautiful lake of the highlands," to capture their spirit of family. The now four-generation family envisioned, created, grew, and has continually operated the park. The family's touch to detail is visible throughout the rides, the entertainment, the food, and the experiences. Memories were made and are still being made at Lake Winnie. When a new ride was ready to be opened for a new season, the first riders were family members—not to be first in line but to assure safety for all who rode. For those who attended the weekly country music shows at Lake Winnie, it is fair to say this was where outdoor music venues began. In its earliest days, the stage was in the center of the lake. Some years later, it became land-based so attendees could be closer to the performers.

Water always has been the main attraction. Carl Dixon designed the legendary Boat Chute that launched its first riders in 1927. Even now, the water ride is considered the oldest operating mill chute in the country. There are numerous recollections of that first kiss in what was termed "the tunnel of love" as the boats slowly navigated the darkened passageway.

Modeled after the traditional American fair, Lake Winnie had bumper cars, a Ferris wheel, and a merry-go-round; a classic pinball arcade and games of skill; and the smell of freshly popped popcorn, which recalls another memory. At Lake Winnie, large carp always have munched on popcorn tossed by guests into the water. Every winter, the lake is drained, leaving only a shallow stream of water. For those at preopening business meetings in the spring at Lake Winnie, there is the surprise of little water, then relief, knowing the carp burrow into the mud awaiting May, when the water and the popcorn-feeding guests return. Personal touches are the difference.

A family member from the family's fourth generation recalled her grandmother giving paintbrushes to her and her two cousins, assigning each a merry-go-round horse to paint. Her takeaway: I would never have been so daring to allow three youngsters to go at it on the horses. One must wonder: Where are those painted horses today? The foundations of Lake Winnepesaukah are etched in the memories of a family who for 100 years has shared memories that always brought fun with a touch of business thrown in. Family matters at Lake Winnie. The owners, the experiences, and the memories are still being made. Looking to the next century at Lake Winnepesaukah—"Come on, get happy."

—Tom Griscom

ACKNOWLEDGMENTS

When one undertakes the writing of 100 years of a business' history, two groups of indispensable people first come to mind: our employees and our guests. Without the loyalty and support of both, this book would not be. We have had the privilege of employing entire families, hiring 14 year olds who later came to be managers after outstanding work, and have kept up with many through the years who credit Lake Winnie as where they learned their work ethic. The guests have shared their smiles, brightened our days, and kept us humble with reminders of any missteps. Their remembrances of "remember when" evidence that we have done our job in creating fond memories.

Several people deserve special gratitude for their diligence in making this book a reality: Conly King, whose enthusiasm for amusement parks is contagious and his attention to detail lifesaving; Meagan Brownfield, whose organizational skills allowed it to be; Carter Dickinson, who never expected her high school history project about her great-grandmother and grandmother to be expanded into a book; and Taylor Dickinson Cordeiro, whose editing is invaluable. And to all the other employees who not only encouraged the process but tolerated the missed meetings and myopic focus for a period, I thank you.

Without the intentional appreciation and accumulation for and of our history by my great-grandparents (Carl and Minette Dixon), grandmother (Evelyn White), mother (Adrienne Rhodes), father (Buddy Rhodes), and aunt (Tootsie Harless), this book would not be possible.

While sorting through hundreds of boxes of records, scrapbooks, and pictures has been tedious, there have been hundreds of "pearls" found, lessons personified, and an understanding of the character it takes to build, grow, and sustain a business gained. I am deeply appreciative of my heritage. The images in this volume appear courtesy of the Lake Winnepesaukah Archives.

Introduction

This book began somewhat reluctantly, considerably late for the anticipated publication, and more out of a sense of obligation to commemorate 100 years in business. It concluded quite differently as a personal journey through the tightly interwoven fabric of a family business through four generations.

The story of the business is told in these pages through both narrative and pictures of the history of Lake Winnepesaukah, one of a few remaining family-owned and -operated amusement parks in the country, and the only known to be consistently run by the females in the family. While this is unique, so is the fact Lake Winnepesaukah has passed through four generations, far above the national average of less than three percent of businesses that operate into the fourth generation.

What is not expressed by the pictures, or the narrative, is the ethos of hard work, resiliency, fair dealing, and appreciation for those who helped along the 100-year journey spanning the Great Depression, World War II, and the COVID pandemic.

Going through business documents, I witnessed firsthand the character traits of courage and patriotism taught in history classes. Via old ledgers and financial statements, I saw how my great-grandmother gave school principals tickets amidst the Great Depression. In the face of World War II, my grandmother kept her ration coupons for the company and family separate. I learned that when the United States was deep in World War II, a portion of Lake Winnepesaukah's proceeds went to war efforts, and the park played host to US Army, Navy, and Marines recruitment efforts. At the height of American casualties after D-Day, she organized patriotic singing at the park.

After the war, when troops returned, she hired many and allowed them to live on the grounds at a bare minimum rent. They became a reliable and long-standing workforce who performed carpentry, welding, plumbing, and maintenance for a generation.

I have seen firsthand what my mother means when she refers to the "Lake Winnie family" of employees—records of payouts for employee diapers, eyeglasses, and doctor visits as loans never expected to be repaid.

What is striking to me is that Lake Winnepesaukah and the family behind it are not unique in their support of our country or our customers and employees. This is the fabric of how America was made—by the hard, honest, noble work of everyday Americans across the country. How appropriate for this series to be titled Images of America.

Yes, it is a business, and yes, we are a family that operates the business. Both have differences of opinion and viewpoint. Like other families, we have experienced painful family times. What I have learned is that it is how we reconcile these that is important.

What began as a journey to chronicle the 100-year history of Lake Winnepesaukah has concluded with my personal appreciation for the values the family members have successively upheld and passed down, for I realize that is the true fabric of a business thriving well into the fourth generation. The history is interesting, anecdotal, and all from the archives. The lessons learned are timeless.

One

The 1920s

The Lore of the Land and the Lake

The Roaring Twenties were full of hope and opportunity in America. The "war to end all wars" was over, and optimism and confidence filled the air. Americans were expanding the boundaries of innovative thinking: Mickey Mouse was created, Charles Lindberg flew across the Atlantic, and Babe Ruth was the hero of sports fans. Women gained the right to vote. The popularity of the automobile and radio was changing both how Americans worked and spent their free time.

It was against this backdrop in 1924 that Carl Orville Dixon, a 35-year-old famed race car driver and entrepreneur who owned a coal and ice business and an auto repair shop, in addition to being among the first men to have a license to drive in Chattanooga, became enamored with a tract of land surrounding a lake. In the early 1900s, the property was a hunting club known for the natural spring-fed lake, only 20 feet deep, as well as an abundance of wildlife on the premises. Dixon had other plans: he envisioned a place for families to come for recreation of all types. In 1924, he and his wife, Minette Heiner Dixon, bought the property, against the "better advice" of his friends, and renamed the lake Winnepesaukah, a Cherokee word meaning "beautiful lake of the highlands" as homage to the Indigenous people. The lake later served as a camp for Confederate soldiers during the Civil War. Following the Civil War, a gristmill was built.

On May 30, 1925, Carl and his wife, Minette, opened the park and offered public boating, fishing, and swimming in the lake. Local newspapers reported 5,000 people in attendance on opening day, which buoyed Dixon's seemingly endless ideas for enhancing the property. Given the park could only be reached by traversing miles of dusty dirt roads, this is most astonishing, but it verified Dixon's belief that the public was ready for, and the economy could support, more recreational activities.

Expansion happened immediately. In 1926, the largest swimming pool in the South, measuring 200 feet long, 100 feet wide, and complete with six diving boards at a staggering cost of $35,000 at the time, opened to the public. The water source was the lake, and an elaborate system of filtration was used that replaced the water every 12 hours with fresh water. In 1927, Dixon designed and built the Boat Chute, the park's first ride. In 1929, a kiddie plane ride, horseshoe pits, and a baseball field were added activities. From these simple beginnings, a business that has entertained millions for 100 years was born.

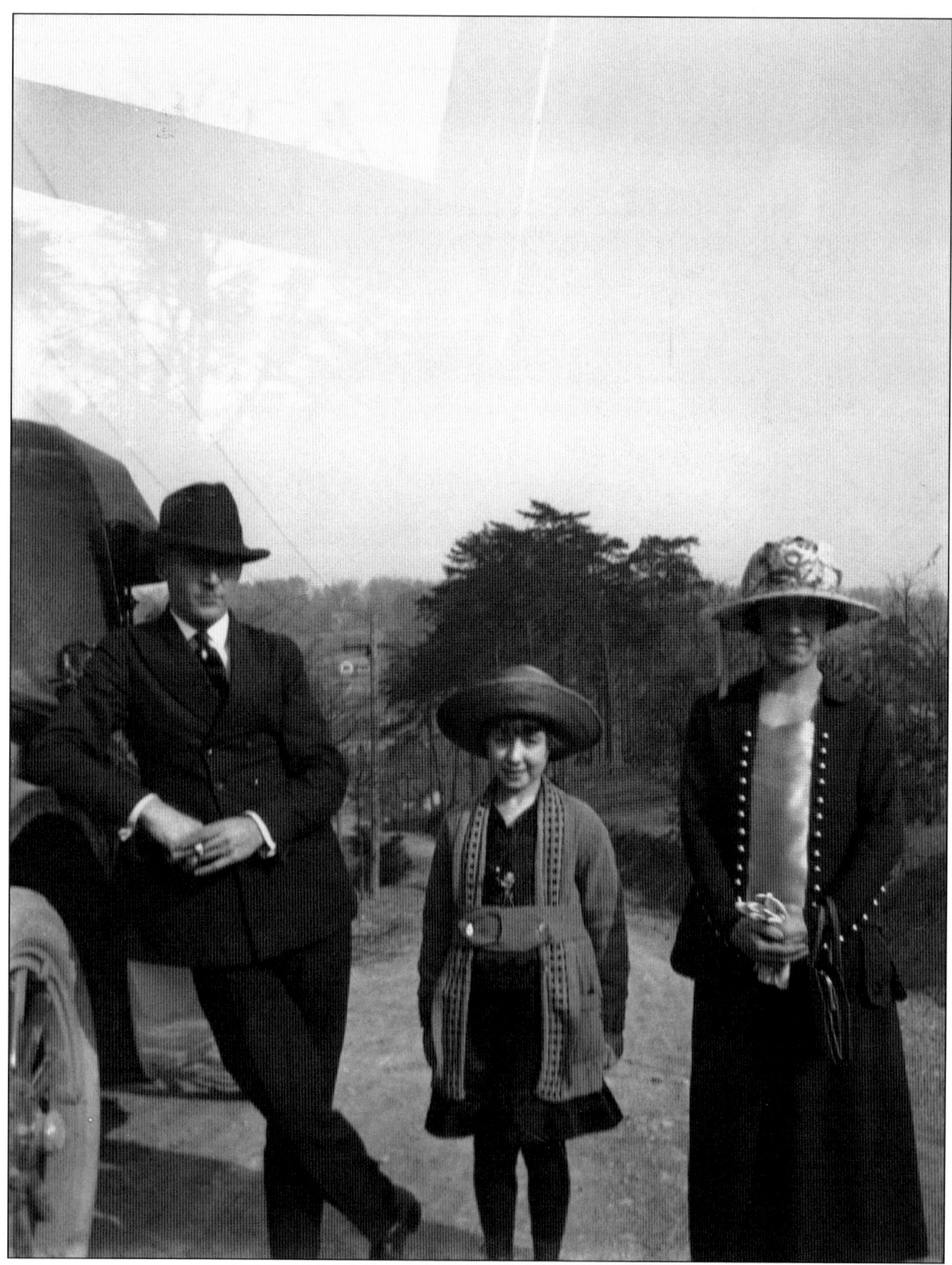

Minette and Carl Dixon are pictured with their only child, Evelyn Virginia Dixon, around the 1920s. Carl, who was among the first people in the Chattanooga area to have a driver's license, leans against his own car, which was a rarity for the time.

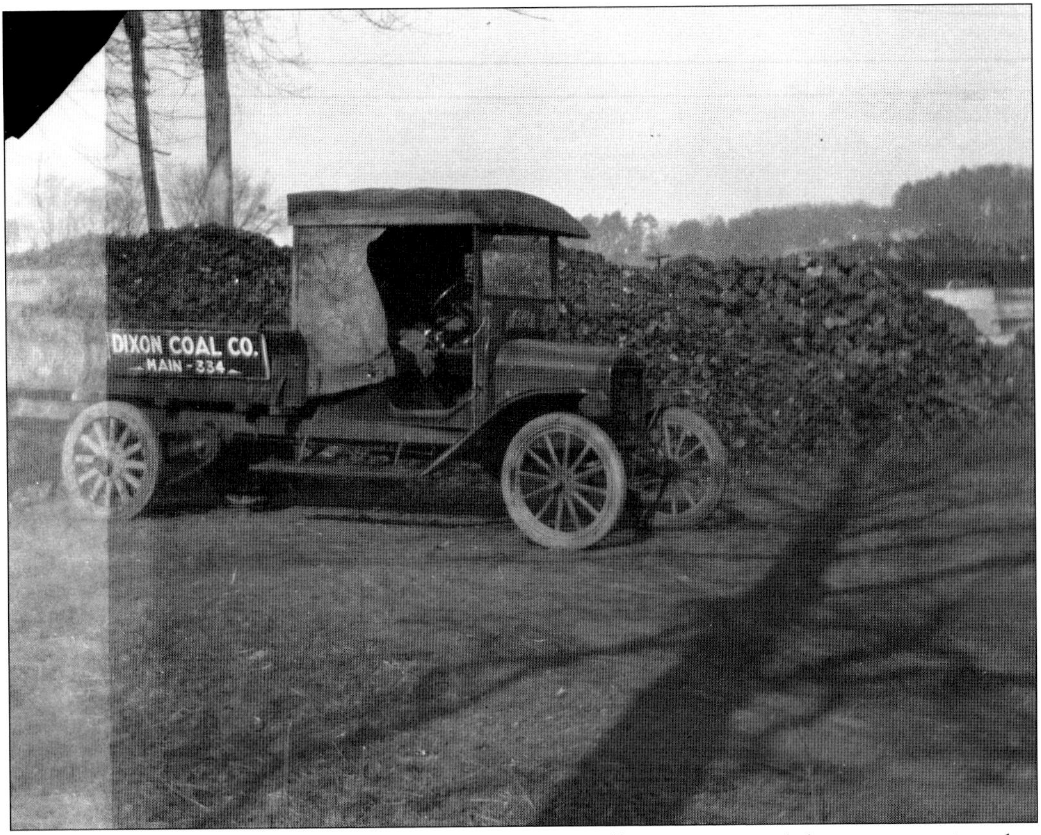

Dixon Coal Company and Dixon Ice Company, as well as an automobile service station that Carl also owned, was located a few miles away from Lake Winnepesaukah. In the 1920s, local newspapers frequently carried advertisements for all four businesses. Pictured is the truck Dixon used to deliver coal.

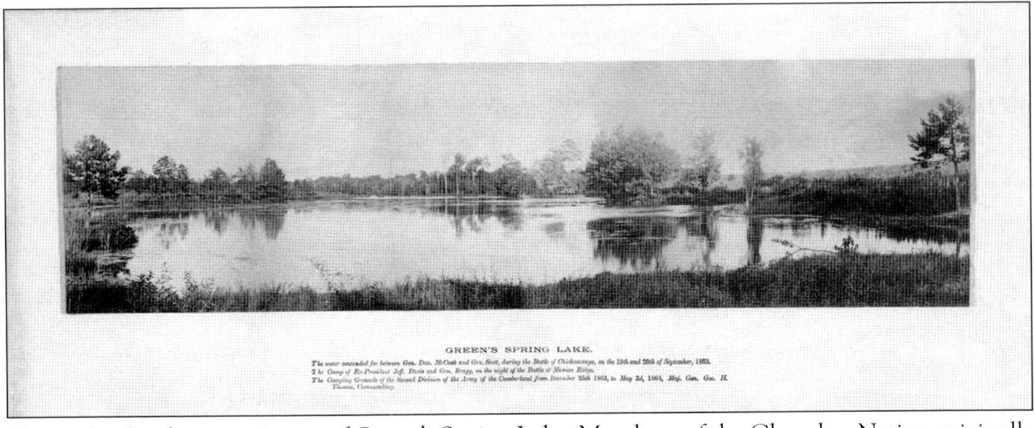

This is the first known picture of Green's Spring Lake. Members of the Cherokee Nation originally used the spring-fed lake and formed an earthen dam around the springs. It was first known as Green's Spring Lake and powered a gristmill for area farms. During the Civil War, it was a meeting place for Gen. Braxton Bragg and Confederate state president Jefferson Davis on the night of the battle of Missionary Ridge. It was later a campsite of Maj. Gen. George H. Thomas from December 25, 1963, to May 3, 1864.

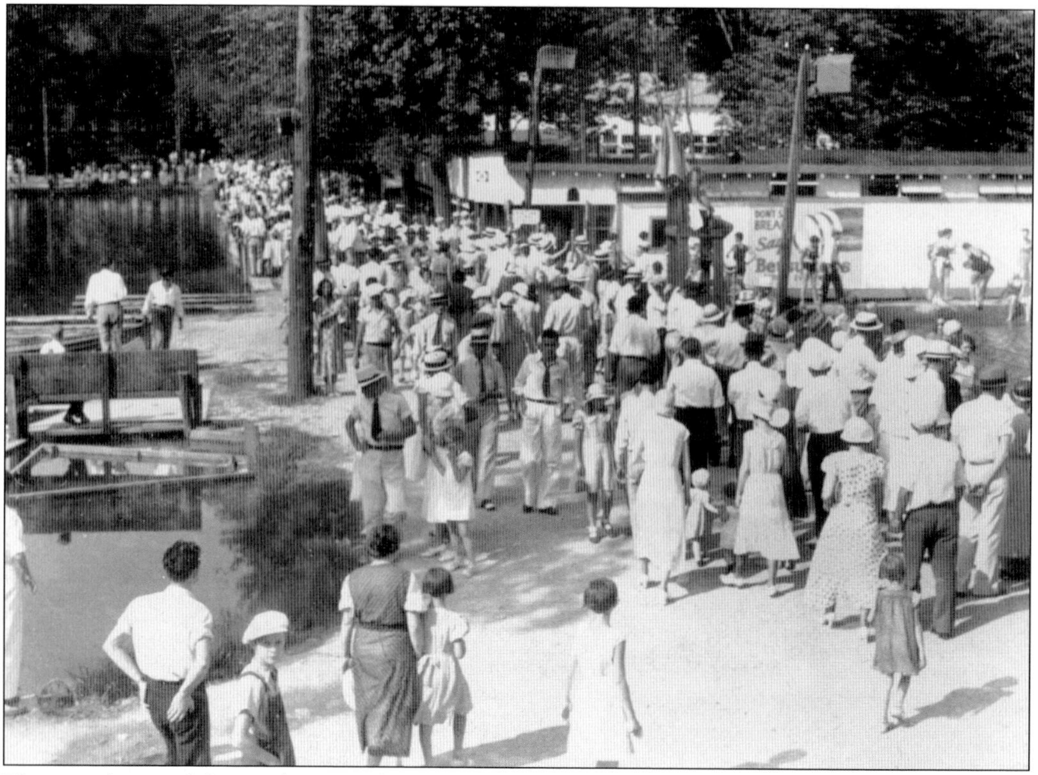

The popularity of the newly opened Lake Winnepesaukah is evident in the crowds that gathered to stroll the grounds and gather to boat, fish and swim, and picnic. This picture shows how close to the lake (left) the pool was built (right). The docking system in the lake accommodated both canoes and rowboats for the enjoyment of customers.

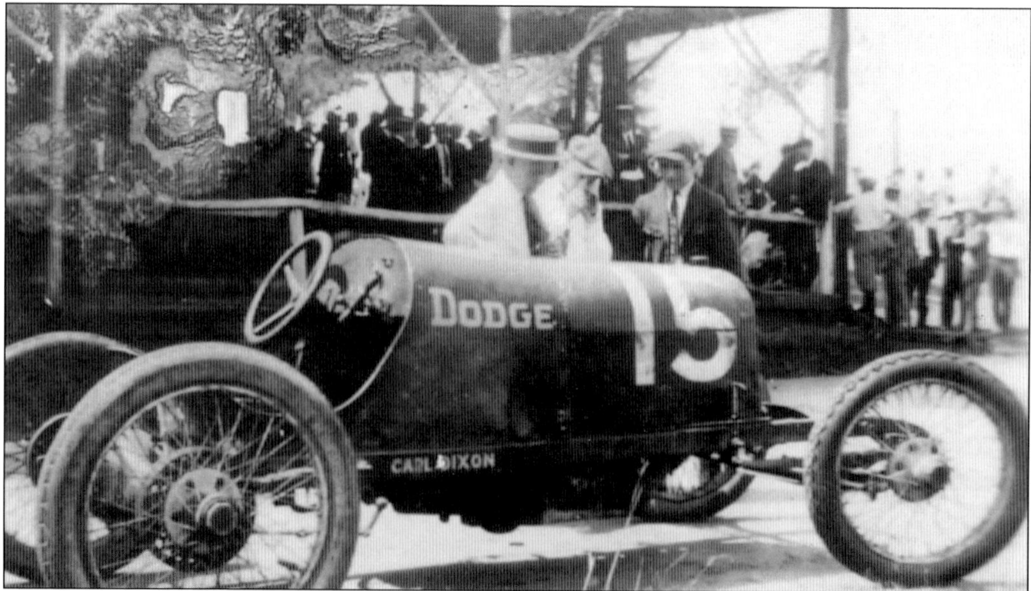

It is known that Carl Dixon raced in the Indianapolis 500 and at Daytona. While the location of this picture is unknown, it is known to be him showing one of his race cars.

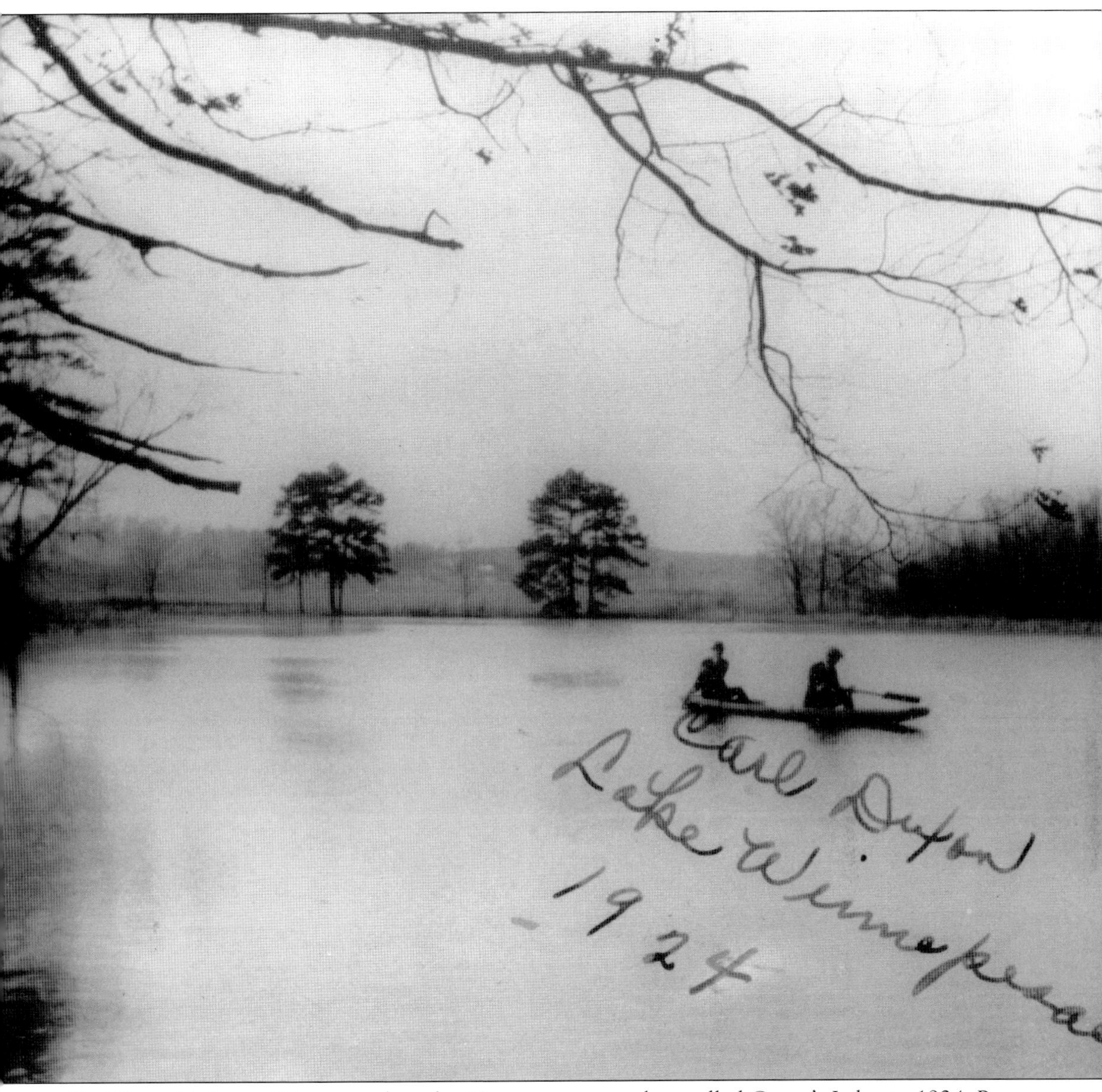

Carl O. and Minette Dixon purchased a 70-acre property, then called Green's Lake, in 1924. Part of the legendary lore of the lake was that Indian warriors and their maidens, on summer nights, went out to these springs to pledge their vows anew. This scene when Carl and Minette first viewed the lake from the water via canoe seems to harken to that time. They renamed the lake to Winnepesaukah, a Cherokee name meaning "beautiful lake of the highlands." They envisioned creating a family swimming and picnic park.

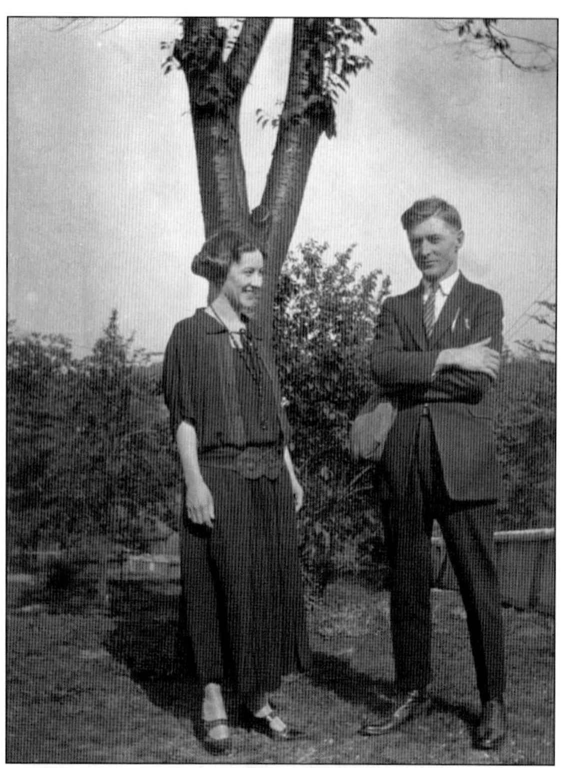

Together, Carl and Minette Dixon opened Lake Winnepesaukah in 1925 against the "better advice" of their friends and offered the public bathing, boating, and fishing. The year 1925 would be the only season when swimming was permitted in the lake, as the following year a large swimming pool was built so the lake could be used for shows, stunts, and boating.

During the opening season in 1925, high diving, sliding, and swimming were allowed in the lake, with a male lifeguard for the men and a female lifeguard for the women. Ladies were admitted for free on opening day, Saturday, May 30, 1925.

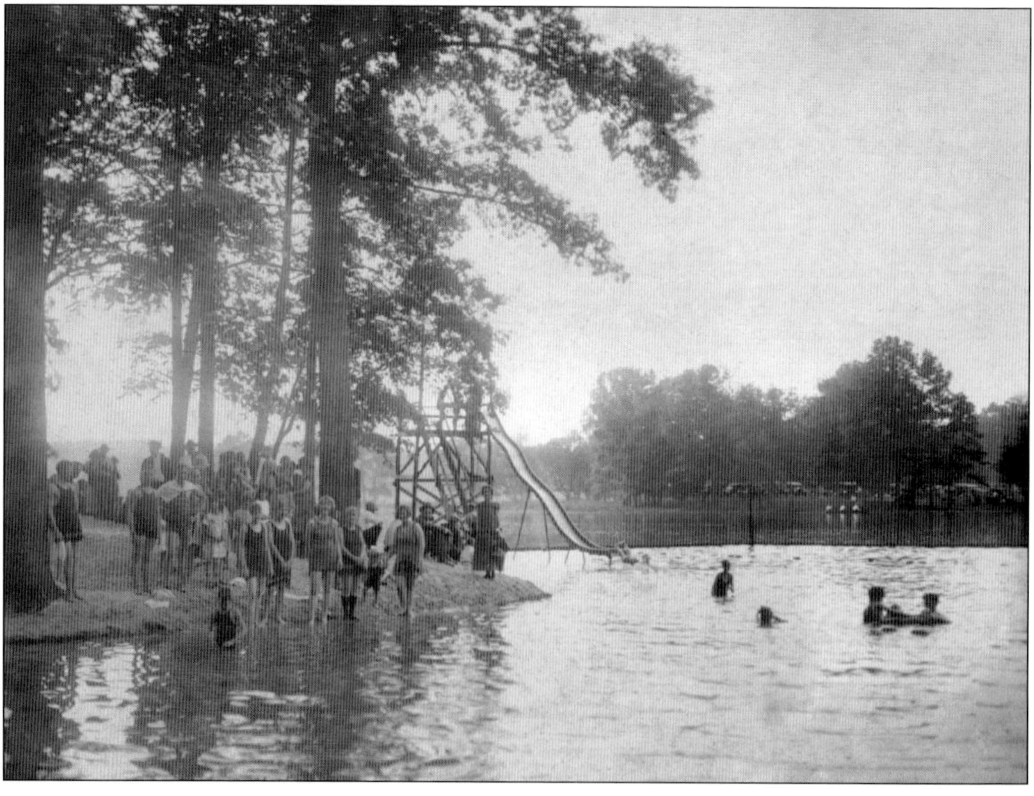

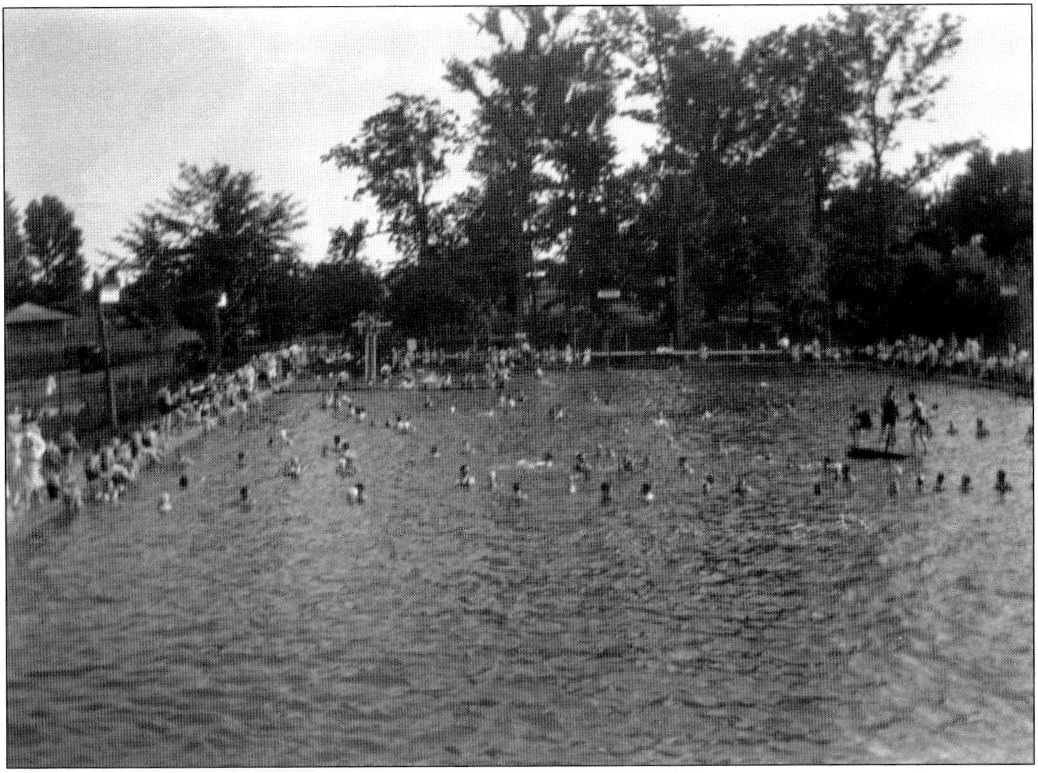

The 1926 season was highlighted by the construction of a new, $35,000 swimming pool measuring 100 feet wide and 200 feet long. Opening day saw more than 1,200 swimmers. A local newspaper, the *Chattanooga News*, noted, "There are slides and trapeze bars and rings and springboards. The diving tower is provided with six springboards, all at regulation height. The water spills into the pool through a unique process of skimming the warm water off the top of the lake, then filtering it, chlorinating it, and thorough circulation. The water in the pool is changed entirely every 12 hours. It is continuously flowing in and draining out."

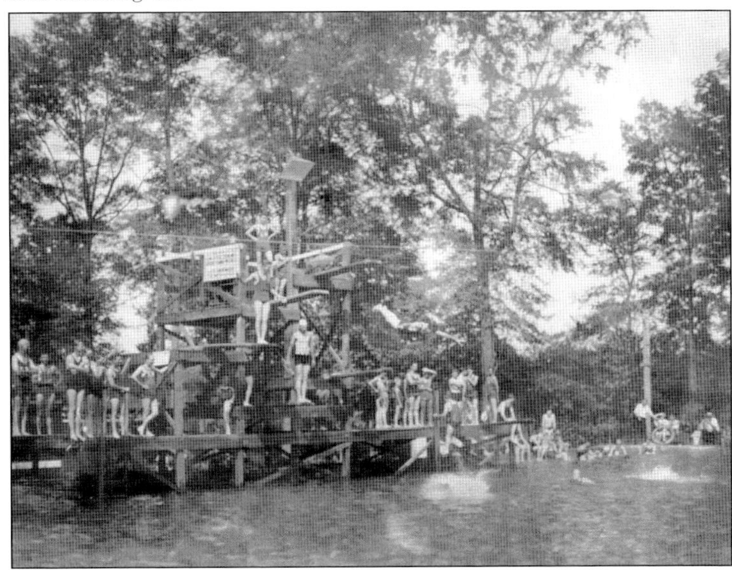

The pool featured six multistory wooden diving boards. The boards were all installed at regulation heights, with the objective of holding competitive diving meets. The numerous city, regional, and even international meets held over the next 38 years did indeed include diving competitions. Carl Dixon was especially proud of the electric lights he installed to enable nighttime use of the pool.

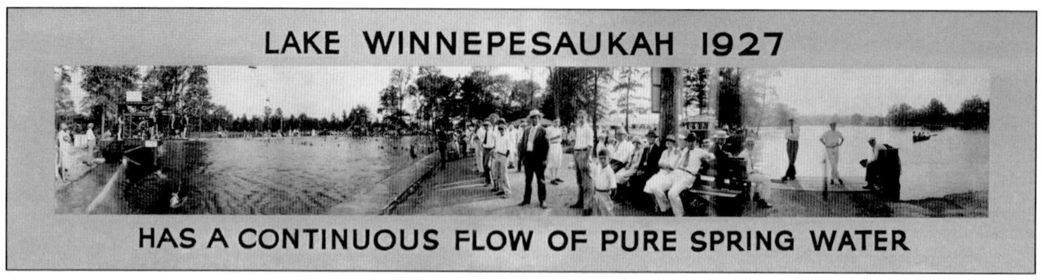

A newspaper clipping from June 25, 1926, states that "the lake has been there for 75 years." It was originally built to get power for a gristmill. More than 25 springs are yielding 30,000 gallons of water an hour in the 15-acre lake. This panel shows a view of the lake adjacent to the newly built swimming pool.

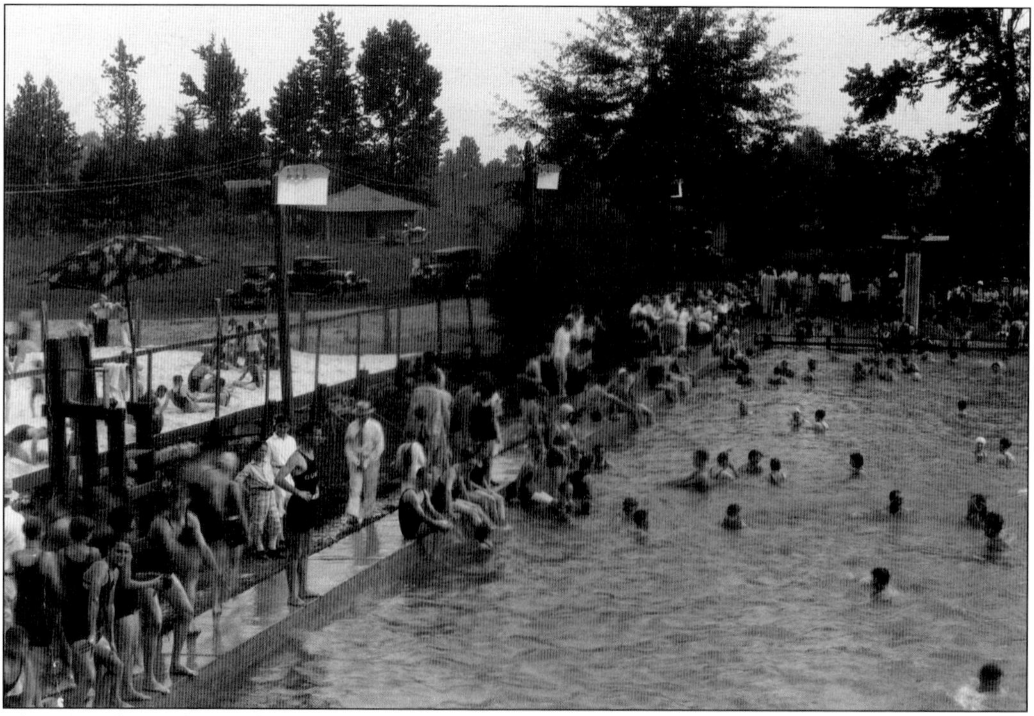

This view shows the pool from 1927, featuring a 40-by-50-foot sand beach on the left made of clean beach sand sourced from Florida. Other optional activities included baseball and tennis.

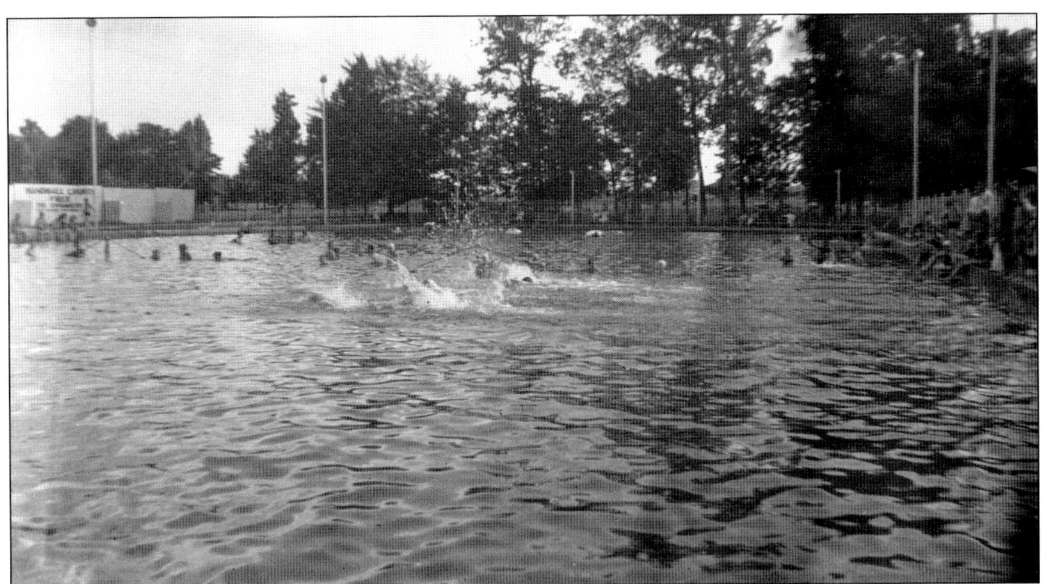

In 1927, Mid-South Swim Meets were held for the first time. They would continue to be hosted at the park until 1964, the final year the pool was open for swimming.

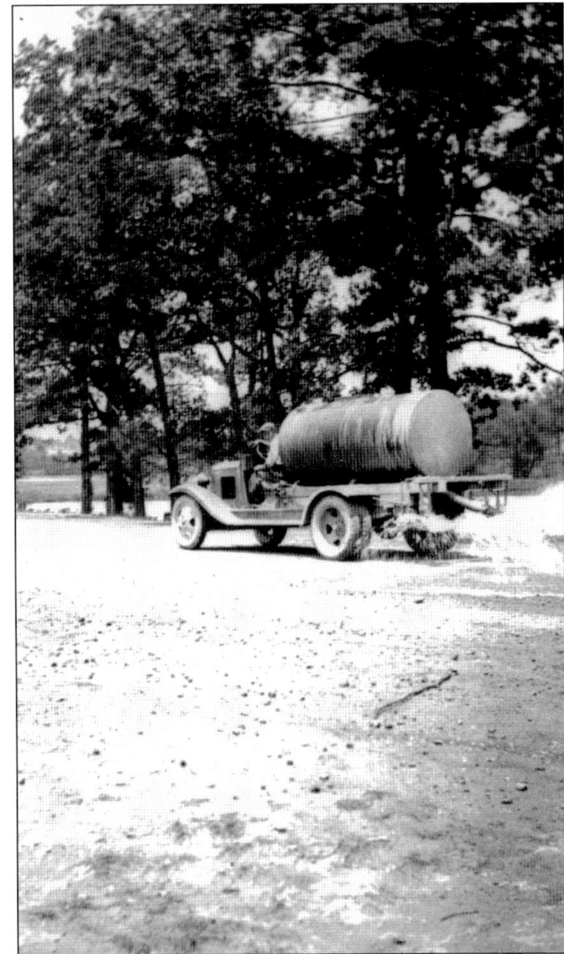

A water truck drove up and down Green's Lake Road to keep the dust on the road tamped down. The *Inland Hopper* paper reported, "The Catoosa and Walker County Road Commission have shown due interest in the importance of Lake Winnepesaukah, and the beautiful road leading to the lake grounds will be oiled next week [June 25, 1926]."

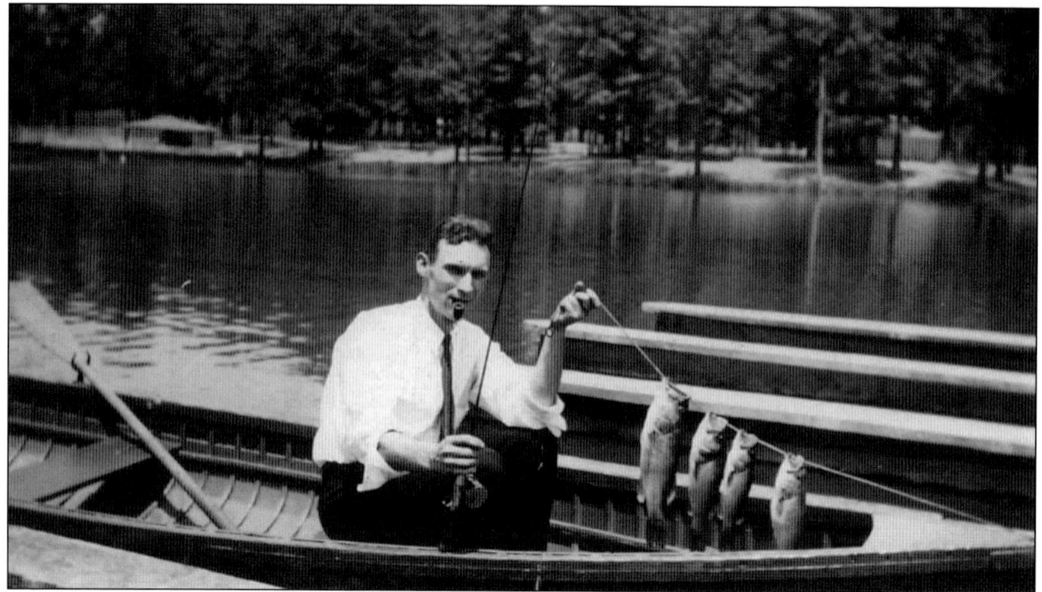

Carl Orville Dixon was an avid outdoorsman who loved fishing and hunting from an early age. In 1927, Dixon issued permits to fish in the lake. He limited each person's catch to 10 brims and five basses, with all under 10 inches in length to go back into the lake.

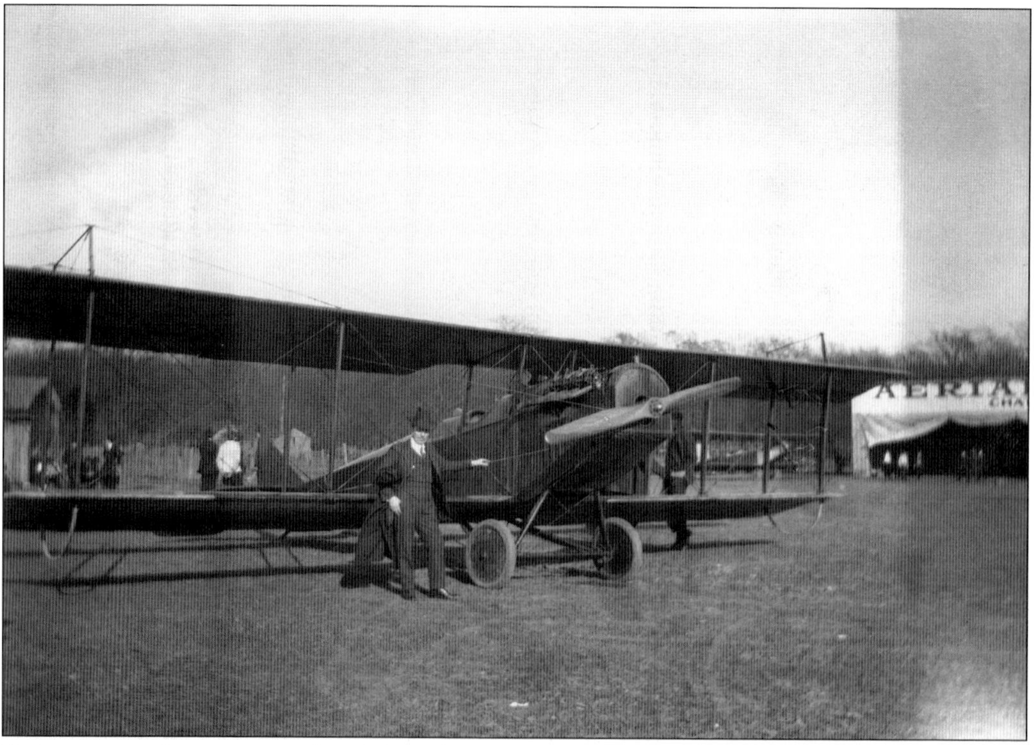

Flying was another example of Carl Dixon's entrepreneurial spirit. This interest later inspired him to book aerial shows over the lake. Anecdotally, he was known to fly, though no pictures of him flying have been preserved.

Carl Dixon was a famed automobile racer who also competed in the Indianapolis 500. This picture shows how he transported his race car. He competed in several races at Lake Winnie while the park was open.

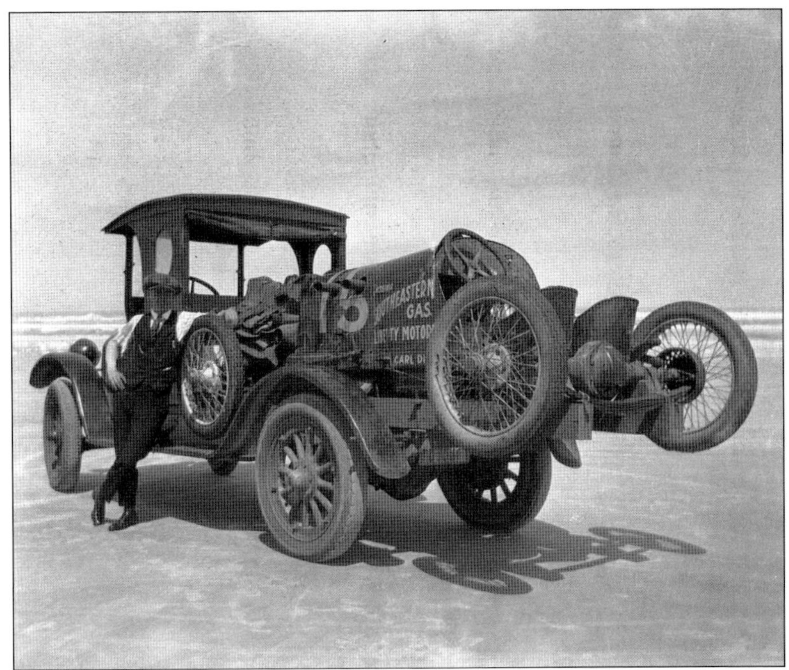

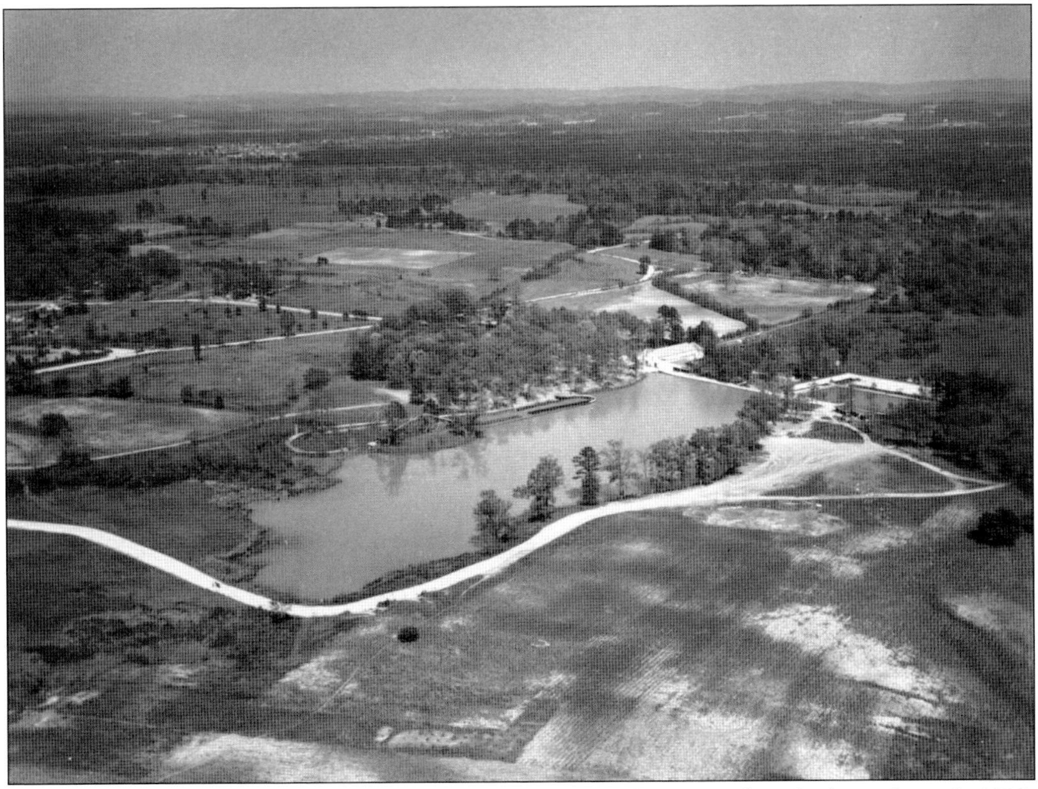

This picture shows an aerial view of the property. The park increased its facilities through 1929, adding the Boat Chute, three horseshoe pits, and a kiddie plane ride, along with a fully complete baseball field.

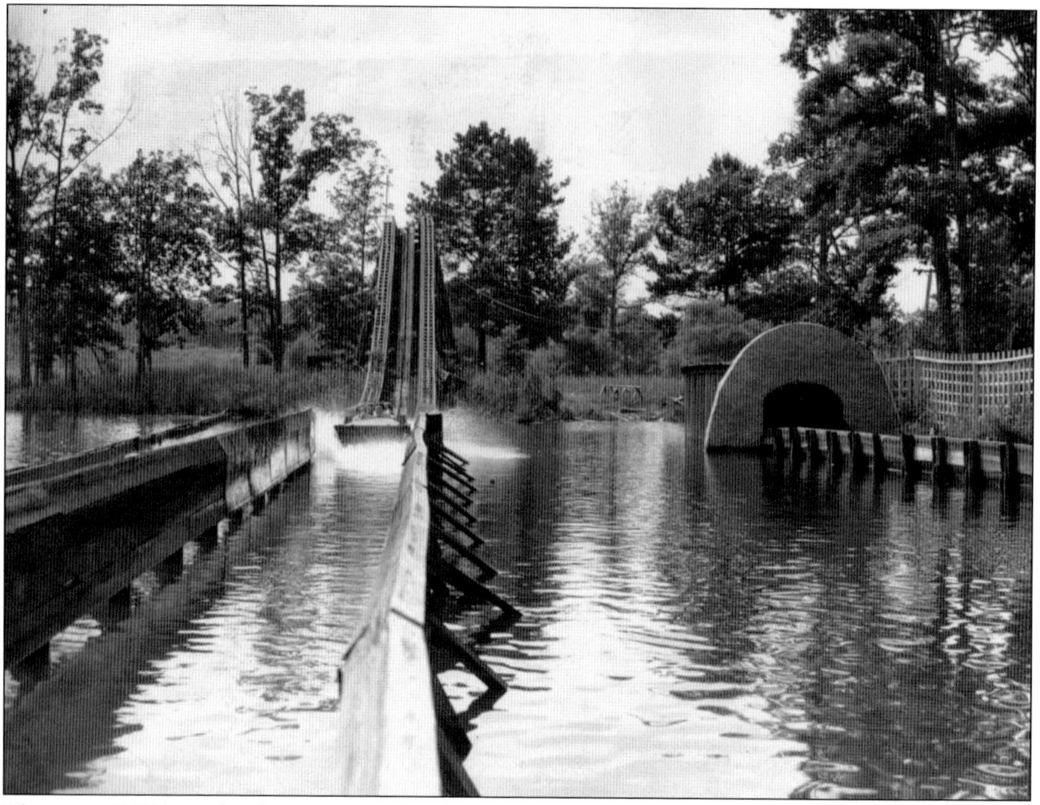

The year 1927 was the first summer for the Boat Chute, which was designed and built over the winter by Carl Dixon and was the first ride in the park. It also became the most copied ride of its kind in the United States. Dixon trained workers at the park in the construction of the ride. Fifty years later, his daughter, Evelyn, designed and built a house under the tall hill of the ride.

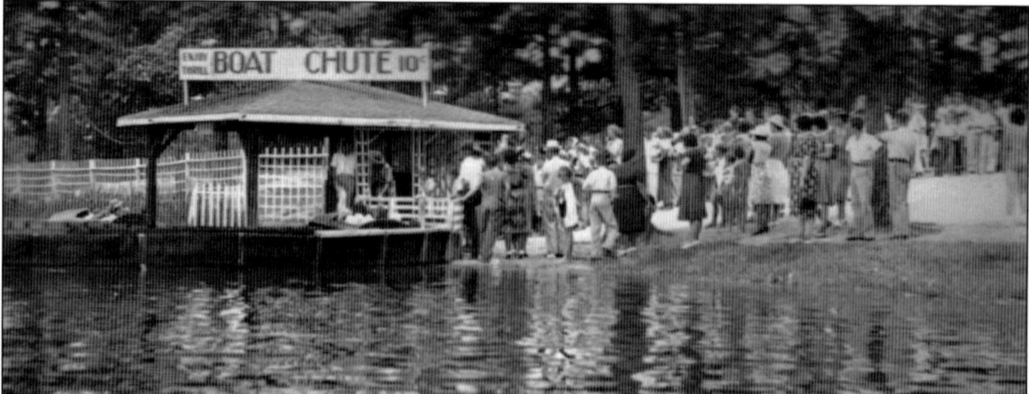

The dock, or entry for the ride, was originally located on the side of the lake. It too, was designed by Carl Dixon and built by workers at the park.

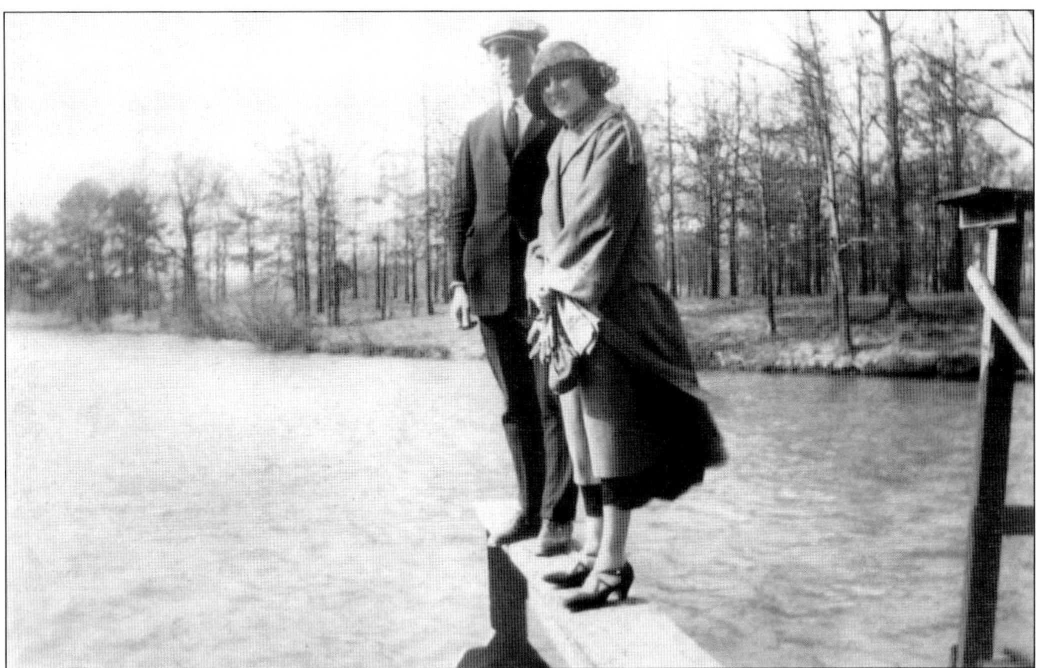

After the park opened to the public, one of Carl and Minette's favorite pastimes was boating. Here, they stand on the boat dock, admiring the progress of the recreation attraction they are building.

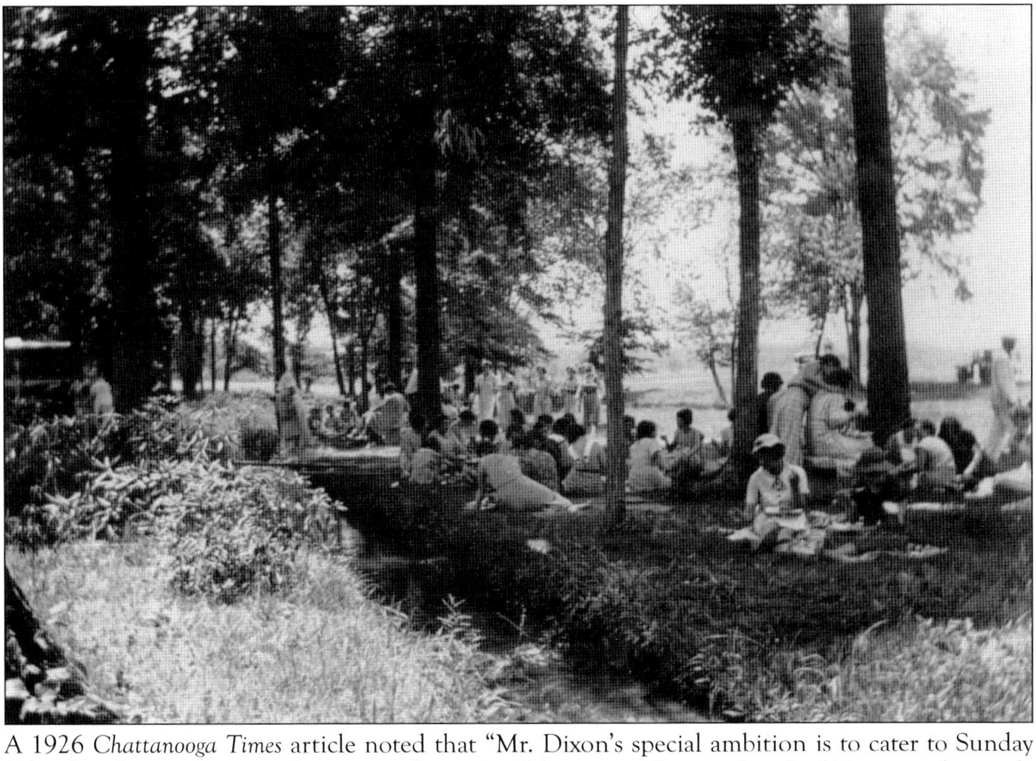

A 1926 *Chattanooga Times* article noted that "Mr. Dixon's special ambition is to cater to Sunday School and community gatherings and picnics. The new and up-to-date facilities can adequately accommodate a limitless number of parties."

OPENING DAY

AT

LAKE WINNEPESAUKAH

"The Beautiful Lake of The Highlands"

Sunday, May 15th, 1927

Bathing Boating and Fishing

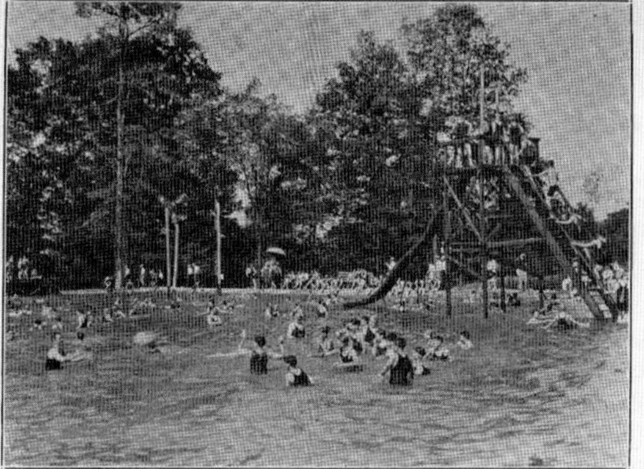

15 Min. from Market Street

One of the Largest Concrete Pools In the South

CONTINUOUS FLOW OF FRESH WATER

No Charges for Use of Picnic Grounds, Tables or Base Ball Diamond

Opening day was advertised in the newspapers as well as on posters placed around town. The "fresh spring water" was a point of pride, and the local water company reported being impressed with the water filtration system Carl Dixon designed.

Two

The 1930s

Only the Strong Survive

Nationally, the 1930s were marked by the Great Depression, which radically changed the face of the economic and social climate in America. Unemployment was close to 25 percent when Roosevelt was inaugurated in 1933. Family income reduced dramatically, and many out-of-work men had to rely on their wives and children to find jobs.

Carl Dixon continued to implement his ideas for growth at his beloved park. He added a miniature golf course in the winter of 1929. A sandy beach by the pool was added, along with a new bathhouse with lockers for all the swimmers and sunbathers. In 1931, a large casino was built to hold dances on Wednesday and Saturday nights. On other days, the building was used as a roller-skating rink. A shooting gallery, Skee-Ball games, and a driving range were built.

In April 1933, Carl Dixon died as a result of a asthma attack he obtained from filing the skate wheels in the skating rink. Minette Dixon was left to run the thriving young business herself. She was thrust into this at a time when women were not allowed to open bank accounts, apply for credit, or commit to a mortgage without a male signature. Where Carl left off, Minette carried on. She rolled up her sleeves, relied on her German heritage of inner resolve and determination, and got to work.

Her first order of business was to execute the plans Carl had put into place for the 1933 season. The summer featured air shows, circus acts, boxing exhibitions, and water races in addition to the other attractions already in place. At some point, she decided to embrace the challenges of the business world and continue Carl's vision. And continue she did, for in the face of the Depression, she not only ran but expanded the park.

Sideshow acts such as a "human cork" floating in the lake, fire divers, motorcycle jumps, beach-wear fashion shows, treasure hunts, hypnotist acts, balloon acts, and motorcycle races were hosted as well as football games in the fall. Tennis, shuffleboard, handball courts, and barbeque pits in a spacious picnic grove were built. Free swimming lessons were offered, with segregation by male/female for both lifeguards and those taking lessons. Perhaps the most long-lasting tradition begun in 1935 is the fireworks display, which has been an annual Fourth of July tradition since. This was followed by a bridle path for horseback riding in 1937 and six electric motorboats for use on the lake. In addition, the lake was stocked with rainbow trout and bass for fishing.

In 1936, a public address system that allowed announcements over the entire park grounds was added. This was later utilized to broadcast President Roosevelt's fireside chats.

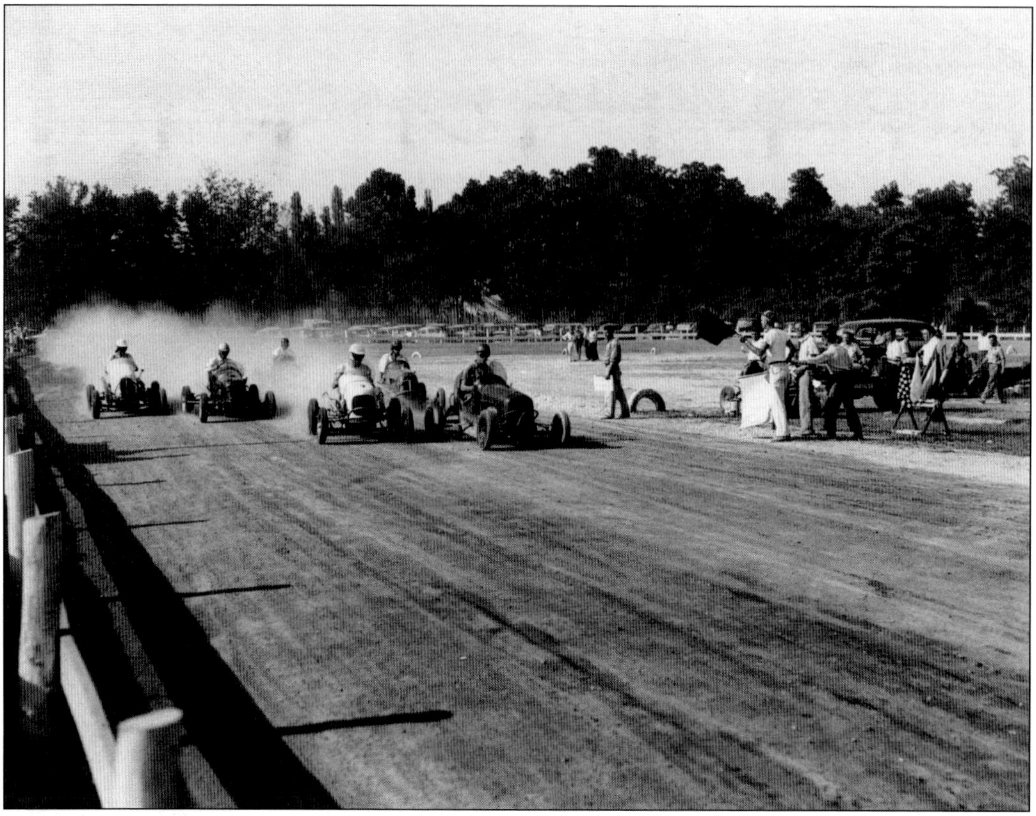

In the late 1920s and early 1930s, Lake Winnepesaukah hosted local automobile races. The area, once a racetrack, is now a field where fireworks are shot on the Fourth of July; however, one can still see the area marked as a racetrack.

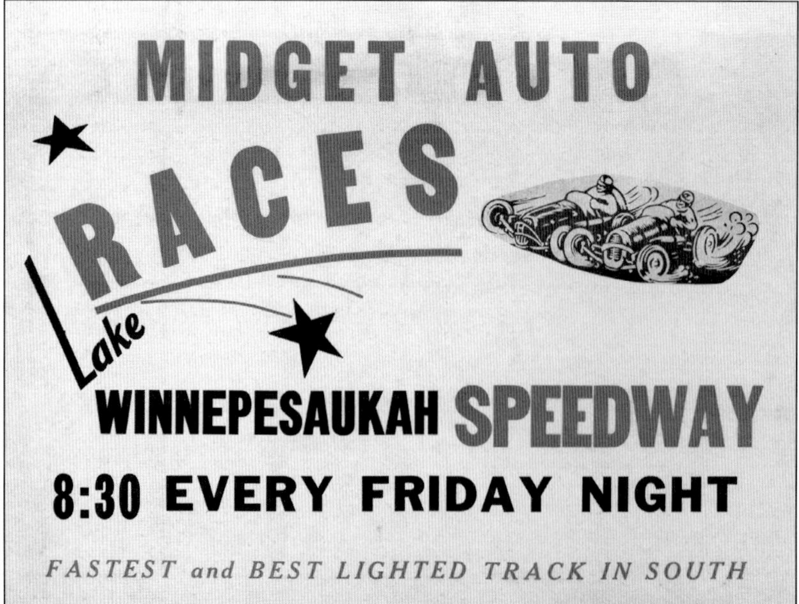

This poster invites all spectators to the midget car races held on the racetrack every Friday and Saturday in the 1930s. Posters were posted around town while the artwork also served as an advertisement in the newspaper. All racing enthusiasts were invited to participate.

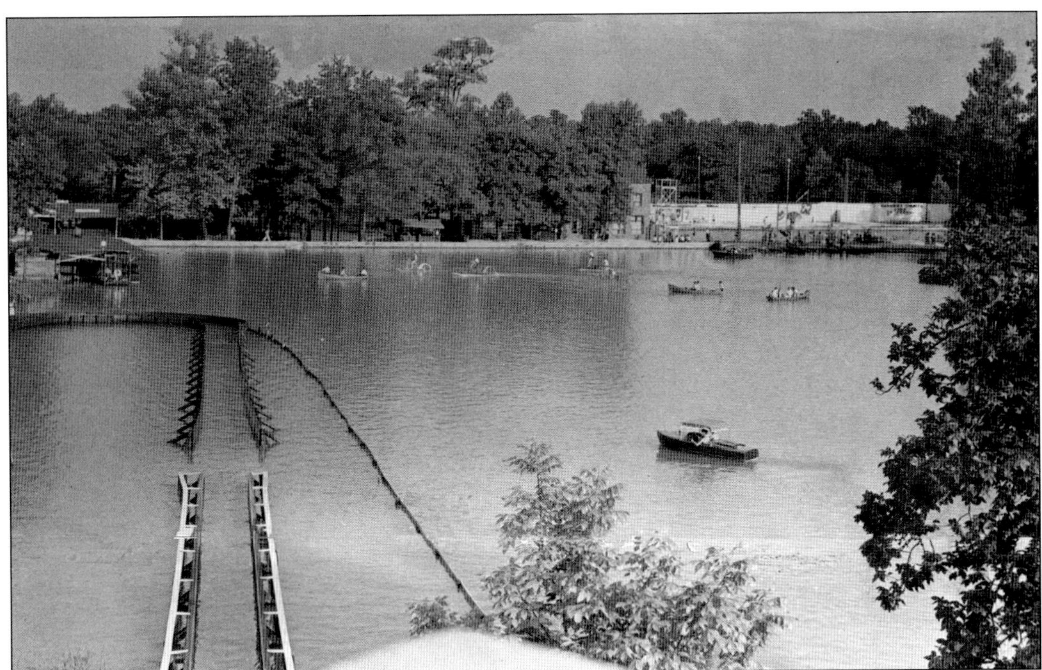

This view from the summit of the Boat Chute shows many of the attractions of the day: canoeing, water bikes, the rowboat dock, electric boats, and the swimming pool in the distance. This was an advantage of all swimming being only in the pool—the lake could be utilized for other recreation.

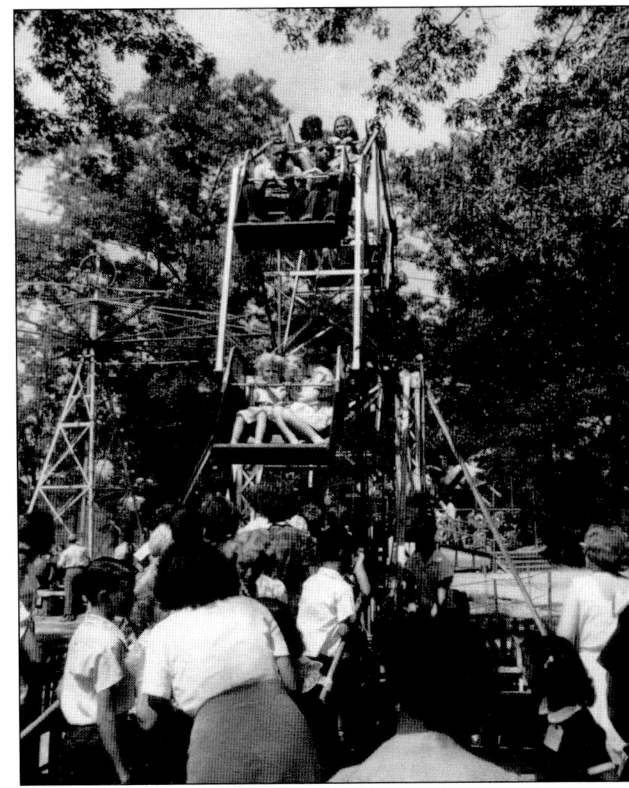

A kiddie Ferris wheel was added in 1936. This attraction was so well received by both younger and older guests, it led to a new Ferris wheel and two new kiddie rides the following year.

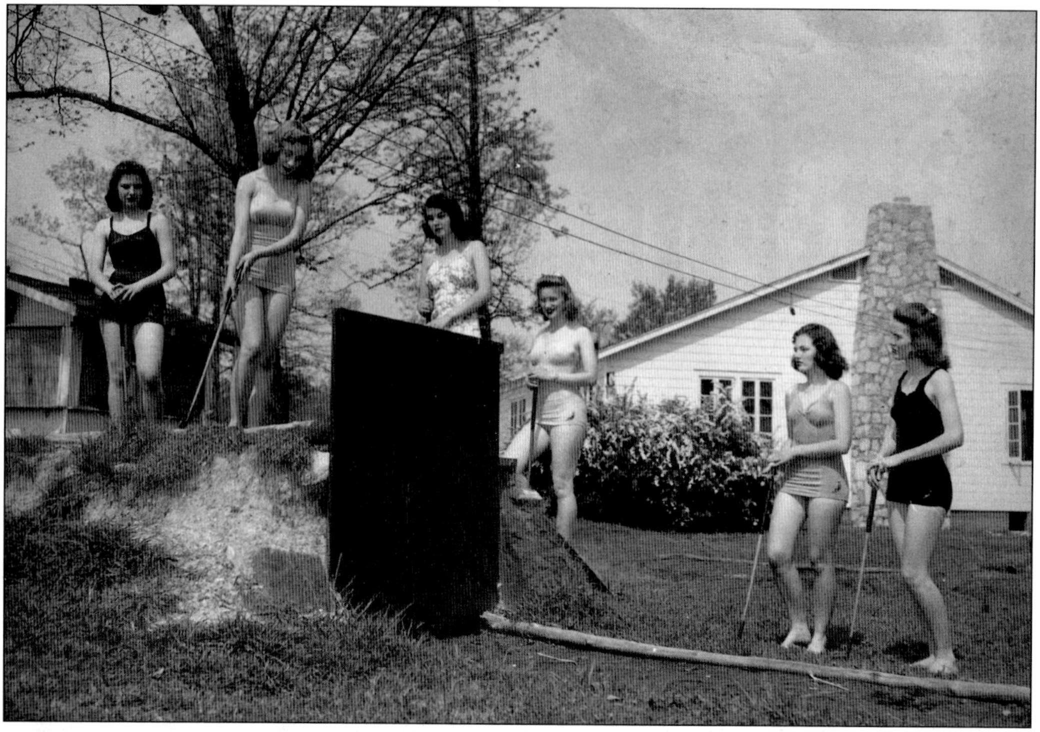

In 1930, Carl Dixon installed one of the trickiest miniature golf courses in the state, which included water hazards, water jumps, and long tunnels. The course was the first built after the original Tom Thumb course on Lookout Mountain. (Lake Winnepesaukah Amusement.)

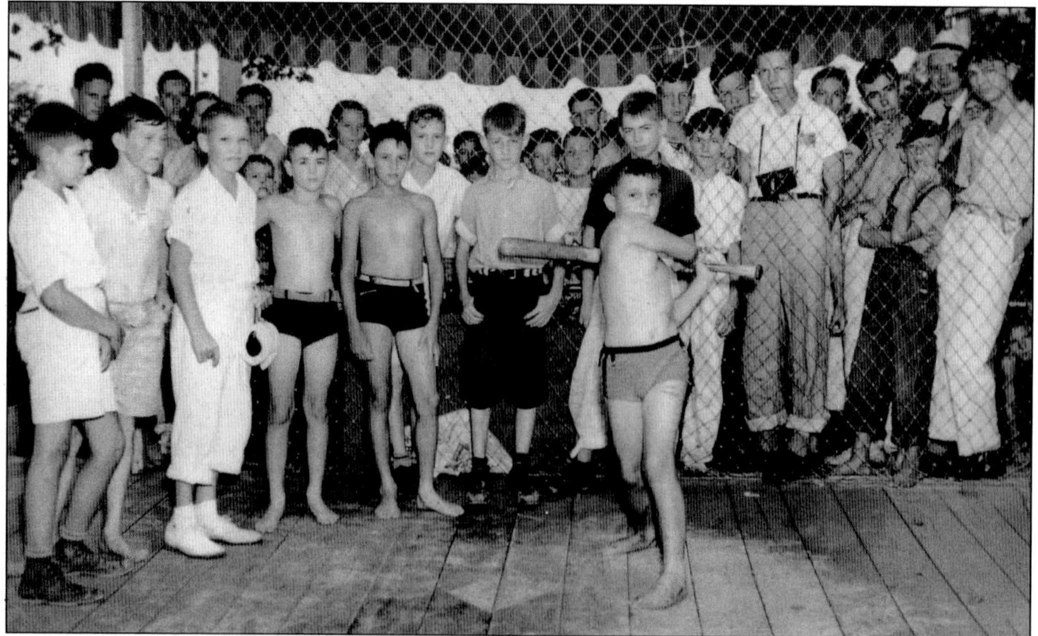

Batting cages were a popular attraction for baseball fans. Carl Dixon installed lights so games could continue into the evening. Minette Dixon worked tirelessly to fulfill her late husband's plan for a complete resort. (Lake Winnepesaukah Amusement.)

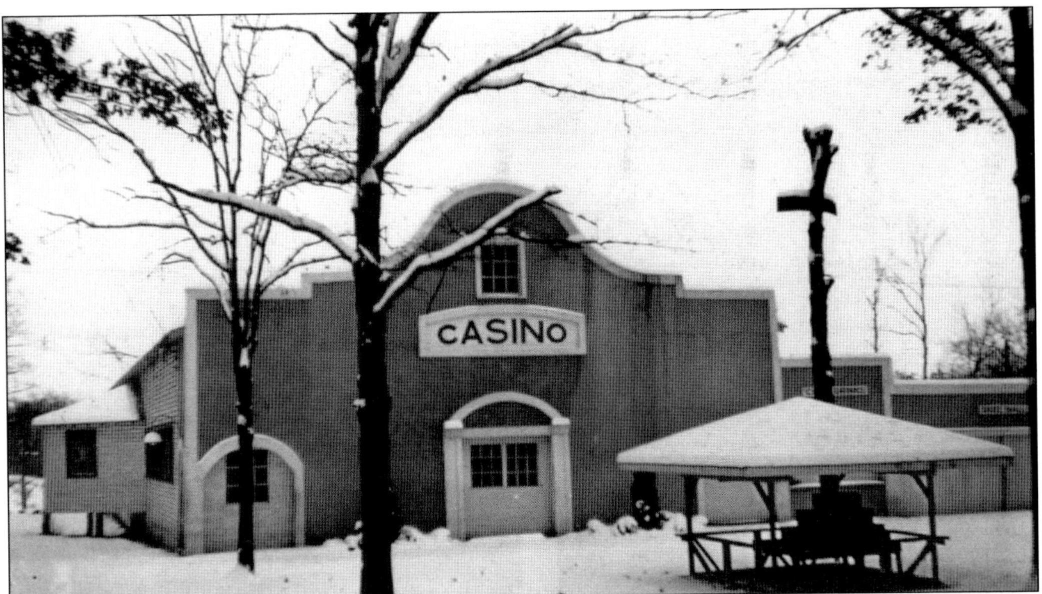

In 1931, a large casino was built on the property, where dances were held on Wednesday and Saturday nights, with music furnished by Jimmy Cox and his orchestra. The remaining nights the casino was used for roller skating, Skee-Ball, and a shooting gallery. (Lake Winnepesaukah Amusement.)

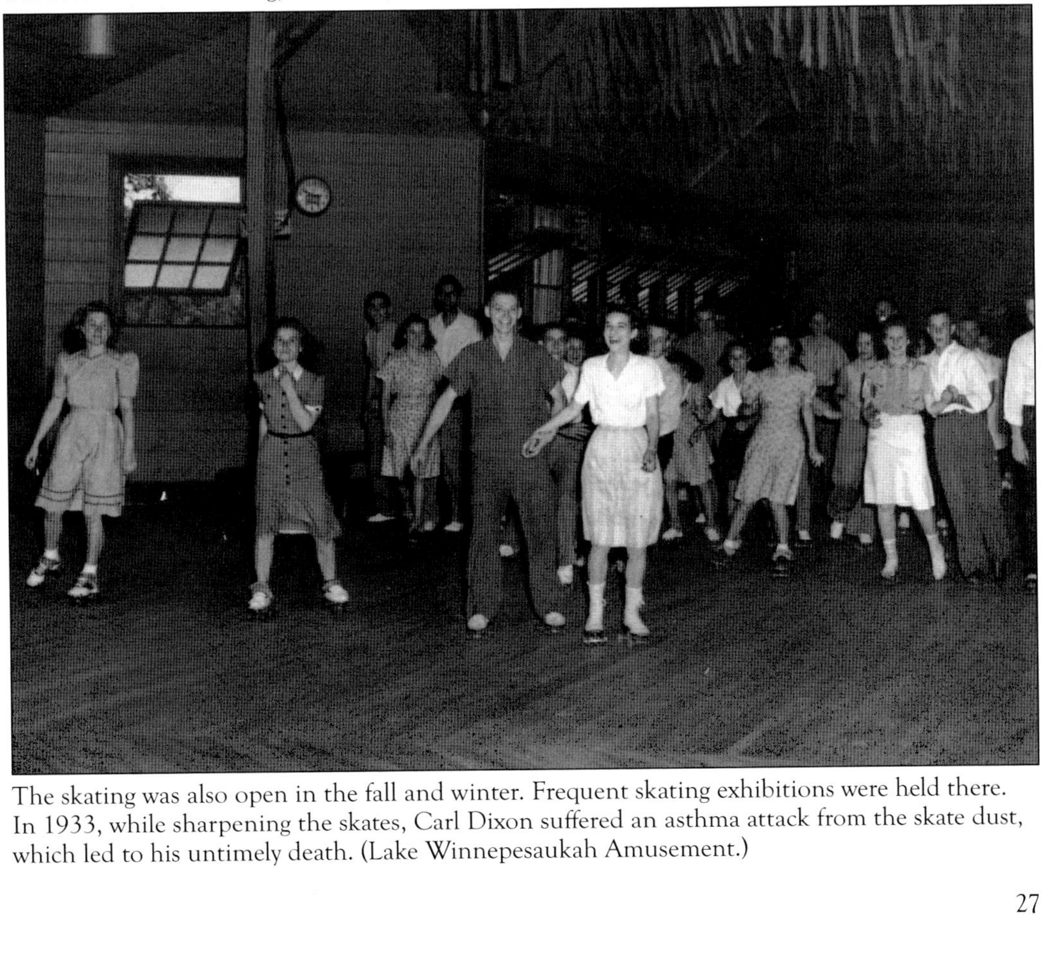

The skating was also open in the fall and winter. Frequent skating exhibitions were held there. In 1933, while sharpening the skates, Carl Dixon suffered an asthma attack from the skate dust, which led to his untimely death. (Lake Winnepesaukah Amusement.)

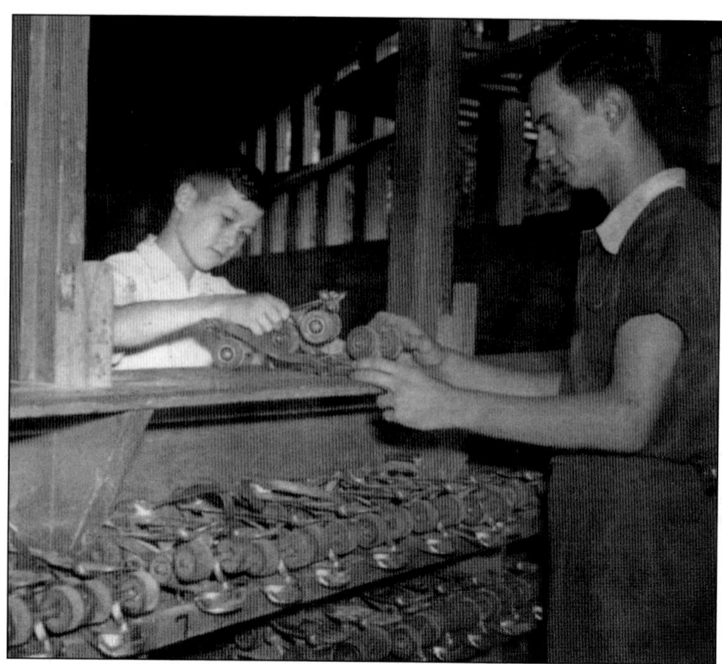

Skates could be rented by all ages for a nickel. Roller skating was a favorite pastime for children and couples. Professional skaters frequently came and gave exhibitions for spectators.

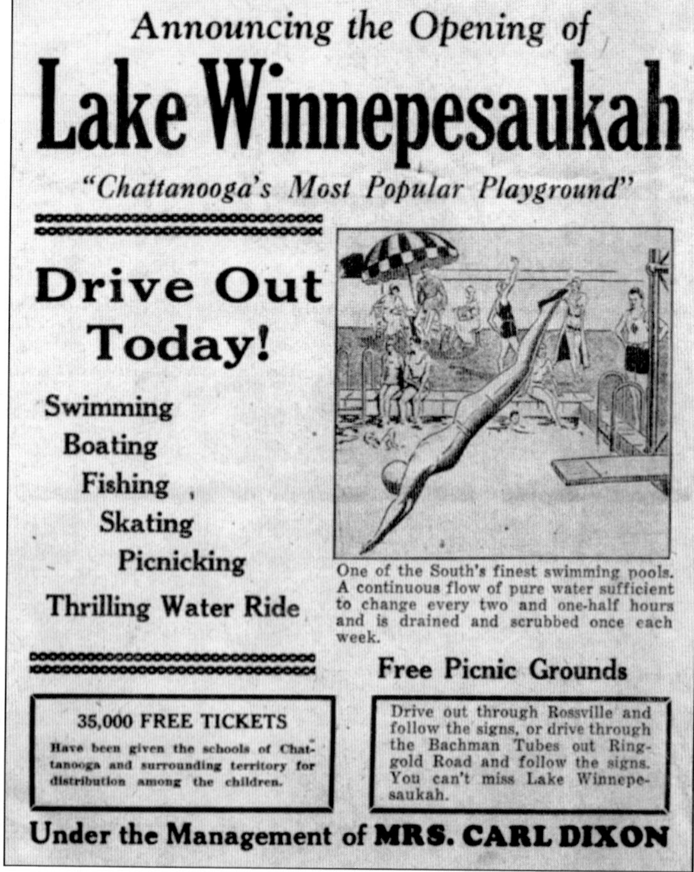

Minette Dixon, who took the helm after Carl died in 1933, was keen on seeking out the local children to visit the park. She wrote to every school principal in the area giving tickets in support of education. Support of education continues today with the Student Achievement Program, which allows any elementary school student to be admitted to the park free on Tuesdays.

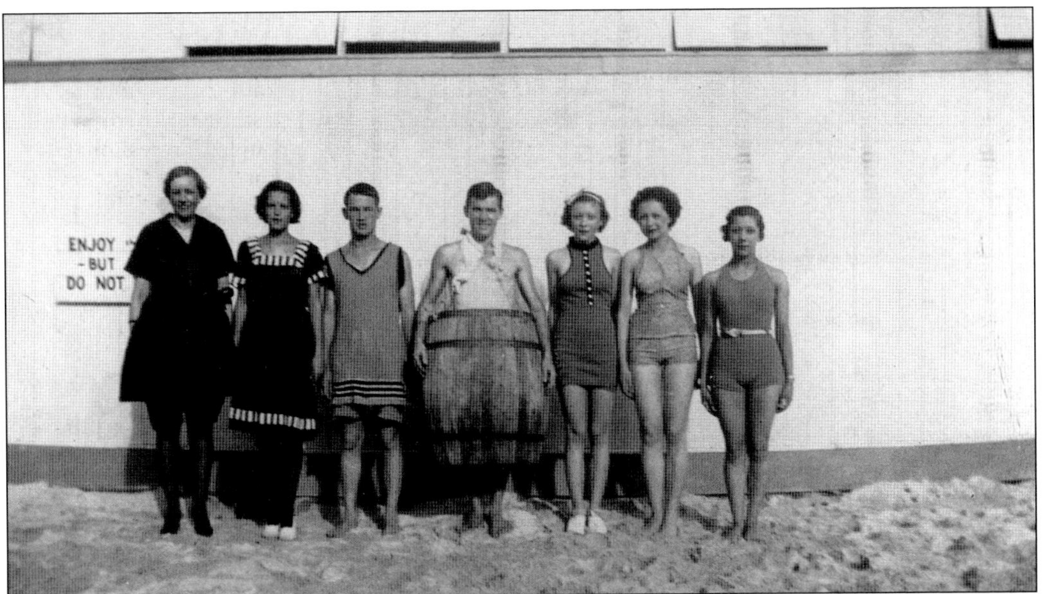

The 1930s featured an array of performers each season. Stunt exhibitions, air shows, and water shows were featured with such talents as fire diving, barrel racing, and beach fashion contests.

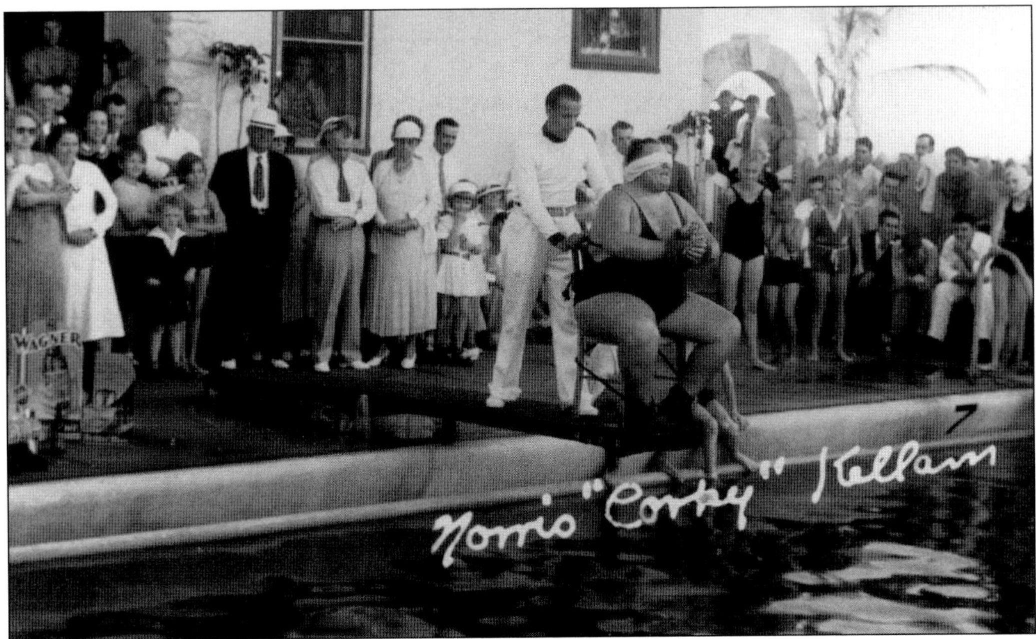

A host of unusual characters came to Lake Winnepesaukah during the 1930s. Thousands of Chattanoogans rushed to Lake Winnepesaukah to see balloonists, prize fights, automobile and boat races, tight-wire acts, wrestling, circus acts, air shows, beauty contests, and fire dives. In 1934, Norris "Corky" Kellam, a self-described 322-pound "human cork," swam in the lake for 62 hours straight.

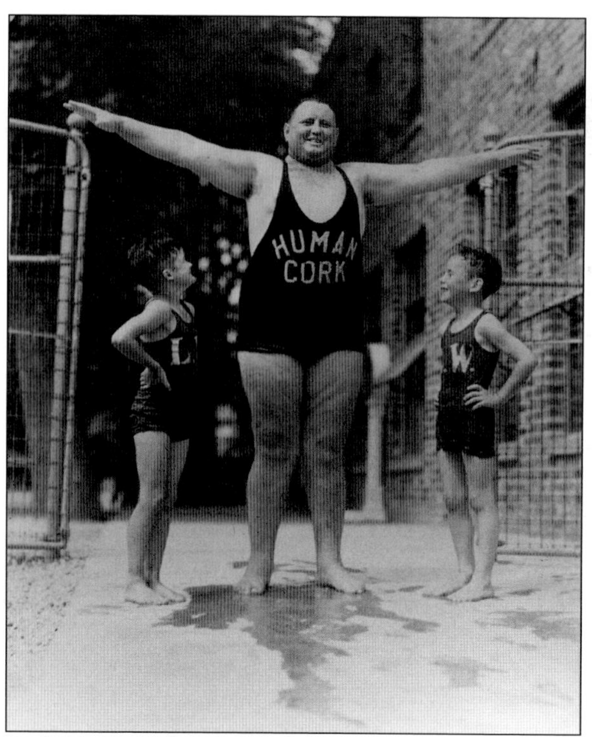

Corky Kellam prepares to dive into the chilling spring-fed waters of Lake Winnepesaukah on July 4, 1934, to break his record with 73 continual hours in the water. Spectators lined the dam four people deep to see his aquatic stunt.

Crowds were plentiful to participate as well as observe boating on the lake. Family history states that the canoes were made of hollowed-out pine, similar to those the native Cherokee would have used on the lake.

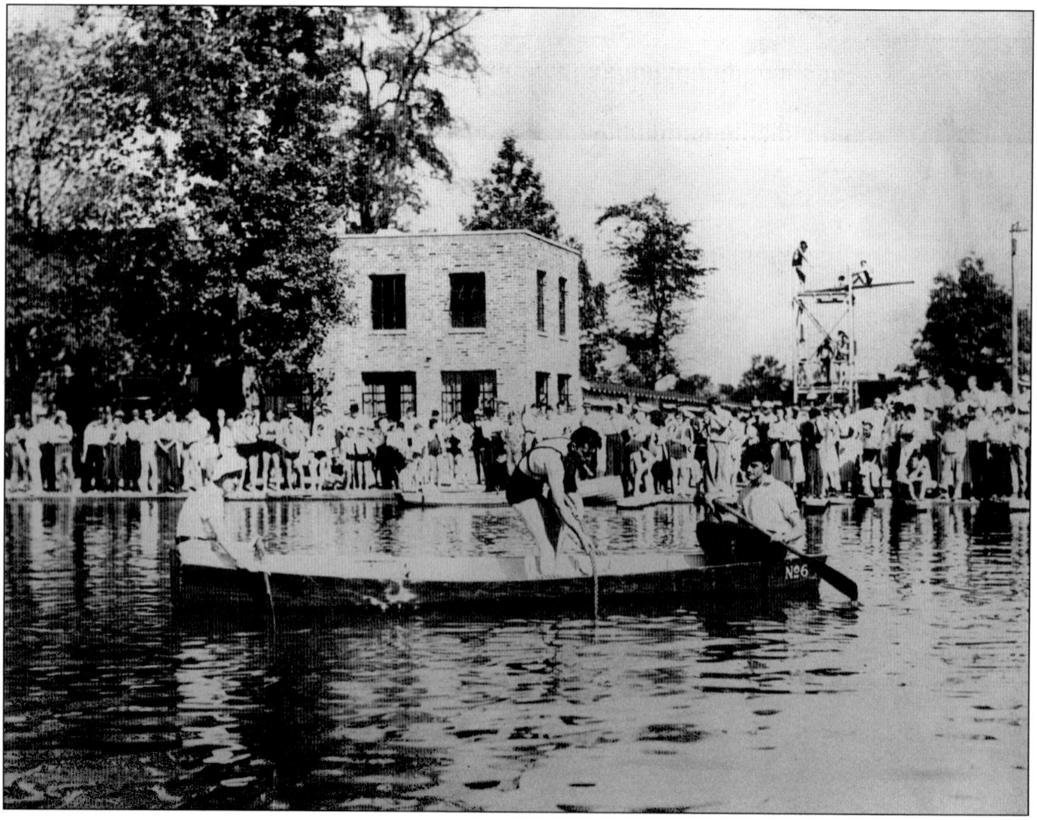

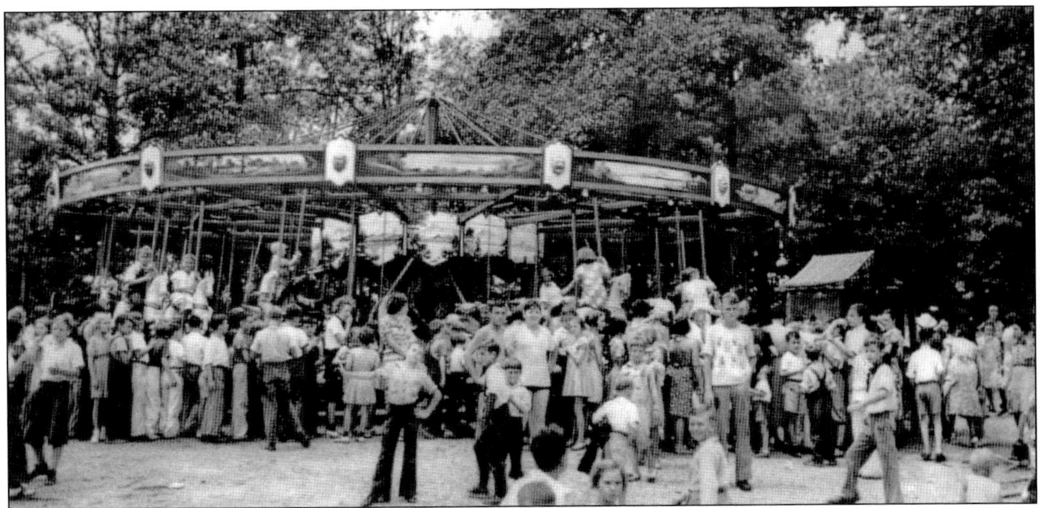

The year 1935 marked the first Kiddie Day at Lake Winnepesaukah. Rides were 5¢ each for children under 12. Note the central location of the merry-go-round, which was added in 1935.

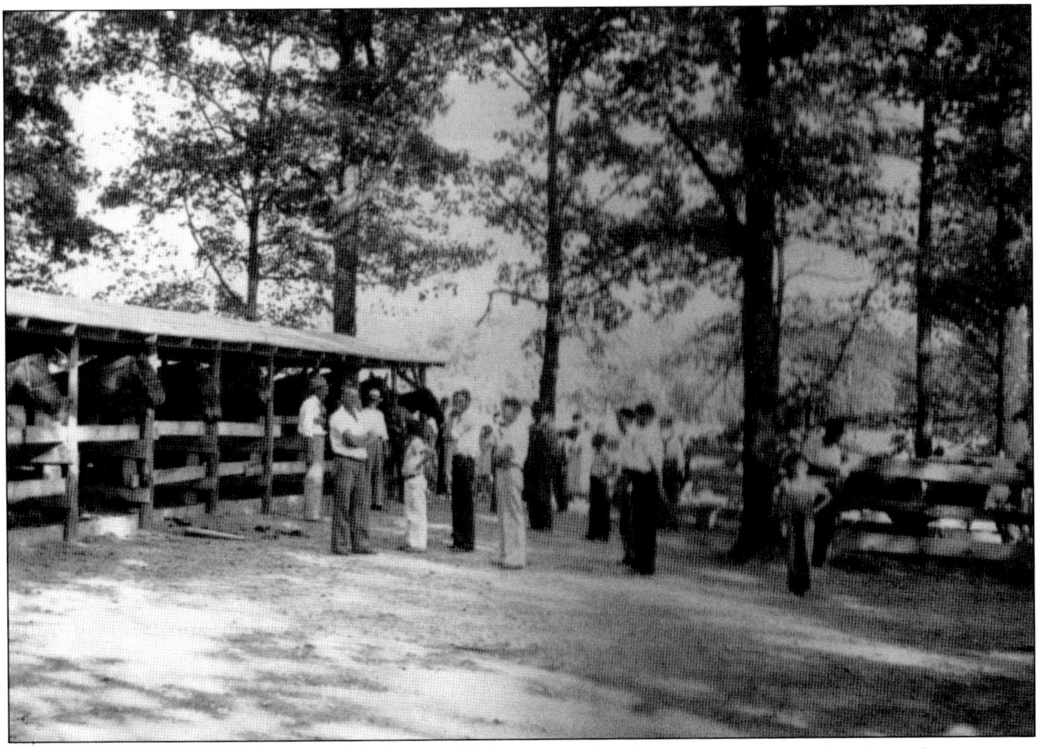

A bridle path and a barn were added in 1937. Horseback riding was soon another popular pastime at the park. Evelyn White loved to ride; her daughter Adrienne met with a lesser enthusiasm when she fell from the hayloft and broke both her arms.

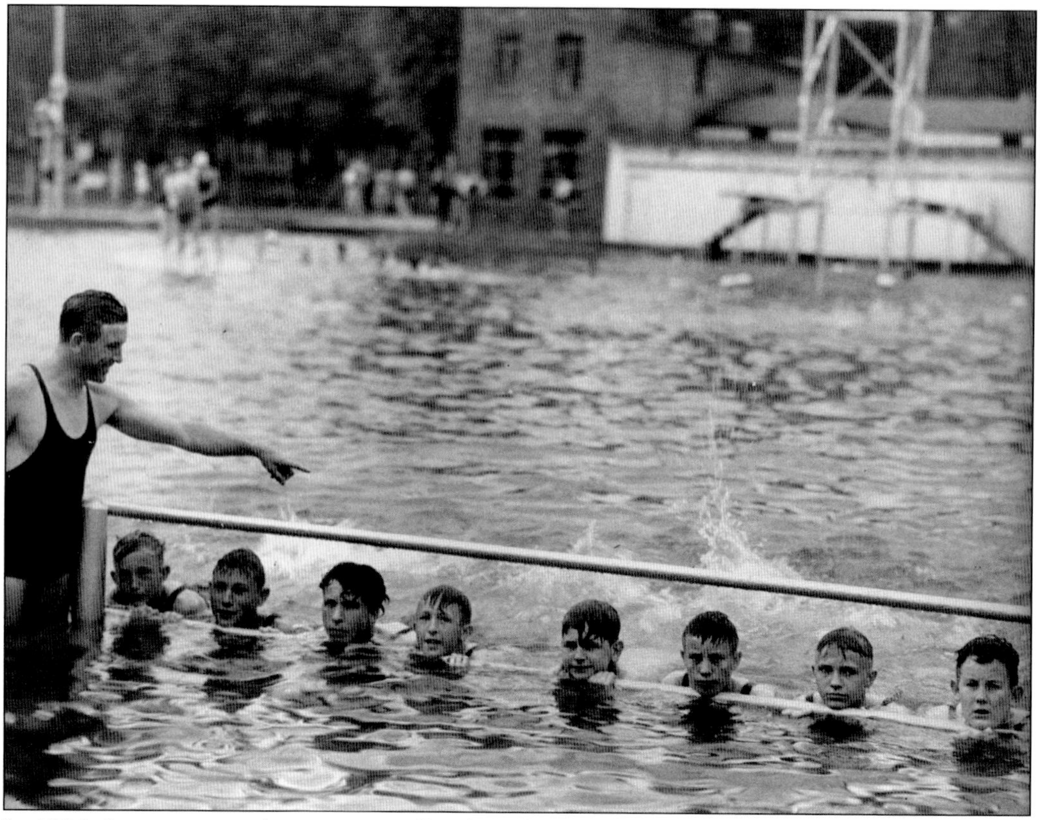

In 1936, free swimming lessons were offered: six lessons over six days. Male students were taught by male lifeguards and female students by female lifeguards.

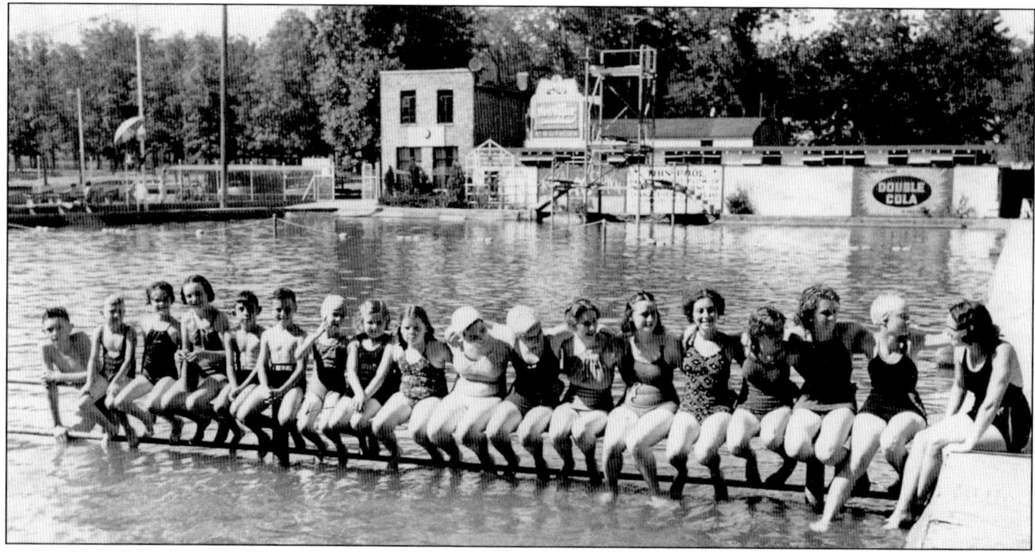

Lake Winnepesaukah offered Red Cross swim instruction and certification. Discount swim cards were offered to students. In May 1936, swimming and diving contests for school students were held, with elimination matches held each Sunday. The winners of the eliminations then competed in the finals for the grand prize on the last Sunday of May.

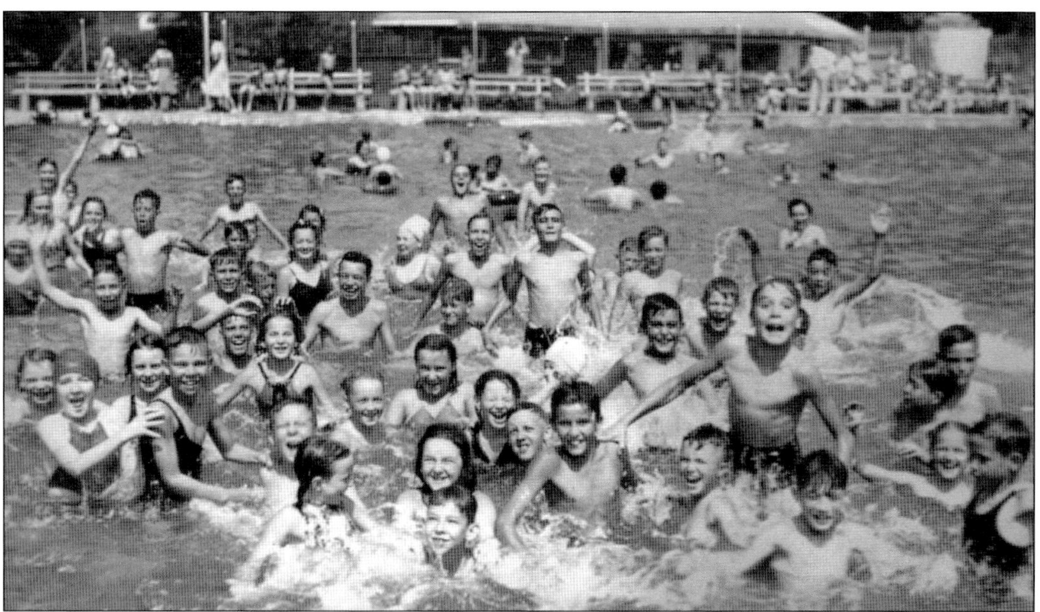

When the pool was not being used for swim meets, swim classes, or stunt shows, it was pure water fun. The year 1936 had a record heat wave of 104 degrees. A total of 104 silver dollars were thrown in the pool, and children dove for them for extra fun.

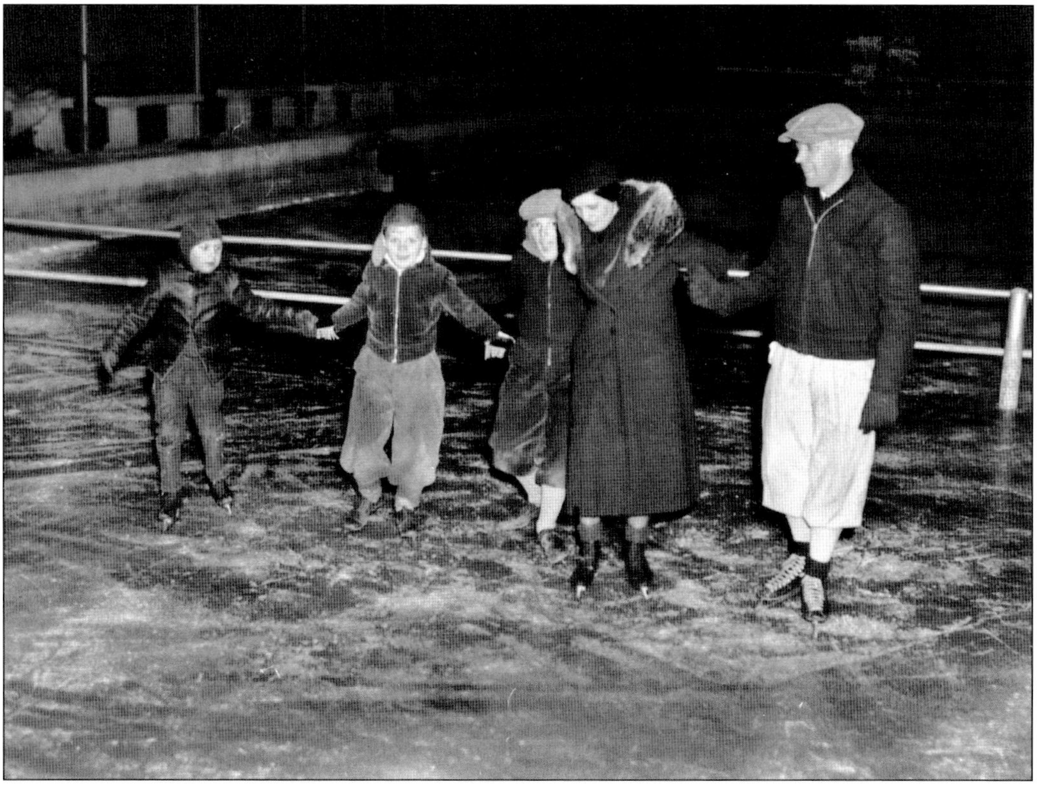

In 1936, the pool froze over in the winter, and people skated on it. Two log fires were lit in the bathhouse, and free coffee and cookies were served.

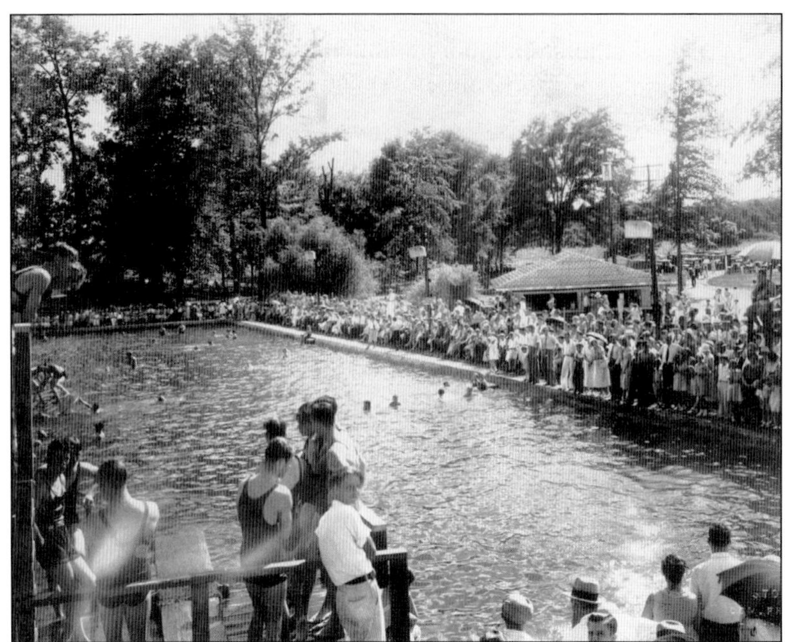

The pool was a major attraction for swimmers, divers, and spectators. Facilitated by the electric lights, many large regional meets went into the evening hours.

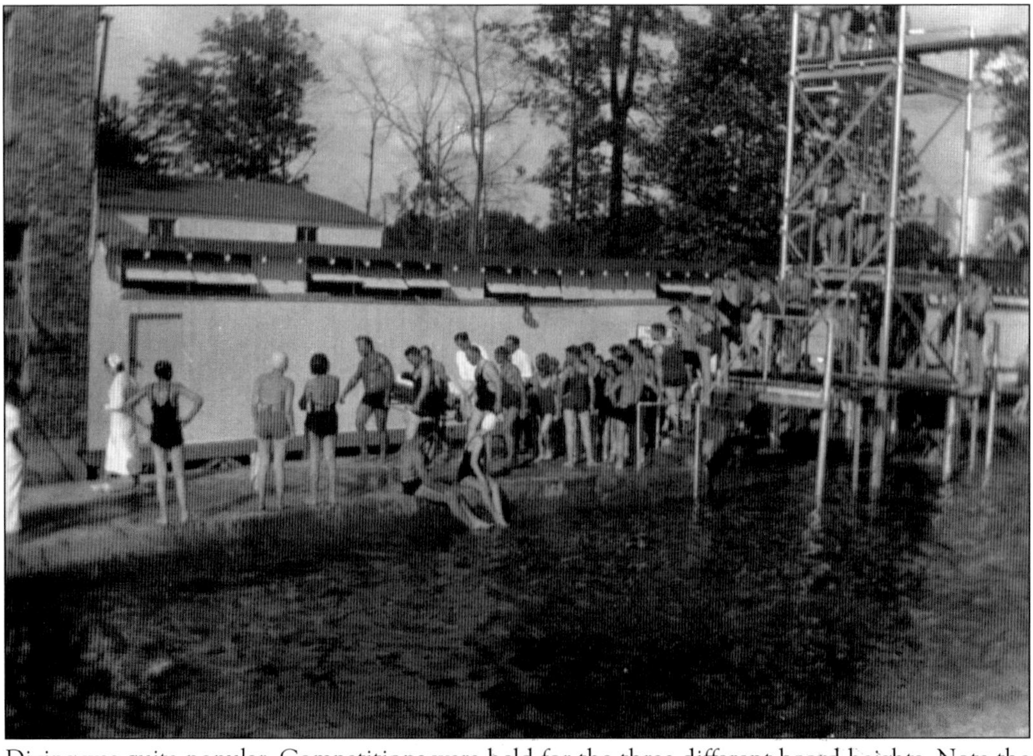

Diving was quite popular. Competitions were held for the three different board heights. Note the nurse on the left—a nurse was always on hand for safety.

Shown is the sand beach at the edge of the swimming pool and the bathhouse beyond that. It is noted in company fact sheets that every "stick of lumber" used in the building was made on the place. The trees were felled and selected and a portable sawmill set up. Over 1,000 people could be accommodated; dressing rooms for the women face left, and those for the men face right.

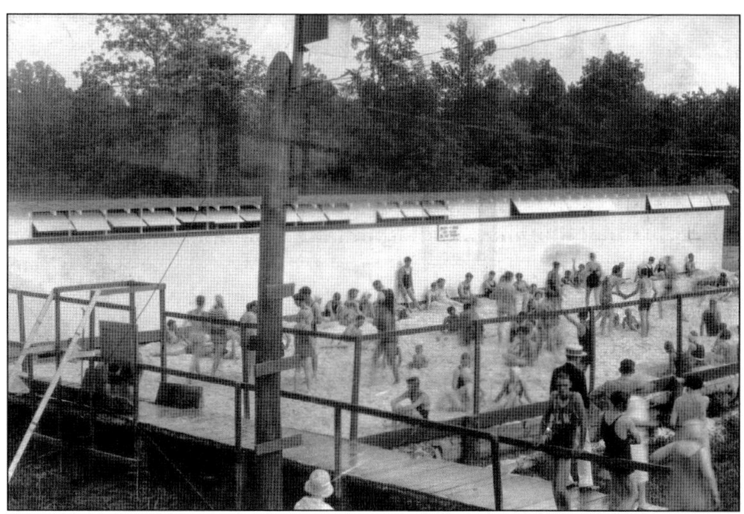

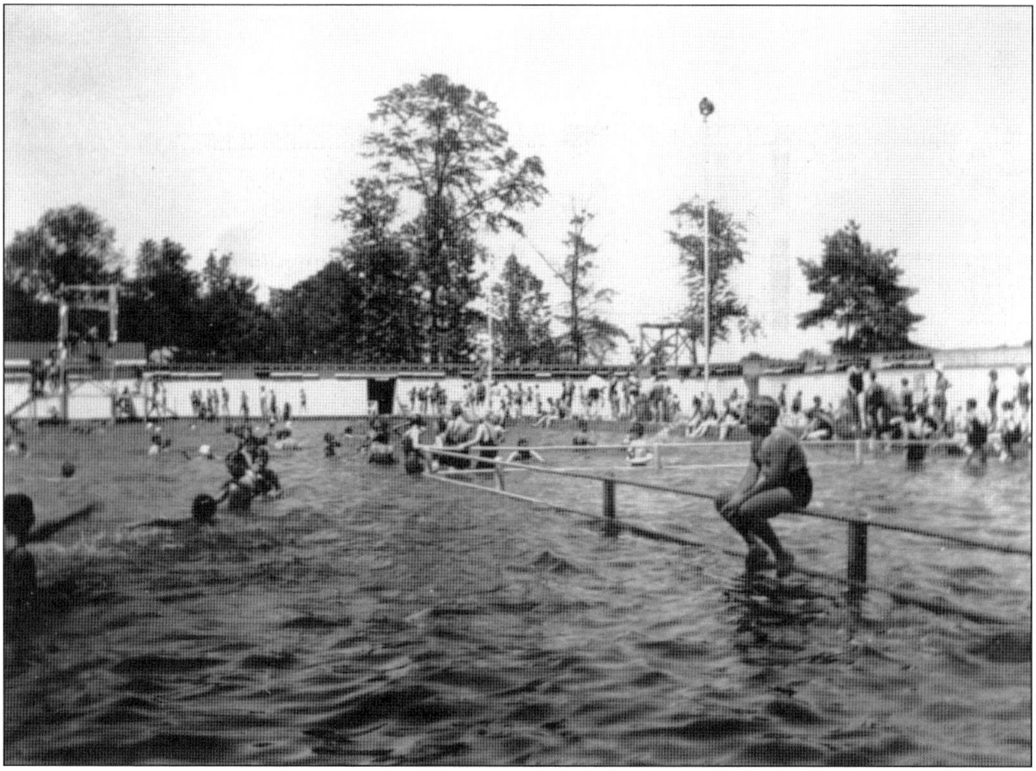

Shown in this picture is the fenced designation of the shallow end of the pool on the right where children swam, the middle area for older children on the right, and the deepest area for divers and swimmers at the heart of the pool. The white sand beach is on the far right. Those swimmers who came to swim were given a two-inch-square piece of cloth each day to pin on their suit to know they had been counted for the day.

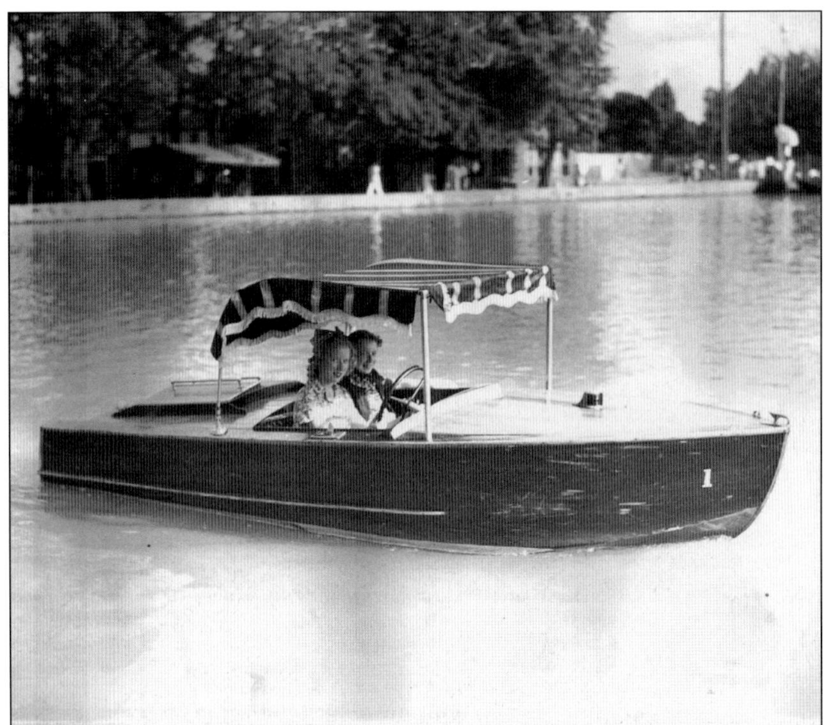

The 1939 season opened with six new electric boats (pictured), rowboats, water bikes, and the Boat Chute. Minette Dixon went to great lengths to source boats that had a top to offer protection from the sun.

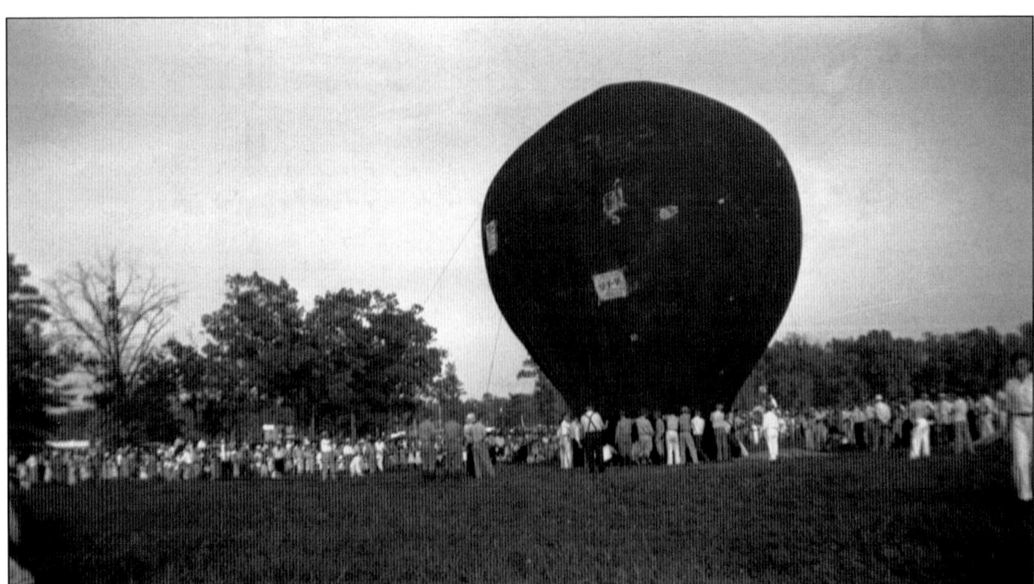

The 1939 season also featured a balloon ascension over the lake. Thomas Blake, one of the world's outstanding daredevils, performed aerial acrobats while ascending in the balloon and then parachuted to Earth from 3,500 feet.

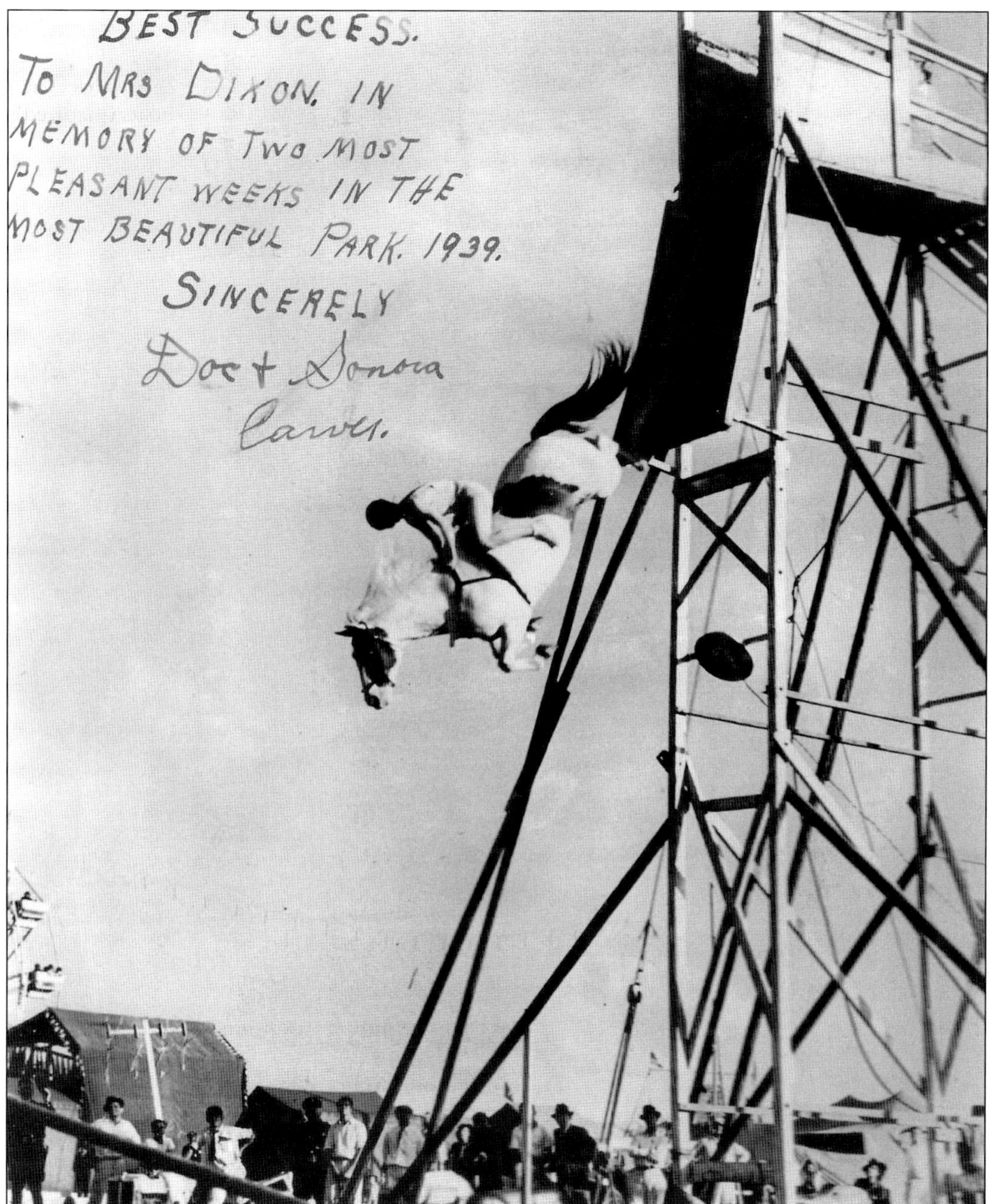

Sonora Carver and her world-famous diving horse performed for eight days in 1939. Carver, who was blind, and her horse Red Lips dove from a 40-foot tower into a pool of water. Senora Carver used no whip, spur, or belt for the five-second drop.

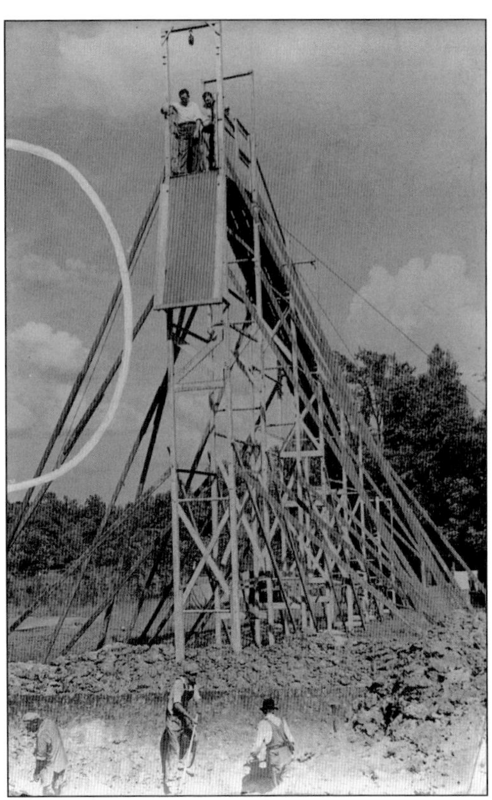

A special 40-foot-tall ramp was built by the workers for the exclusive purpose of Red Lips and Senora Carver's dive. They jumped from where the men are standing at the top of the ramp into a 20-by-30-foot pool, which the men dug.

Red Lips and Senora Carver brought a huge crowd to Lake Winnepesaukah. Guests were astounded not only by the jump, but also by the shallow 11-foot pool they dove into.

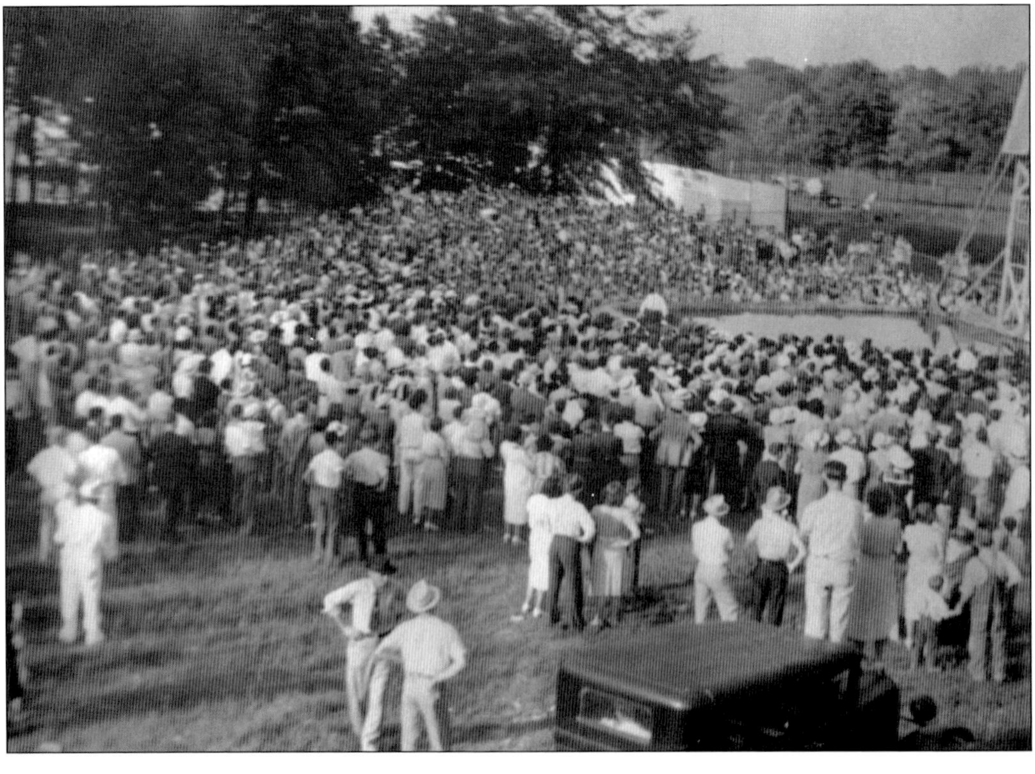

Three

The 1940s

Supporting the War Effort

America was at war. The attack on Pearl Harbor in December 1941 made that real and changed the life and lifestyle of every American for the next four years. Food and gas were rationed. The war effort affected but also united all Americans. Over six million women entered the workforce through campaigns such as "Rosie the Riveter." In 1942, Congress authorized women to serve in the Navy, and the Women's Army Corps (WAC) and Women Accepted for Volunteer Emergency Service (WAVES) were established. Locally, the average yearly salary in Chattanooga was $1,300.

Minette Dixon continued her efforts to promote Lake Winnepesaukah and bring fun to families during a stressful time. In 1941, a Ferris wheel was added. The following year, a penny arcade, shooting gallery, bowling alleys, and an Auto Scooter were added. An amphitheater was built in a shady grove, and it became the site of many productions from plays to concerts. A dining hall was added, and records of the day state it would "dispense every delicacy from hot dogs to chicken a la king." Notes from the year state that picnic season business was down due to "the threat of dreaded infantile paralysis," which caused many picnics to be canceled. The 1942 season brought the addition of a chair swing, the Tilt-a-Whirl, and a kiddie car ride. The casino building that housed the skating rink burned but was replaced the following year with a portable skating rink.

Minette Dixon, like other business owners, navigated the business while dealing with the rationing of products, such as sugar and gas. She ensured the park contributed to the war effort: recruiting movies were shown at the park by the Army, Navy, and Coast Guard. The patriotism of citizens was also evident in the park not only through the broadcasting of President Roosevelt's fireside chats, but also through Sunday afternoon events. Members of the community gathered every Sunday afternoon to "raise their voices in a general singing of patriotic numbers and folk songs," urging people to be conservative with gasoline and ride a bus to the park, which was provided free of charge. The WACS, who were stationed in nearby Fort Oglethorpe, often marched to the park, where they were admitted for free, singing patriotic songs as they marched. The park hosted a war show, with all the receipts going to the Army-Navy relief fund. In 1946, all veterans were allowed to swim and ride for free.

The years following the war brought the addition of Fly-O-Planes and a merry-go-round and continued acts such as balloon ascensions and water sports. Minette Dixon was a speaker at the IAAP (International Association of Amusement Parks) convention.

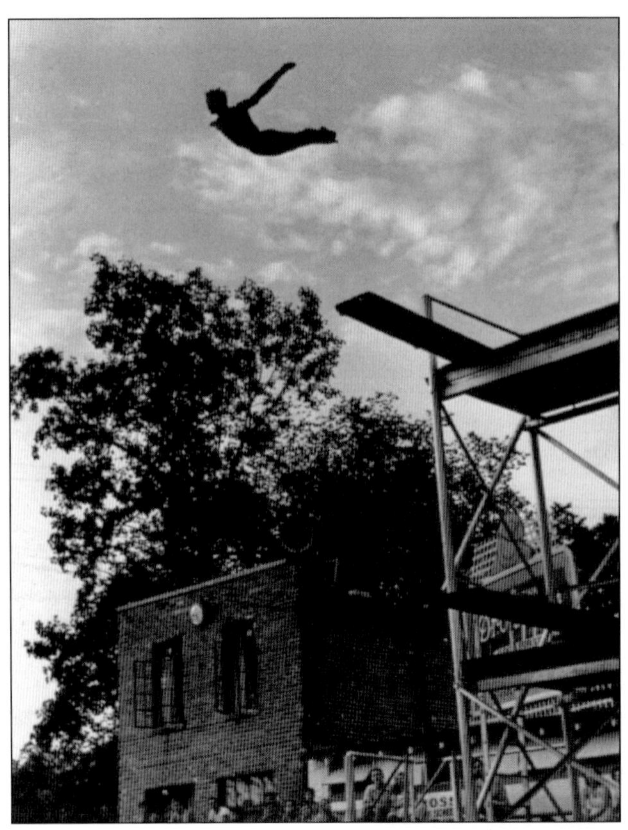

Synchronized diving shows were one of the many shows presented in the pool. Others included slack-wire artists over the pool, trapeze acts, performing bird acts, and a two-year-old swimming and diving exhibition. Most noted of 1940 was Harry Frosboess, "the Swaying Marvel," who performed at the top of a 75-foot flagpole.

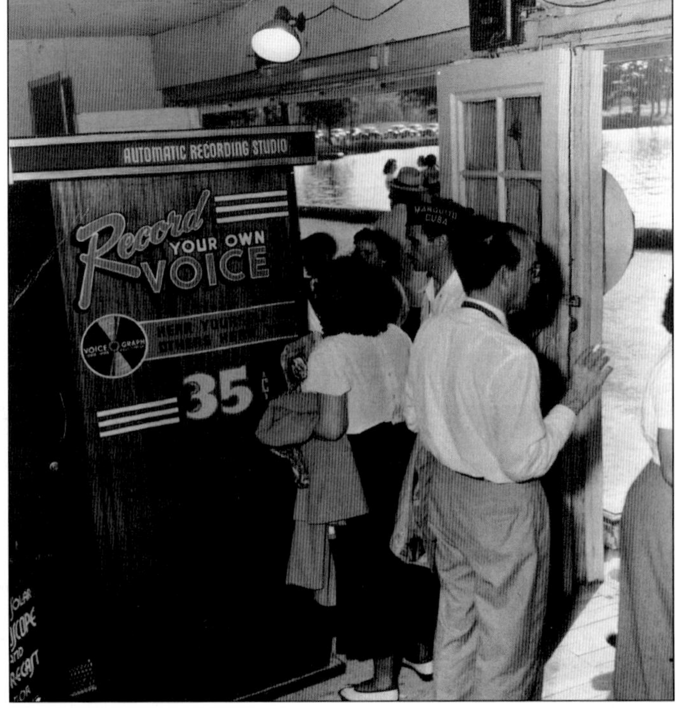

The year 1941 brought the addition of a shooting gallery, a penny arcade, and a restaurant. The arcade featured this voice machine that played back voices—a marvel of the day. The archery range and badminton and handball courts were all reconditioned this year for guests' enjoyment. Different plays were presented free of charge weekly by the Pa Peruchi Players in a new amphitheater adjacent to the lake.

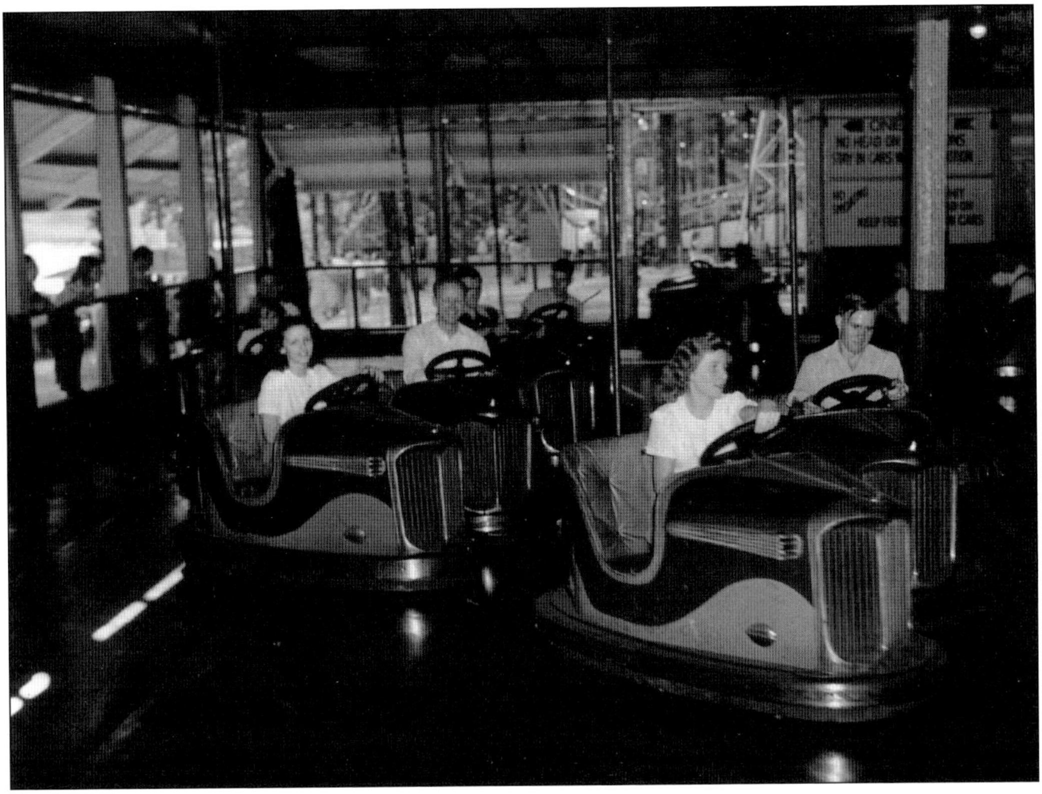

Another new addition to the 1941 season was the new $8,000 Auto Skooter, manufactured by the Lusse Company of Philadelphia. This was a forerunner of the bumper cars. The year featured "Boys Week," which was a weeklong promotion giving all boys one-half off every attraction, or 5¢ for every attraction.

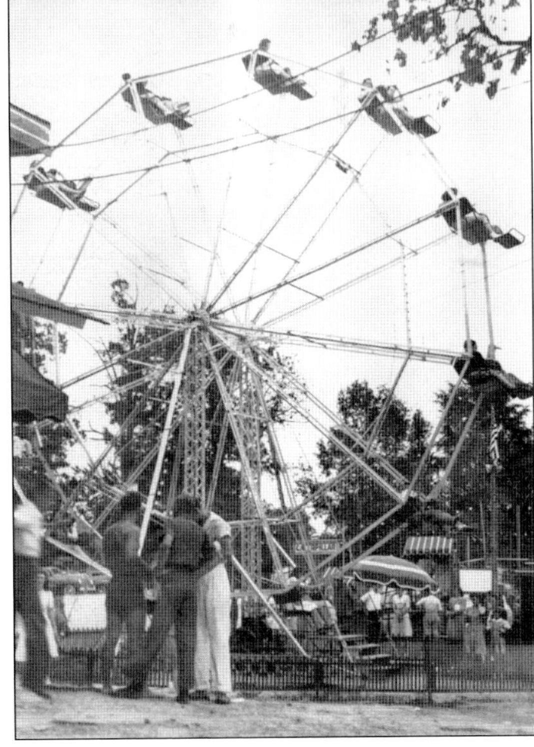

In 1892, George W. Ferris approached management of the World's Columbian Exposition in Chicago with a "crazy idea" for building a gigantic amusement wheel over 200 feet high to rival the Eiffel Tower. The popularity of the Ferris wheel saved the 1893 exposition from financial disaster. William E. Sullivan was inspired by the wheel and created a more practical version of the ride in 1900. Sullivan's Eli Bridge Company is still making the wondrous wheels under the management of his great-granddaughter Patty Sullivan. This Ferris wheel arrived at Lake Winnepesaukah in 1941, following the tremendous popularity of the Kiddie Wheel, which debuted in 1936.

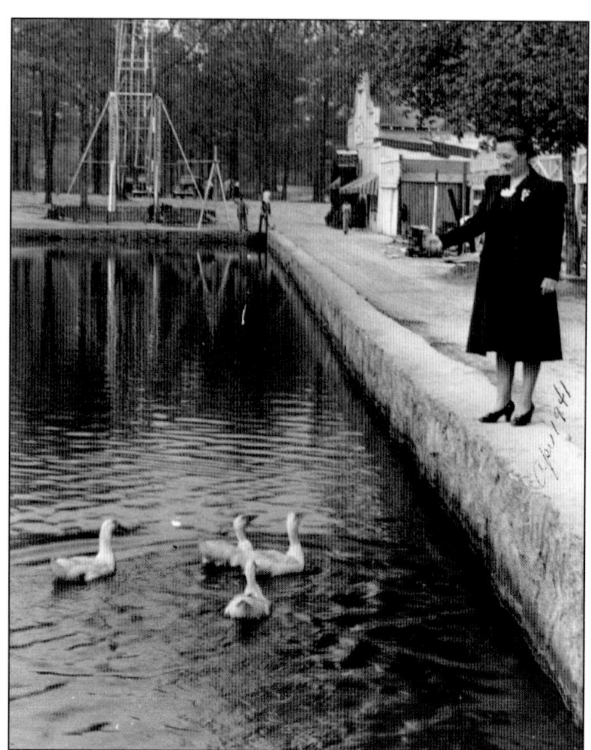

Owner Minette Dixon feeds the ducks who swim on the banks of the lake. The Ferris wheel and the casino are also shown in this picture from 1941. A year later in September 1942, the casino burned to the ground and damage was done to the Ferris wheel and nearby concessions.

The Swing Ride, seen here, was added in 1942. The placement near the lake made it all the more appealing as the chairs whizzed up in the air. The season opened with a high trapeze act, "the Skylarks," and a lion act.

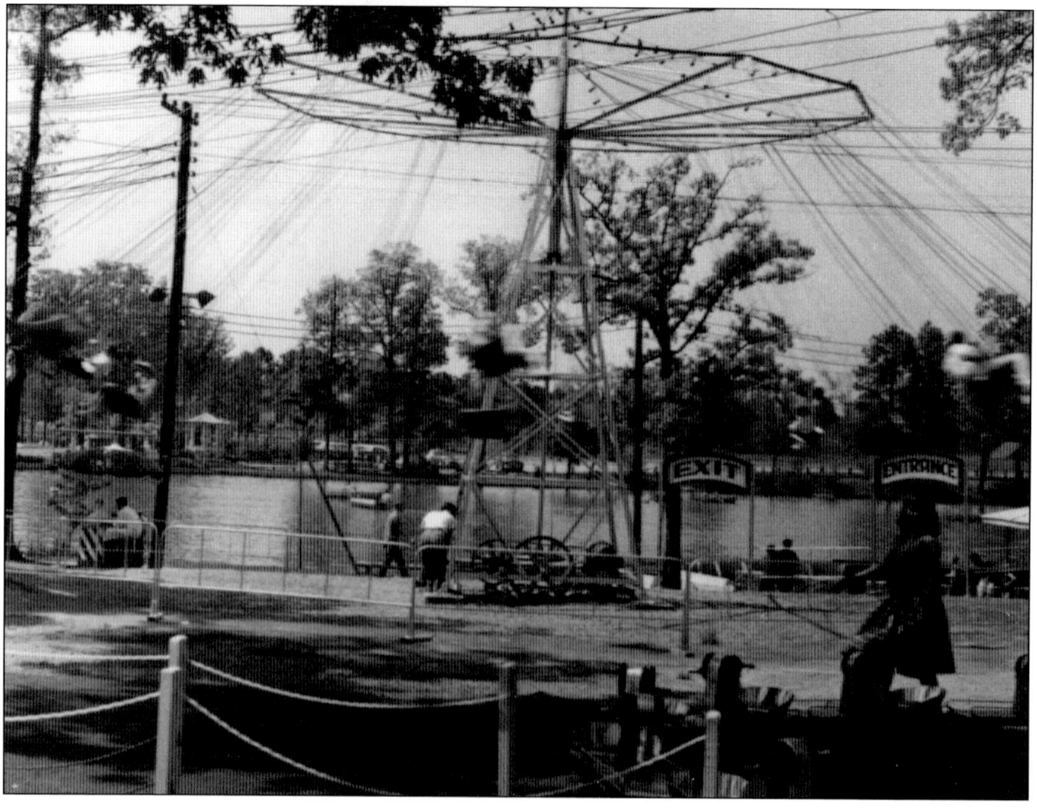

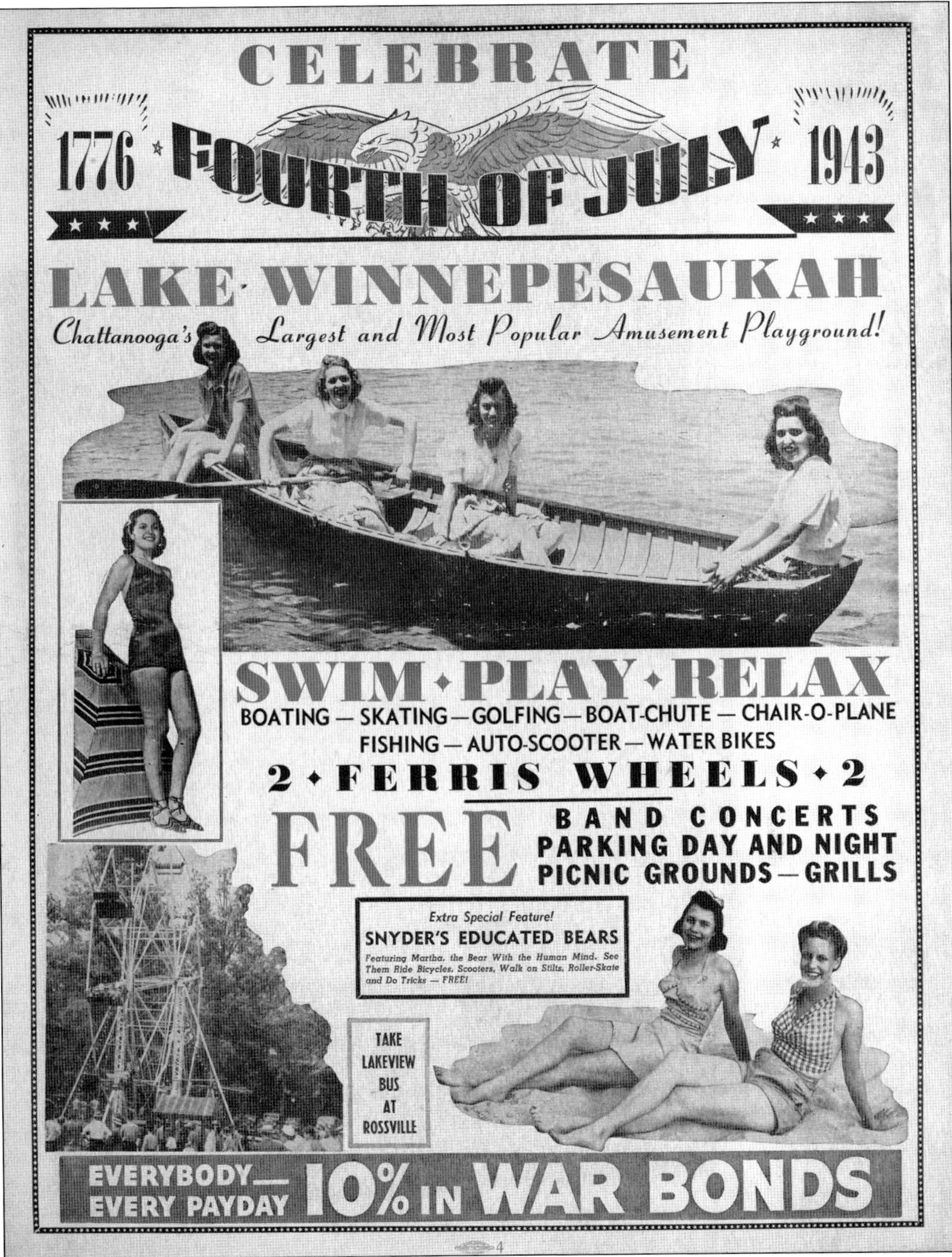

The 1943 poster seen here promotes the Fourth of July at Lake Winnepesaukah. There were two Ferris wheels—one for adults and one for children. The park offered free bus service to the park as gas was rationed. The "Educated Bears" was a trapeze act that was performed frequently. In addition, there was a "Stratosphere Man" aerialist act. Lake Winnepesaukah put on a 99¢ war show, with all receipts going to the Army-Navy relief fund.

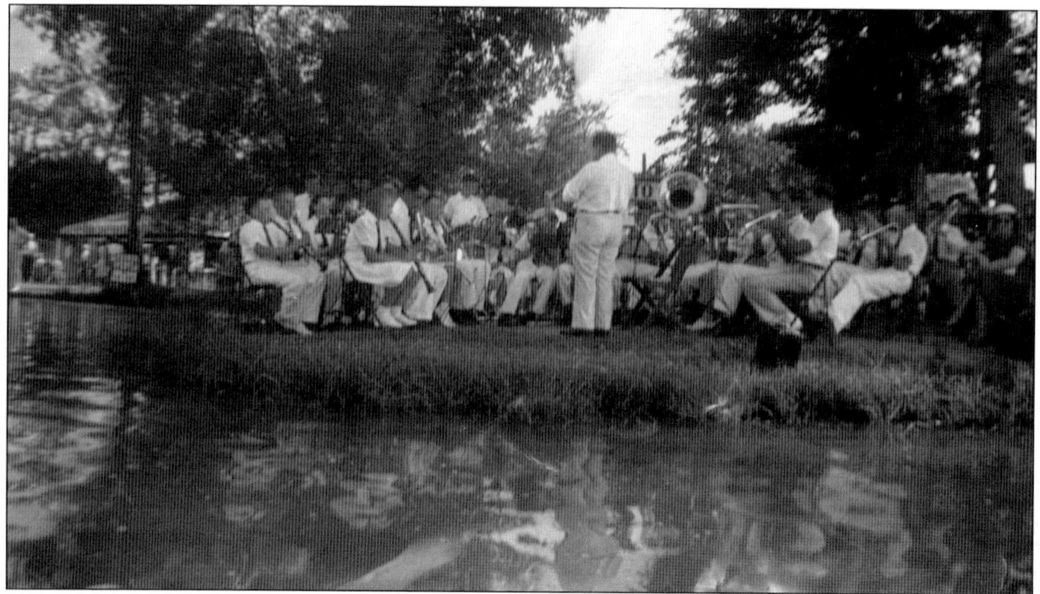

The Lakeview High School Band played on Saturday, May 28, 1943, under the direction of Sgt. Luther Jones, who was formerly the leader of General Patton's Army band. Two anti-tank guns were on display with men to demonstrate them. Recruiting movies for the Army, Navy, and Coast Guard were shown.

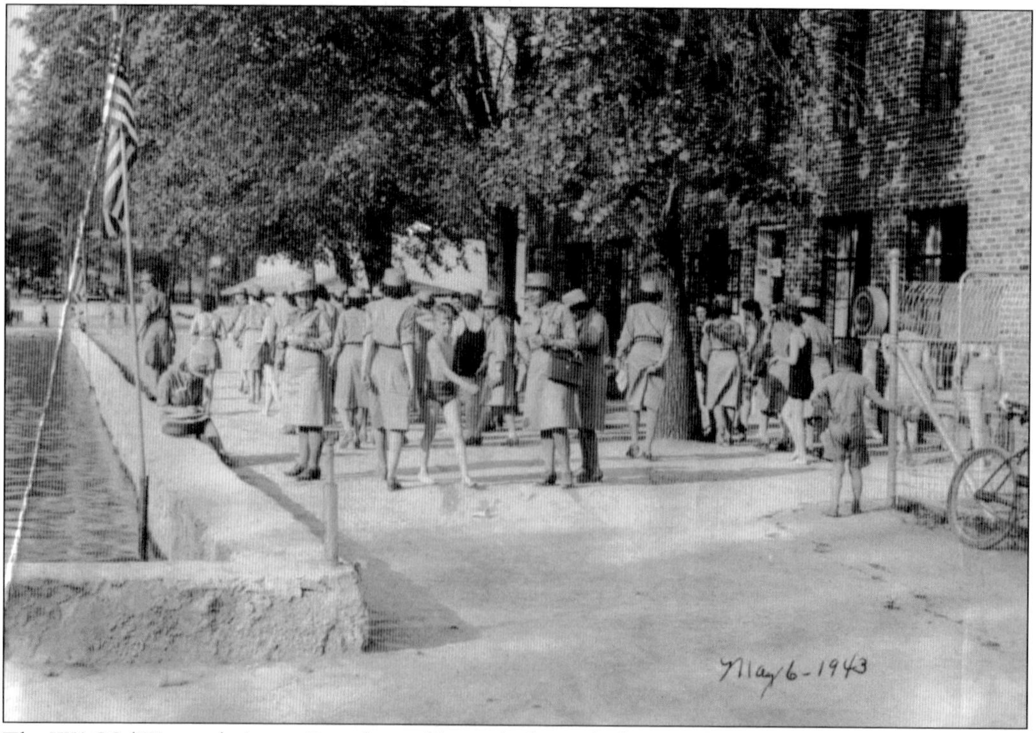

The WACS (Women's Army Corps) would march through the woods from nearby Fort Oglethorpe for visits to the park. Guests would hear them marching and singing for quite a distance. Discounts to the park were given to all servicemen and women and later to all veterans.

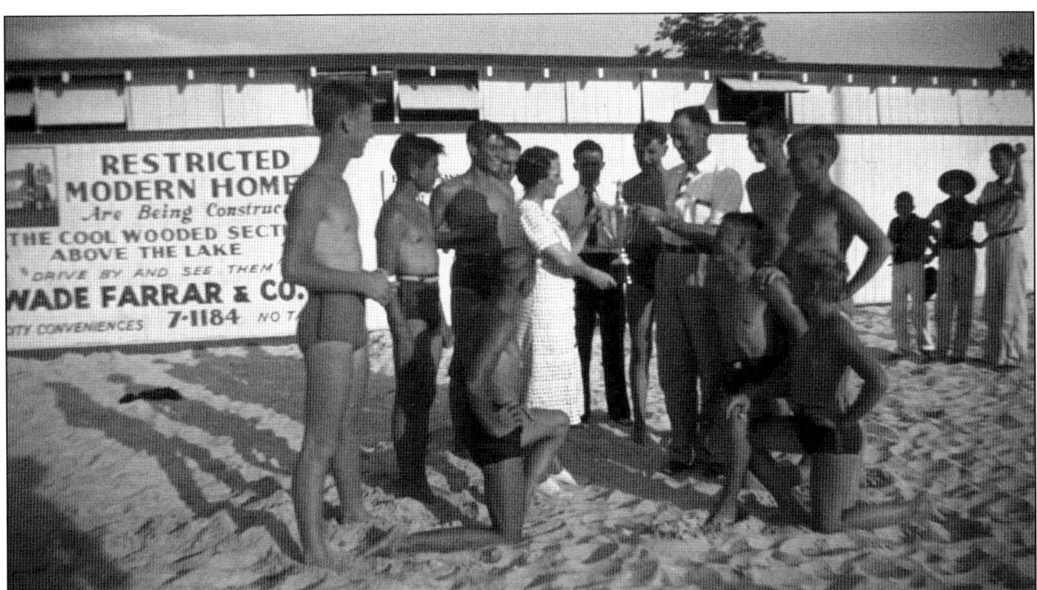

Minette Dixon presented the trophy at the Southeastern Amateur Athletic Union (AAU) swim meet. Lake Winnepesaukah was an active member of the AAU of the United States.

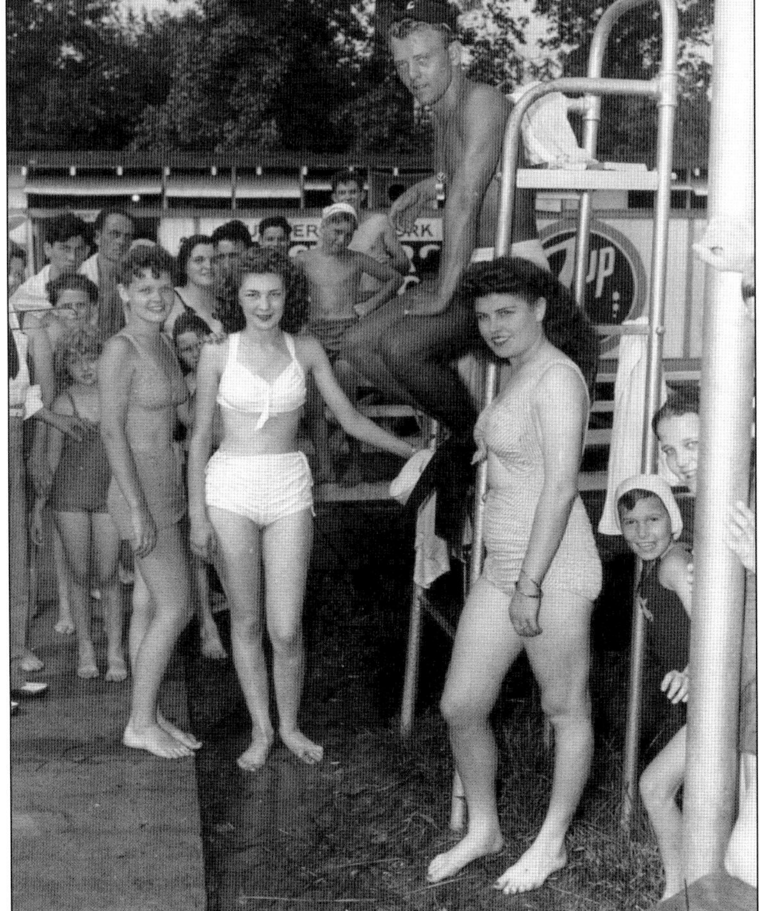

It seems the appeal of a lifeguard is timeless, as this one in 1945 is not lacking attention. Years later, in 1964, Jerry Daniels, a Lake Winnepesaukah lifeguard, was selected as Mr. America.

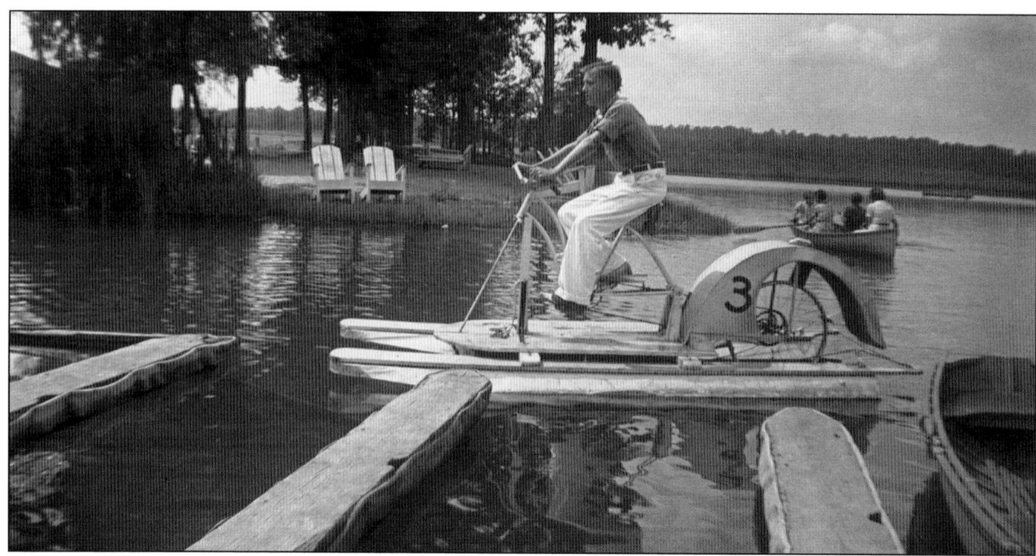

The water bikes were a popular attraction during the 1940s. They added to the fleet of rowboats, motorboats, and canoes available for fun on the water. The 1940s also saw the introduction of plays presented nightly in a new amphitheater located on the grounds.

UNITED STATES OF AMERICA
OFFICE OF PRICE ADMINISTRATION

OUR CEILING PRICES

SANDWICHES

1	CLUB	50¢
2	FRIED HAM AND EGG	35¢
3	BACON AND TOMATO	25¢
4	CHICKEN SALAD	25¢
5	LETTUCE AND TOMATO	20¢
6	PIMENTO CHEESE	20¢
7	HAMBURGER - PLAIN	15¢
8	HAMBURGER - DRESSED UP	20¢
9	BARBECUED PORK	25¢
10	SLICED CHICKEN	35¢
11	HAM - BAKED	25¢
12	AMERICAN CHEESE	20¢
13	JELLY AND PEANUT BUTTER	15¢
14	FRIED EGG	20¢
15	FRANKFURTER - PLAIN	15¢
16	CHEESEBURGER	25¢
17	1000 ISLAND	20¢
18	EGG SALAD	20¢
19	SOUPS - 20¢ - CHILI -	20¢
20	PIE - PER SLICE - 10¢ - A LA MODE	15¢

Name MRS Evelyn Dixon White

Address LAKE WINNEPESAUKAH - MARCH 26-1945

Form OPA 4152-1836

ICE CREAM 10¢ - SHERBET - 10¢

AS FILED WITH THE WAR PRICE AND RATIONING BOARD No. 43-9-1

SALADS Address Ringgold, Ga. - Catoosa County

	TOMATO WITH CHICKEN SALAD	50¢
21	POTATO SALAD	30¢
22	SLICED TOMATOES	30¢
23	COLE SLAW	20¢
24	LETTUCE AND TOMATO	30¢
25	CHICKEN - 45¢ - HEAD LETTUCE	30¢
26	COFFEE - 10¢ - SWEET MILK	07¢
27	ICED TEA - 10¢ - BUTTERMILK	05¢
28	ALL BOTTLE DRINKS	10¢
29	FOUNTAIN DRINKS - IN DINING ROOM	10¢
30	FOUNTAIN DRINKS - AROUND COUNTER -	6¢ AND 11¢
31	TOMATO JUICE 10¢ - ORANGE JUICE	15¢
32	GRAPEFRUIT JUICE	10¢
33	GLASS OF ICE	05¢
34	TWO FRIED EGGS - WITH TOAST AND COFFEE	40¢
35	PLAIN OMELETTE " " " "	50¢
36	BACON AND EGGS " " " "	50¢
37	CHEESE OMELETTE " " " "	60¢
38	HAM OR BACON " " " " "	60¢
39	TWO EGGS POACHED, ON TOAST " "	40¢
40	For Employees Only: MEAT - TWO VEGETABLES - DESSERT	50¢

CHICKEN DINNER - 75¢

Signed by Mrs Evelyn Dixon White (OWNER OR MANAGER)

ERASURES OR CHANGES OF PRICES ON THIS POSTER ARE UNLAWFUL

The 1940s brought rationing for the war effort. A new dining room with table service opened in 1940. This menu from 1943 shows the pricing of the day. At this time, Minette Dixon placed her daughter, Evelyn, in charge of the food department. Evelyn developed the recipes and did the pricing.

This picture shows the new dining room building, called the Luncheonette, and an advertisement read that it would "dispense every delicacy from hot dogs to chicken a la king." The building featured a fireplace and table service. Evelyn's younger daughter Tootsie was a waitress there. While the building has been remodeled numerous times, it is still a fixture at the park today.

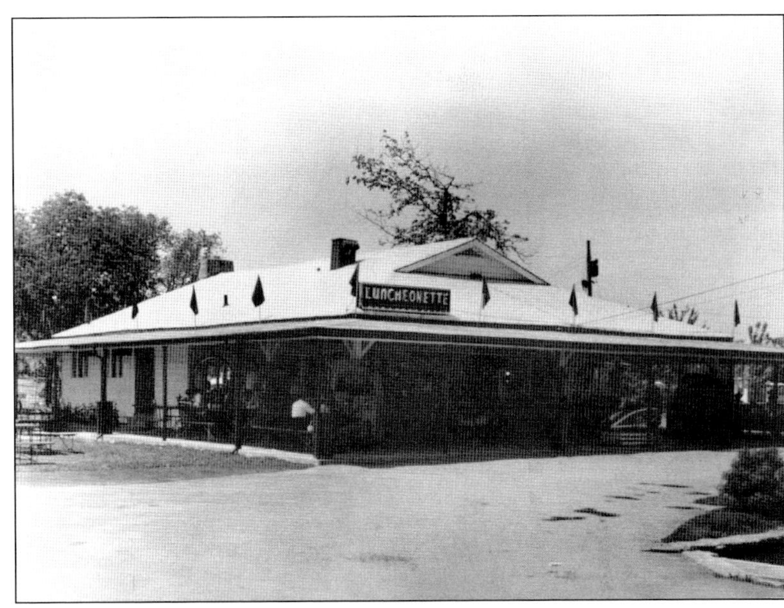

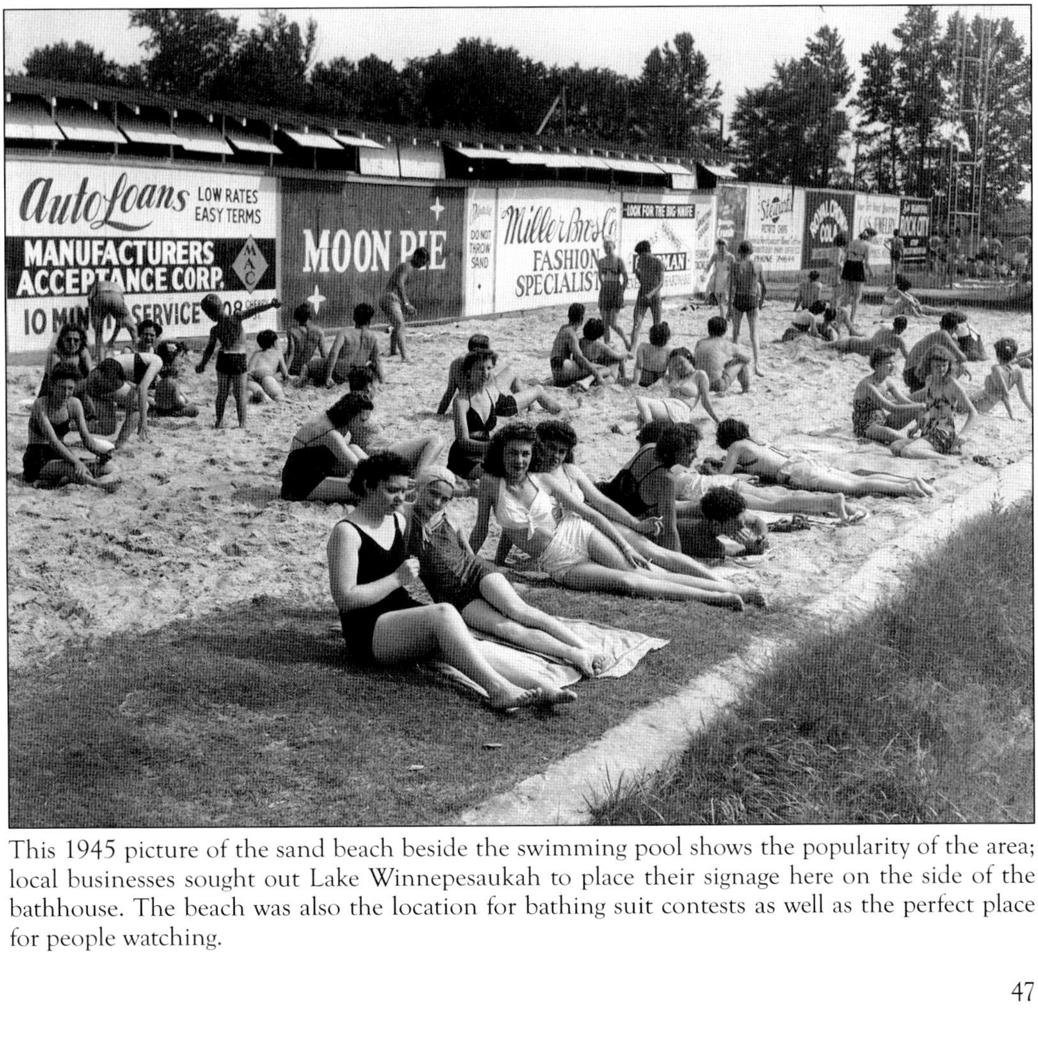

This 1945 picture of the sand beach beside the swimming pool shows the popularity of the area; local businesses sought out Lake Winnepesaukah to place their signage here on the side of the bathhouse. The beach was also the location for bathing suit contests as well as the perfect place for people watching.

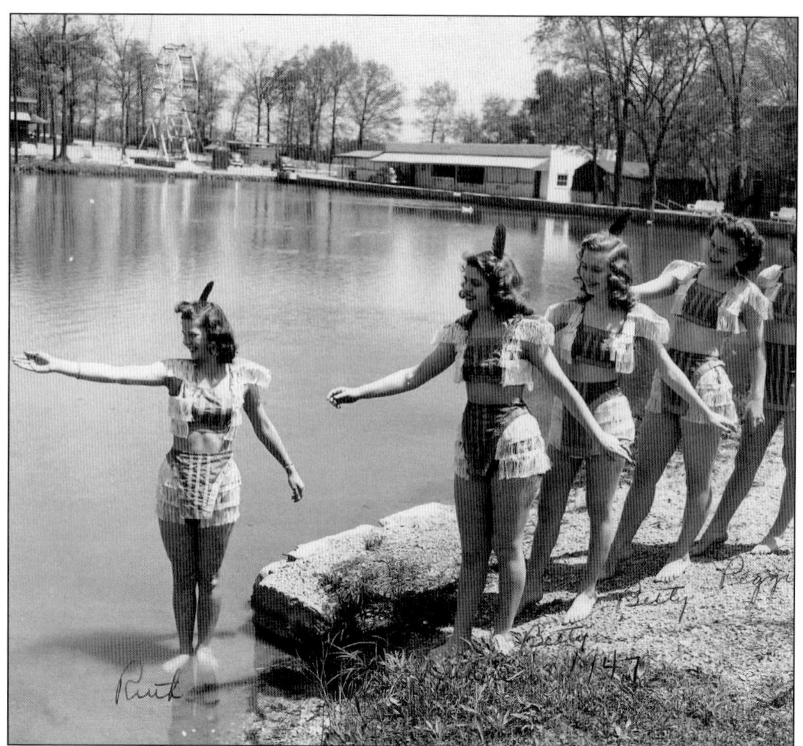

Local as well as traveling dance groups performed at Lake Winnepesaukah. This is a local group that performed an Indian princess dance on the shores of the lake for guests in 1947.

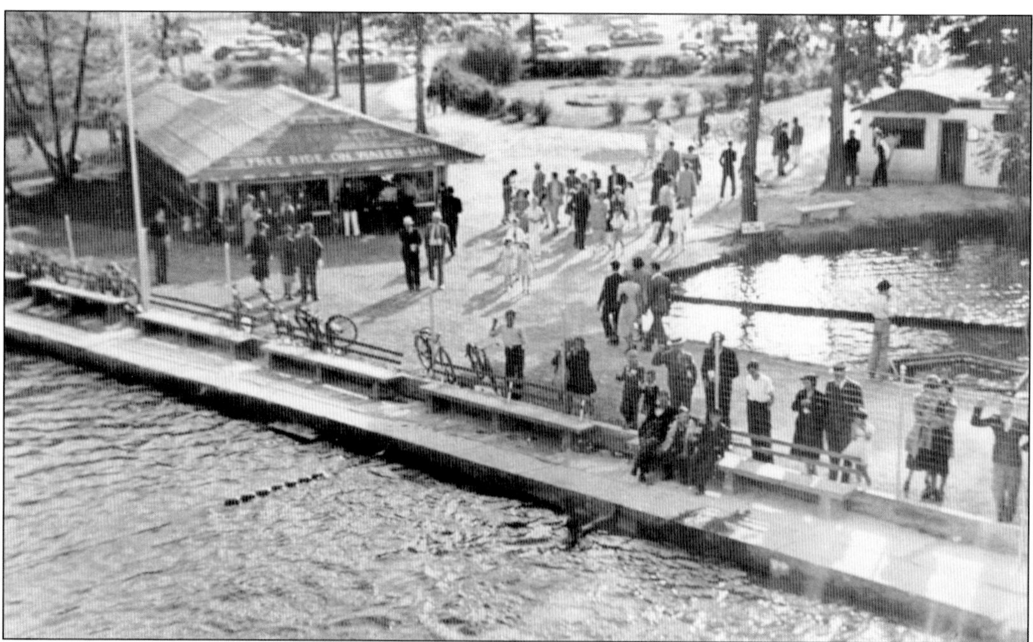

The pool is ready for a swim meet with the lane ropes in place. The lake features boating and water bikes, which customers could use free of charge. Of interest is the proximity of parking in what later became the south side of the park. The next addition in this area was the Luncheonette, where the water bikes building is pictured.

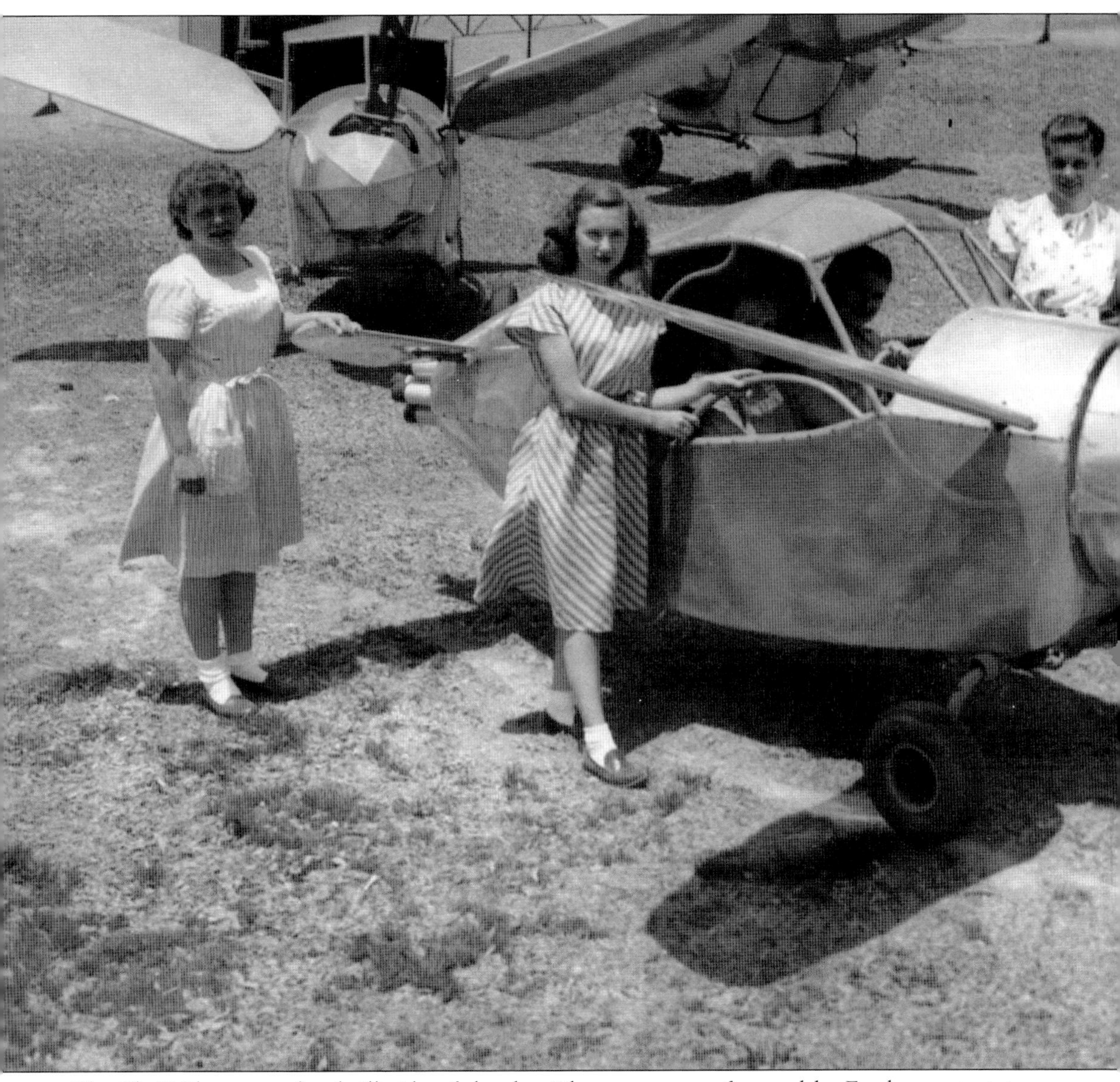

The Fly-O-Plane was the thrill ride of the day. They were manufactured by Eyerly as a training simulator for pilots for the war. Each individual plane was controlled by a passenger pilot and could be turned over if desired. Eight planes carried two passengers each and circled safely at a circumference of 100 feet. Pictured is Adrienne Dixon White (center), granddaughter of Minette Dixon.

NON-TRANSFERABLE — RATION CHECK —
THE UNITED STATES OF AMERICA
OFFICE OF PRICE ADMINISTRATION

CHECK NO. ______ DATE 7-24 1944

TRANSFER TO THE
SUGAR
RATION BANK ACCOUNT OF Economy Wholesale Co. (NAME OF SELLER)
One Hundred & Twenty pounds (AMOUNT IN WORDS)

AMOUNT IN FIGURES 120 POUNDS OF SUGAR

PIONEER BANK
FR-6 CHATTANOOGA, TENN. 87-728

Mrs. Charles White (PRINT OR TYPE NAME OF YOUR ACCOUNT)
Mrs. Charles White (AUTHORIZED SIGNATURE)

Lake Winnepesaukah, like other businesses, was issued a certain number of food commodities as food was rationed during the war. These are checks used by Minette Dixon to purchase food for sale during the war years.

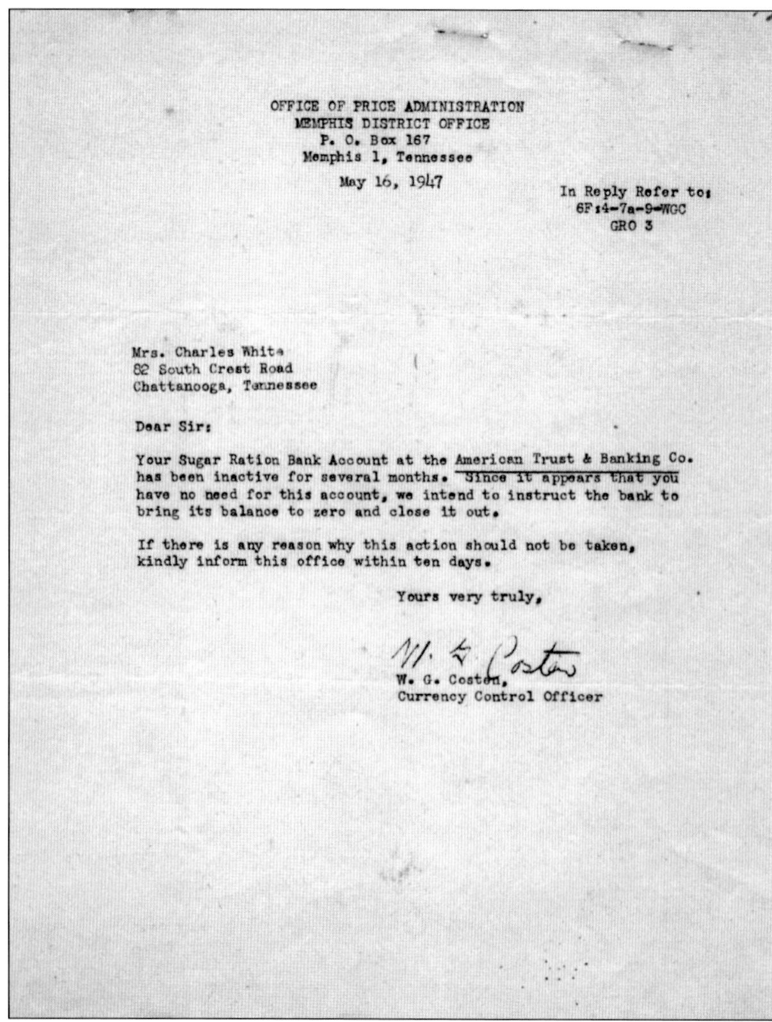

OFFICE OF PRICE ADMINISTRATION
MEMPHIS DISTRICT OFFICE
P. O. Box 167
Memphis 1, Tennessee

May 16, 1947

In Reply Refer to:
6F:4-7a-9-WGC
GRO 3

Mrs. Charles White
82 South Crest Road
Chattanooga, Tennessee

Dear Sir:

Your Sugar Ration Bank Account at the American Trust & Banking Co. has been inactive for several months. Since it appears that you have no need for this account, we intend to instruct the bank to bring its balance to zero and close it out.

If there is any reason why this action should not be taken, kindly inform this office within ten days.

Yours very truly,

W. G. Coston
W. G. Coston,
Currency Control Officer

In May 1947, Evelyn Dixon White received a letter informing her since she had not used her allowance of sugar rationed year-round, she would no longer be able to receive sugar. In essence, she was being cut off from buying sugar, which is a staple in the amusement industry.

LAKE WINNEPESAUKAH

Chattanooga's Finest Outdoor Amusement Park

Luncheon Service

MRS. CHARLES WHITE, Owner

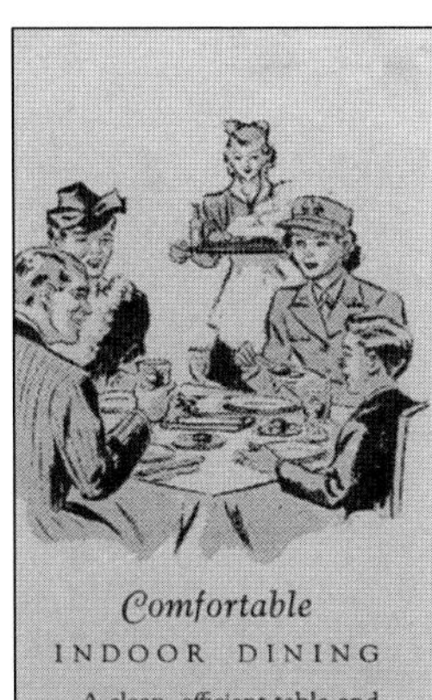

Comfortable

INDOOR DINING

A clean, efficient table and counter luncheon service, providing only the finest foods and beverages. Situated in the heart of the Winnepesaukah playground area. . . . . .

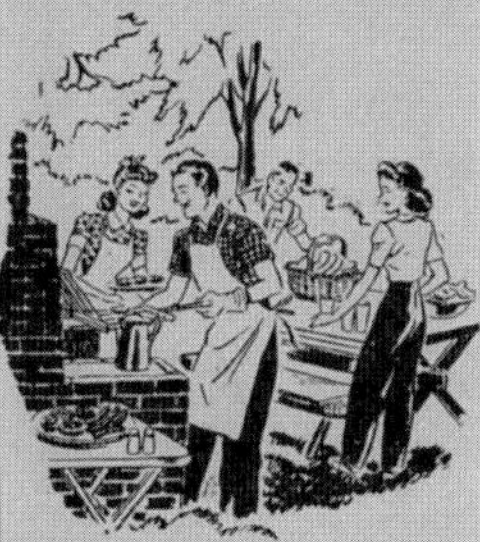

Outdoor

LUNCHEON SERVICE

A supplemental outdoor luncheon and beverage service designed to provide those essentials in your picnic menu which require constant refrigeration and adequate cooking equipment. We will, if desired, prepare your entire picnic luncheon on 24-hour notice. . . . .

Phone 2-6316

CHATTANOOGA, TENNESSEE
Post Office Address:
RT. 2, ROSSVILLE, GEORGIA

May 20, 1947

W. G. Costen
Office of Price Administration
Memphis District Office
P. O. Box 167
Memphis, Tennessee

6F: 4-7a-8-WGC
Gro 3

Dear Mr. Costen:

In reply to your letter of May 16th, I would like to explain that our business is seasonal since we operate the dining room and refreshment concessions in an amusement park. The account was inactive during the winter but we used the sugar ration account at the American Trust & Banking Company both in April and May of this year.

Please do not close out our sugar account at the bank as we definitely can not operate without sugar.

Hoping that this explains why the account was inactive for a few months, I am

Yours very truly,

Mrs. Charles White

Evelyn Dixon White immediately appealed and explained that Lake Winnepesaukah is a seasonal business and that is why the account was not used year-round. She pleads for the allotment to be reinstated, saying, "We definitely can not operate without sugar." This was an anxious time, as the park had just opened for the season. Her appeal was granted.

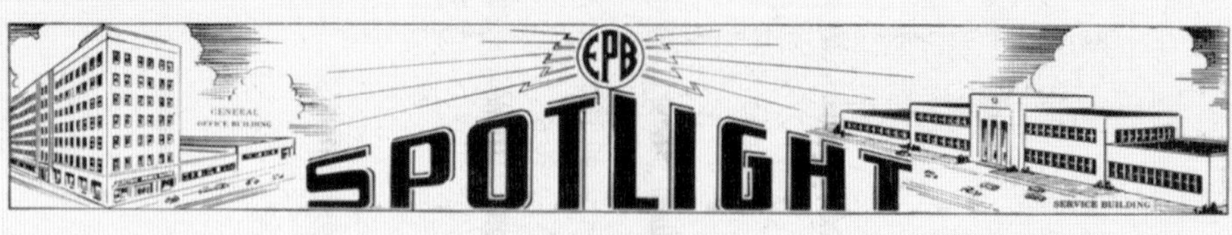

Vol. VII CHATTANOOGA, TENNESSEE, August, 1947 Number 10

Winnepesaukah, Wednesday! . . .

ANNUAL EMPLOYEE--FAMILY PICNIC

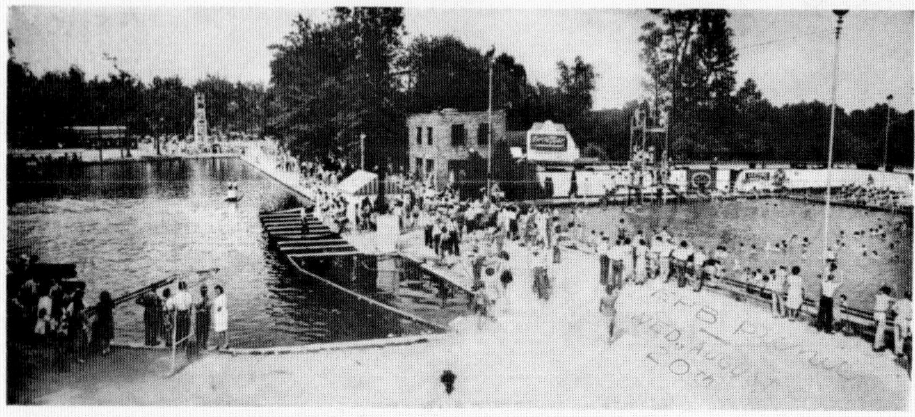

LAKE WINNEPESAUKAH—Be there for sports, thrills, prizes and plenty of good barbecue Wednesday afternoon.

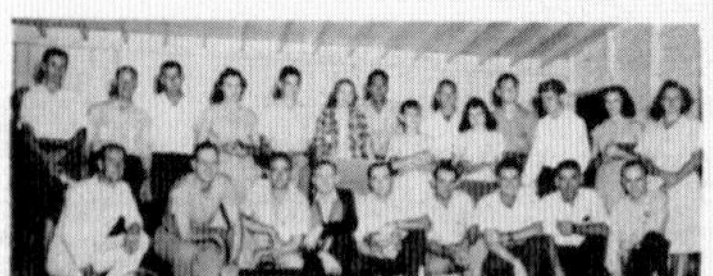

DEFENDING CHAMPIONS—1946 Champions in the various activities who will be out to take home again the big five-pound boxes of chocolates, badminton rackets, horseshoes, fountain pens, dart boards and more boxes of chocolates Wednesday afternoon. If you want to try for prizes even though you didn't check your "questionnaire," see the director of the activity you want to enter and get in there.

Clown Act, Water Pageant, Even Men From Mars Scheduled For Picnic Feature

"Chefs" Renan and Davis Promise Tasty Barbecue to Follow Full Afternoon of Badminton, Golf, Arch- Horseshoes, Boat Races and Many Other Activities

Even a "flying disc" has been contacted and weird little men from Mars will entertain the kiddies, no stone was left unturned by the committee to make the annual Employee-Family picnic scheduled Wednesday afternoon, August 20, even bigger and better than last year's successful outing.

Approximately 1,200 employees and members of their immediate families, single employees and their dates, are expected to enjoy an afternoon of fast-paced activities, dunk in the pool, ride, boat, win prizes and climax the afternoon with heaping plates of tender brown barbecued beef and all of the trimmings.

Piece de Resistance

Chef Joe Renan has already selected the hundreds of pounds of prime beef preparatory to getting the big barbecue pits in operation shortly after midnight before the big day. Betty Davis and her staff of experts havs laid by the huge supplies necessary as "fixins."

The heaping plates of last year were voted in again. In addition to plenty of barbecue there will be tomatoes, onions, potato salad, buns, those good hot beans, slaw, barrels of orange juice and scads of ice cream.

The only change the committee saw necessary was the addition of eating lines to eliminate the

(See Page 3, Column 1)

This 1947 Electric Power Board internal newsletter features information about the company picnic that was held at Lake Winnepesaukah for 1,200 people. The menu included beef barbeque, baked beans, potato salad, and coleslaw. Evelyn Dixon White developed all the recipes and oversaw the food preparation and serving.

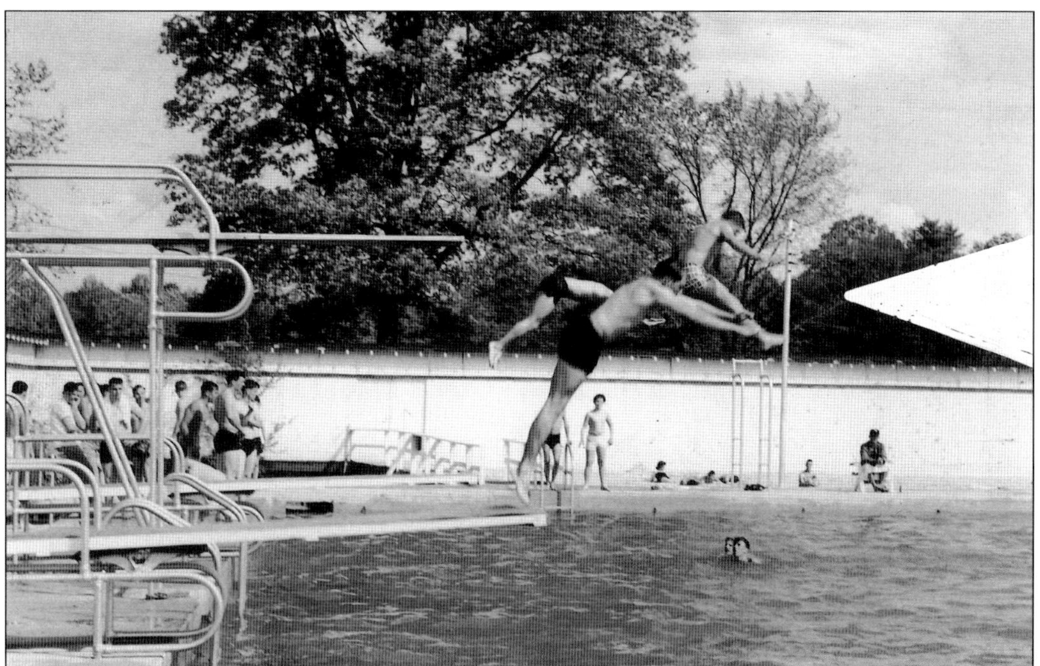

With six diving boards at the pool, Lake Winnepesaukah was highly sought after for diving competitions. The boards were placed at three different heights, thus making a spectacular show for spectators. The second set of three boards was to the right corner of the first set. It is said that the multiple locations and heights sparked the beginning of synchronized diving in the Southeast.

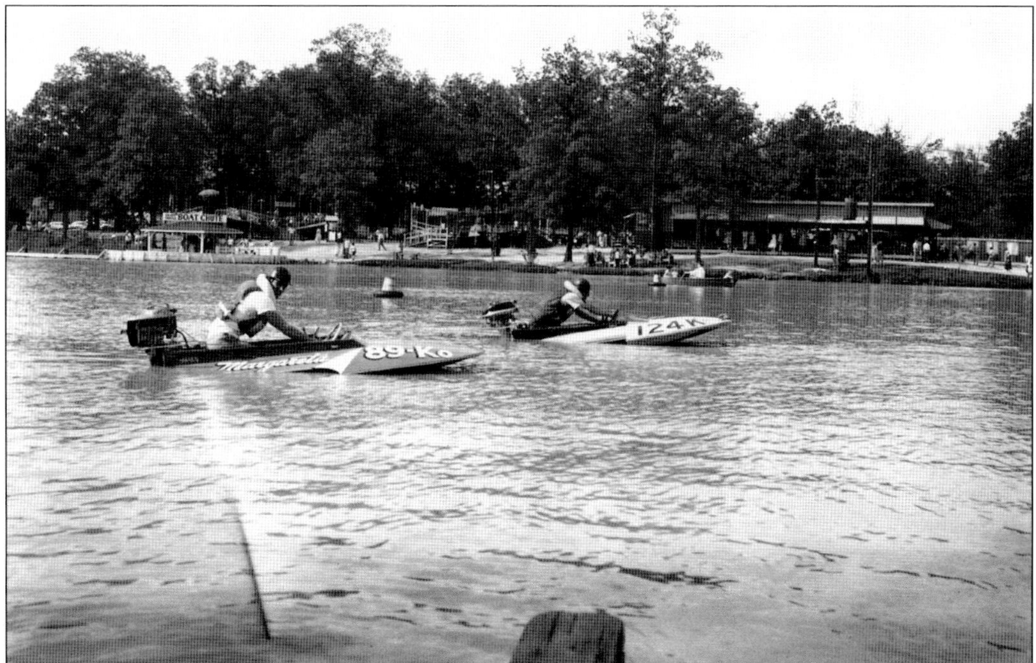

These one-man motorboats raced on the lake in the summer of 1948. Other events that season that brought large crowds included auto races, motorcycle races, a balloon ascension, and an amateur boxing match.

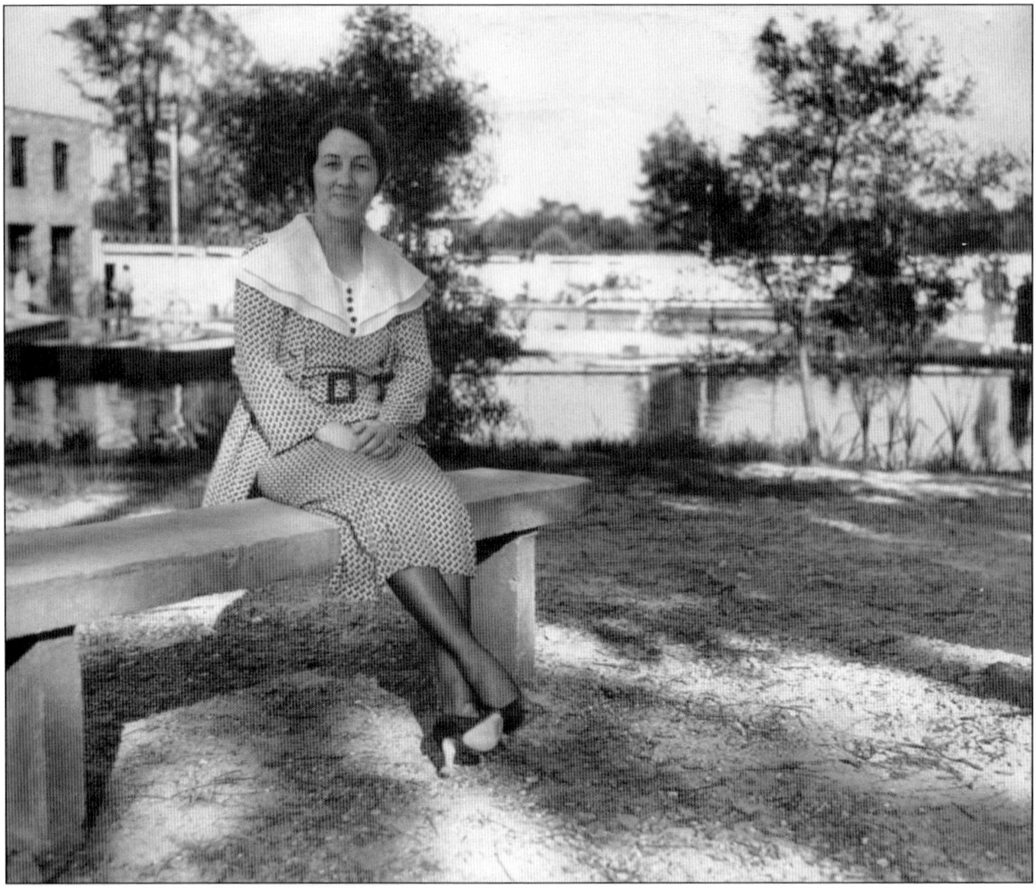

Minette Dixon received many accolades for her business leadership. In 1949, she was named "Woman of the Week" by WDOD radio station and chosen to speak at the International Association of Amusement Parks annual convention in Chicago, Illinois.

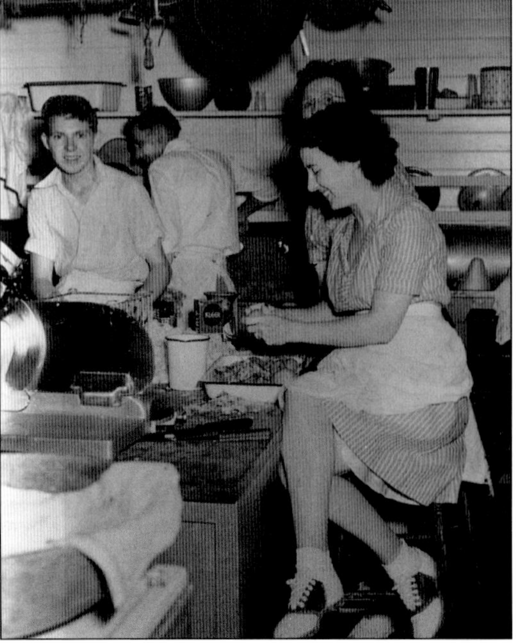

Meanwhile, Evelyn Dixon White remained busy with the food business at the park. She oversaw not only the kitchen purchasing, preparation, and serving for the concession areas, but also the preparation and serving of the tens of thousands of catering guests annually.

Four

The 1950s

The Happy Place to Be

Minette Dixon is now aided by her daughter, Evelyn Dixon White. Evelyn met her husband, Charlie White, at the park when he was a lifeguard in 1933. Evelyn took the lead in developing the recipes used in the catering department and at the food stands. For Evelyn, it was all homemade; she sampled and tasted repeatedly to develop her special recipes for iced tea, lemonade, coleslaw, potato salad, barbeque sauce, and baked beans, all of which were found after her death in her safety deposit box. Charlie, her husband, was a captain in World War II who oversaw large mess halls of soldiers. Hundreds of Army surplus pots and pans were purchased, and she insisted all the barbeque brisket be smoked all night, making serving picnics of thousands of customers a 24-hour job.

Tommy Tomblin, a railroad enthusiast, friend, and business associate, ran the games and retail shop. He convinced Southern Railway to make a smaller model of the *Royal Palm* train, which ran from Chicago down to the east coast of Florida. Tomblin owned and operated Lake Winnepesaukah's "Little Royal Palm," which opened in 1951 and traveled a one-mile track around the park. The following year, a miniature roller coaster, the Little Dipper, was added. In 1953, a long-standing tradition of free country music shows began. Shows were held on a floating stage in the lake. Archie Campbell in his "Grandpappy Show" was the first nationally known entertainer. By 1955, the park had ten major rides, four kiddie rides, a miniature golf course, snack bars, and activities on the lake such as water ski shows, musical groups, parachute jumps, trampoline artists, unicycle acts, and aerialists. A replica of an old-time Mississippi River boat, the *Show Boat*, which traveled the waters of the nine-acre lake, as well as the Scrambler and Kiddie Sky Fighter were all added in 1956.

For the 1958 season, Evelyn White designed the Cake House, a colorful round picnic shelter decorated like a real birthday cake. It was dedicated by children from the Chambliss Center for Children, a long-standing favorite philanthropy of the park. *Our Gang* comedy star Spanky McFarland was a featured entertainer. The year ended on a sad note with the death of Minette Dixon on September 6. Evelyn White was now leading the park with the aid of her daughters, Adrienne and Tootsie.

In 1959, hand cars, a favorite of the area children, were introduced. Also this year, Charlie gave Evelyn a special birthday gift of a new kiddie helicopter ride. The list of performers included the Willis Brothers, Bill Carlisle, and Porter Wagoner, and a new promotion called "Date Night," where a male and female could ride for the price of one after 6:00 p.m., was introduced.

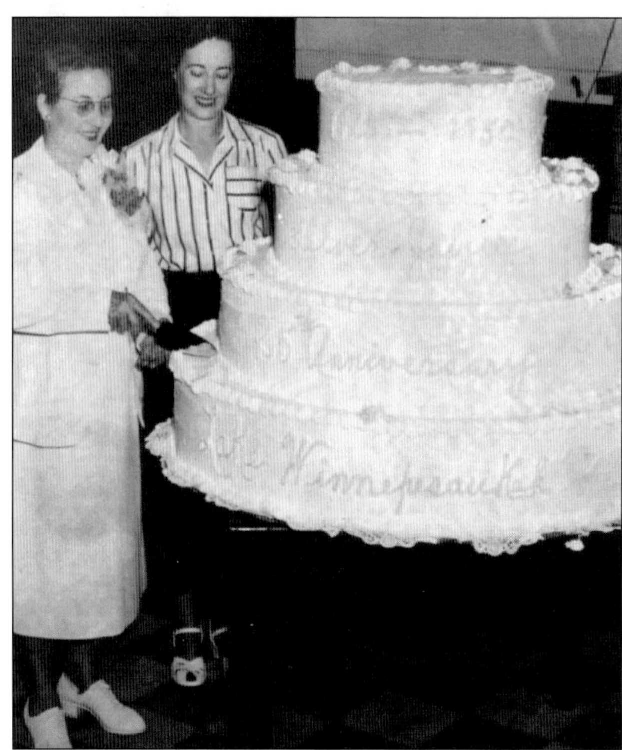

In May 1950, Minette Heiner Dixon (left) and her daughter Evelyn Dixon White (right) celebrated Lake Winnepesaukah's 25th birthday. To celebrate, a huge cake was cut and served to guests. The height of the baby boom years was the 1950s; only 30 percent of enrolled college students were females. Less than five percent of businesses at the time were owned and run by women, as there were significant social and legal barriers preventing this.

In 1950, Evelyn White was officially put in charge of all the catering, food, and drink business. The catering business was increasingly growing, with picnics regularly for over 1,000 people.

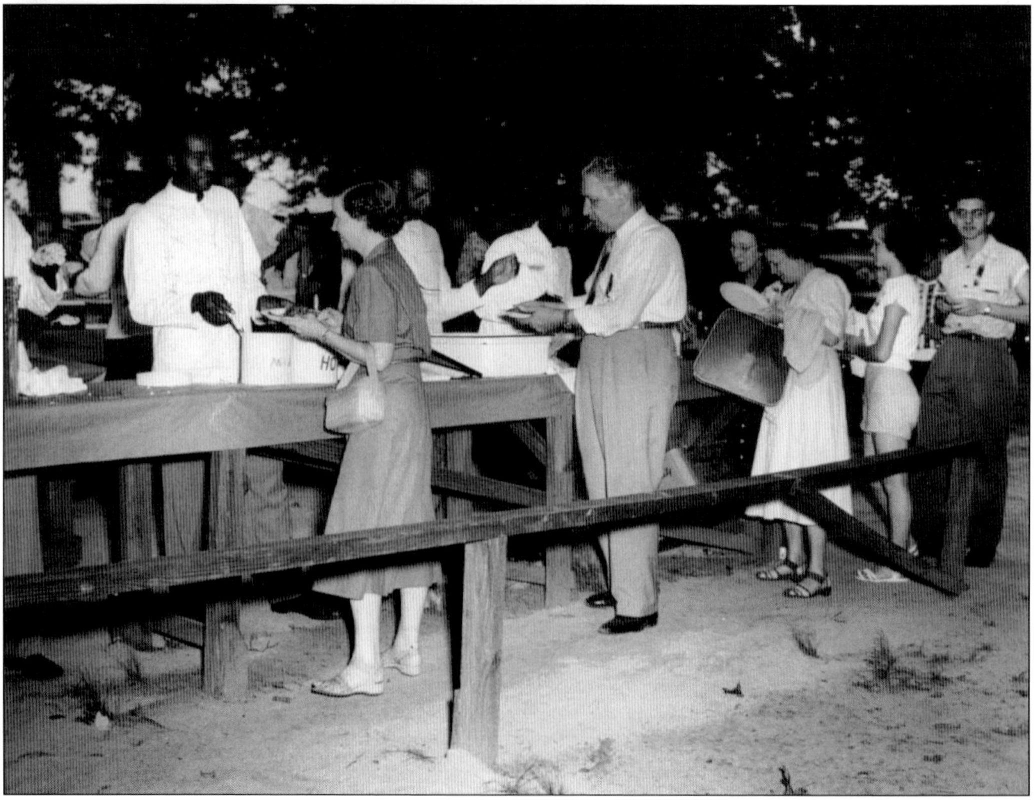

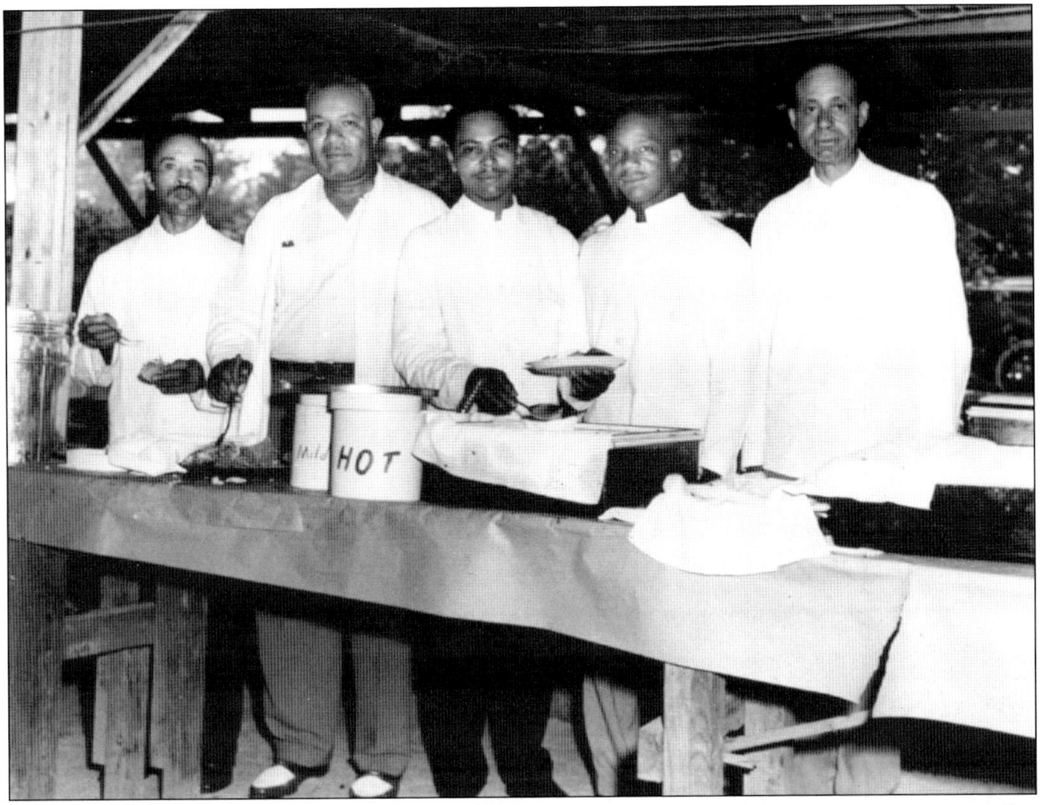

Evelyn White let it be known to area churches that there was an opportunity to raise money by serving picnics at Lake Winnepesaukah. Servers were required to wear white tops and serve the guests whatever they desired. Her homemade lemonade, made with simple syrup and mint, was a particular favorite on a hot summer day.

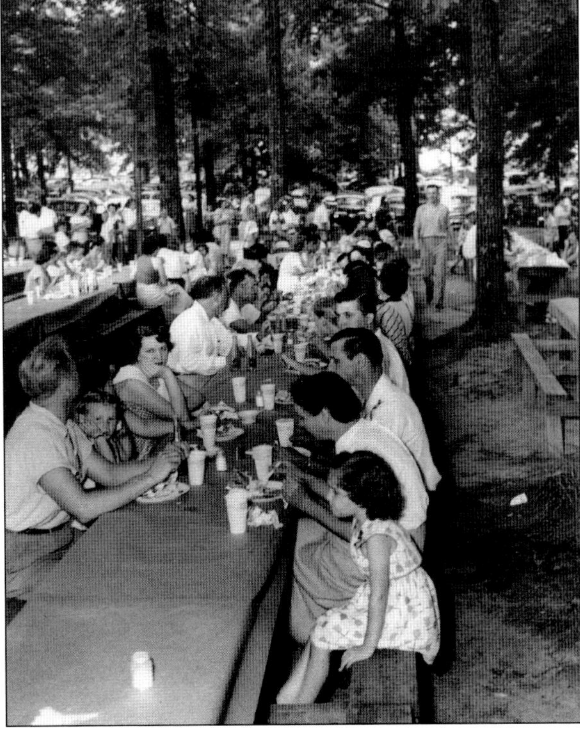

Guests of the company hosting the picnic would line up, often over 100 feet, waiting for Evelyn White's specially curated recipes. Barbeque sauce (in three levels of heat), baked beans, coleslaw, and potato salad were all favorites. She had handwritten recipes for each, with quantities ranging from 25 servings to 1,000 servings.

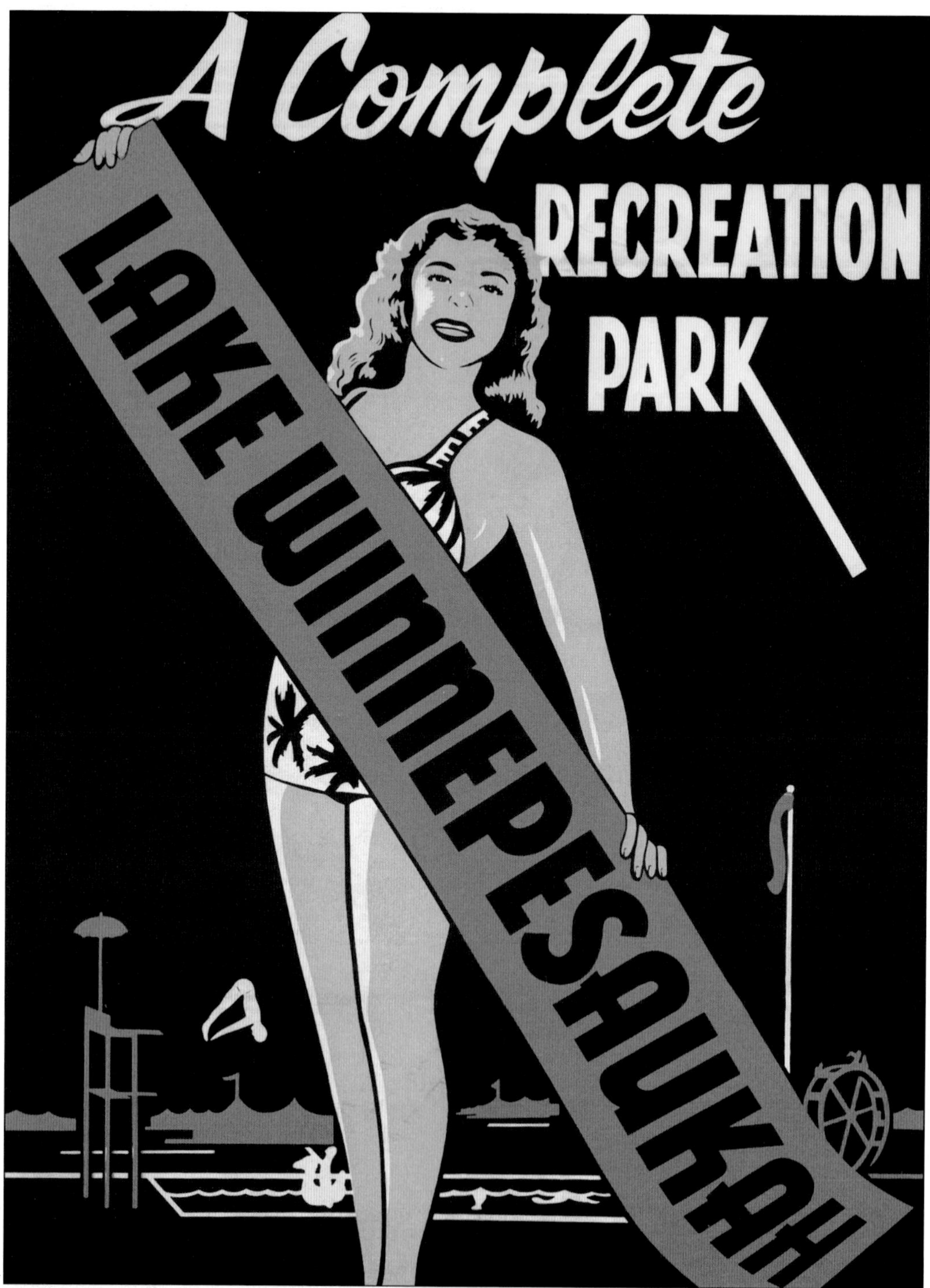

Before shopping malls came into fashion, most people shopped in downtown areas. Chattanooga was the largest city nearby, and many local attractions displayed their advertisements on the garbage cans in downtown Chattanooga. This picture shows an original piece of art that was used to advertise Lake Winnepesaukah in 1950 and 1951.

Minette Dixon drives stakes for the train. A new miniature train ride was added for the 1950 season, and Minette contributed to its build in January 1950. The train was a 1.1-mile ride around the lake.

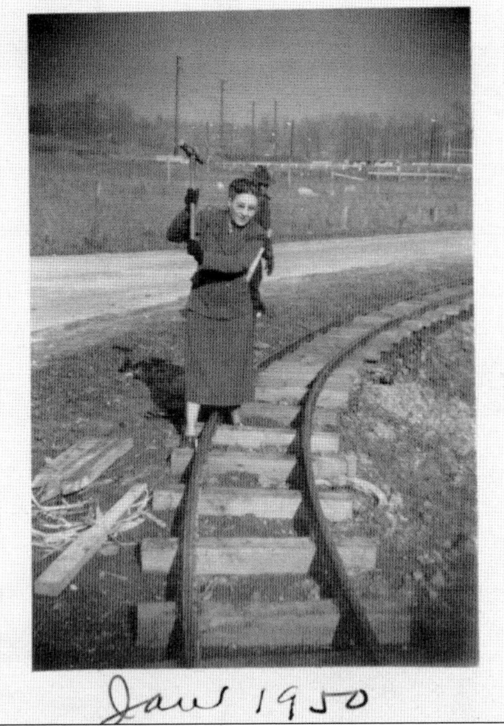

The new train offered seating for 40 people per ride—a large number for the day. It is a miniature diesel-powered train with three passenger cars. The train was made in the Southern Railway shop. The project was led Tommy Tomblin, a park manager.

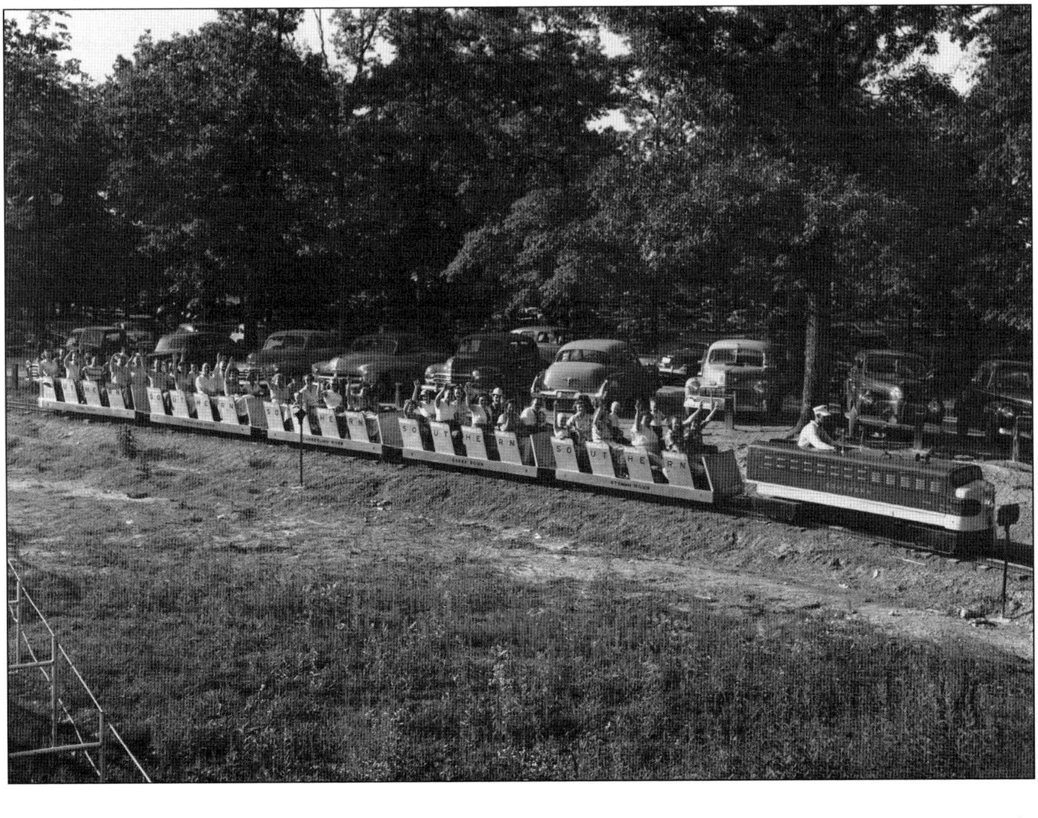

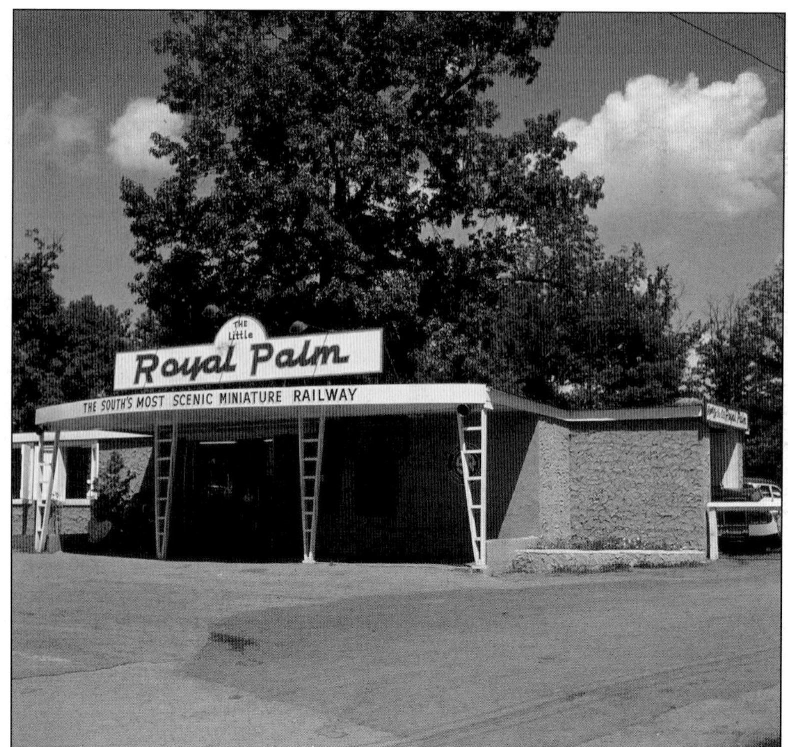

The station was painted in conventional Southern Railway colors. Southern Railway city signs, crossing signals in miniature scale, and a miniature automatic diesel air chime whistle were all made in the Southern Railway shops.

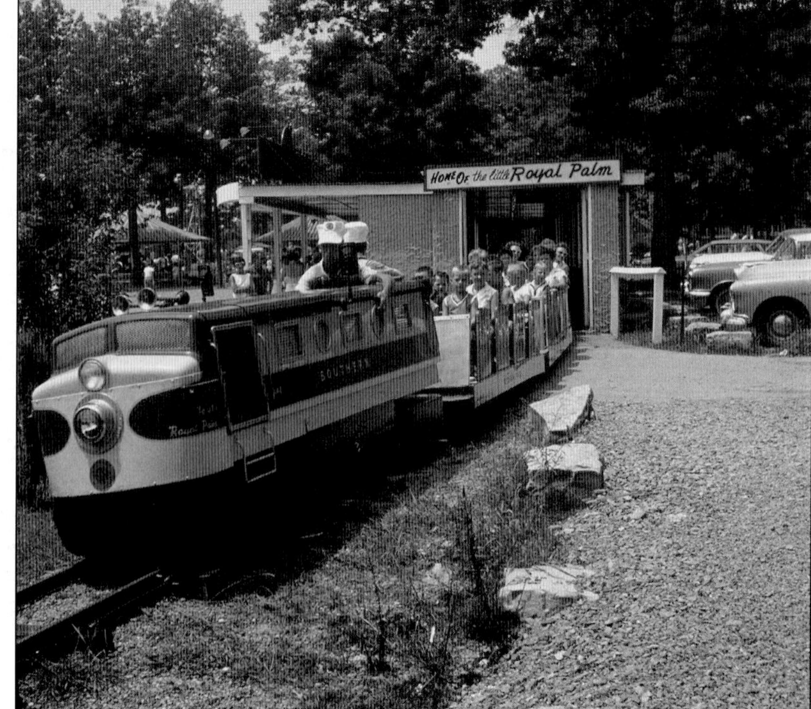

The train boasts a Southern Railway emblem on the nose of the diesel engine. The Southern Railway company painted a "Little Royal Palm" sign that is just like the full-scale and popular *Royal Palm* train of the day.

The public loved the new addition, as evidenced by the consistently long lines. Georgia governor Herman Talmadge sent a congratulatory telegram on its debut.

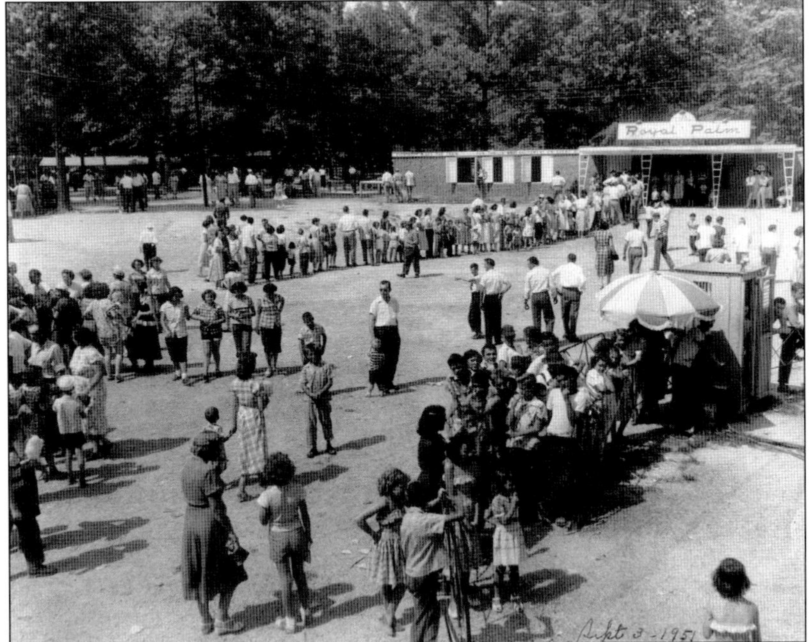

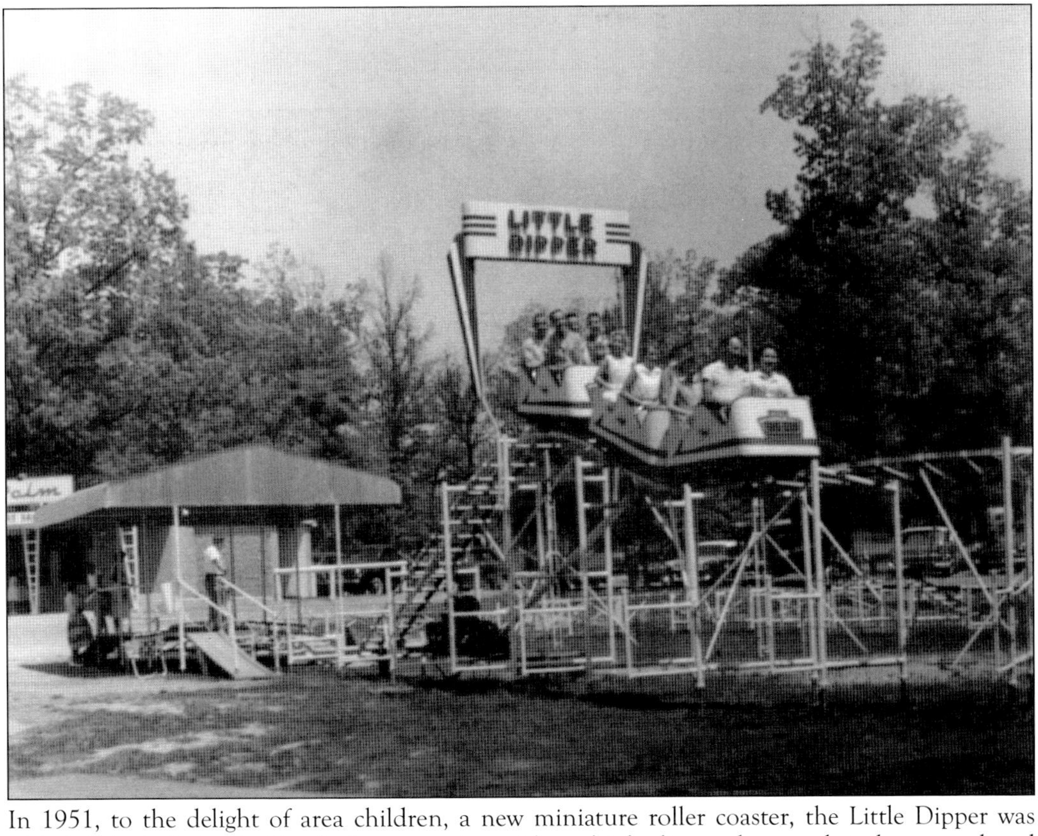

In 1951, to the delight of area children, a new miniature roller coaster, the Little Dipper was added. It had all the thrills of a larger version with multiple dips and turns that always produced smiles and thrills.

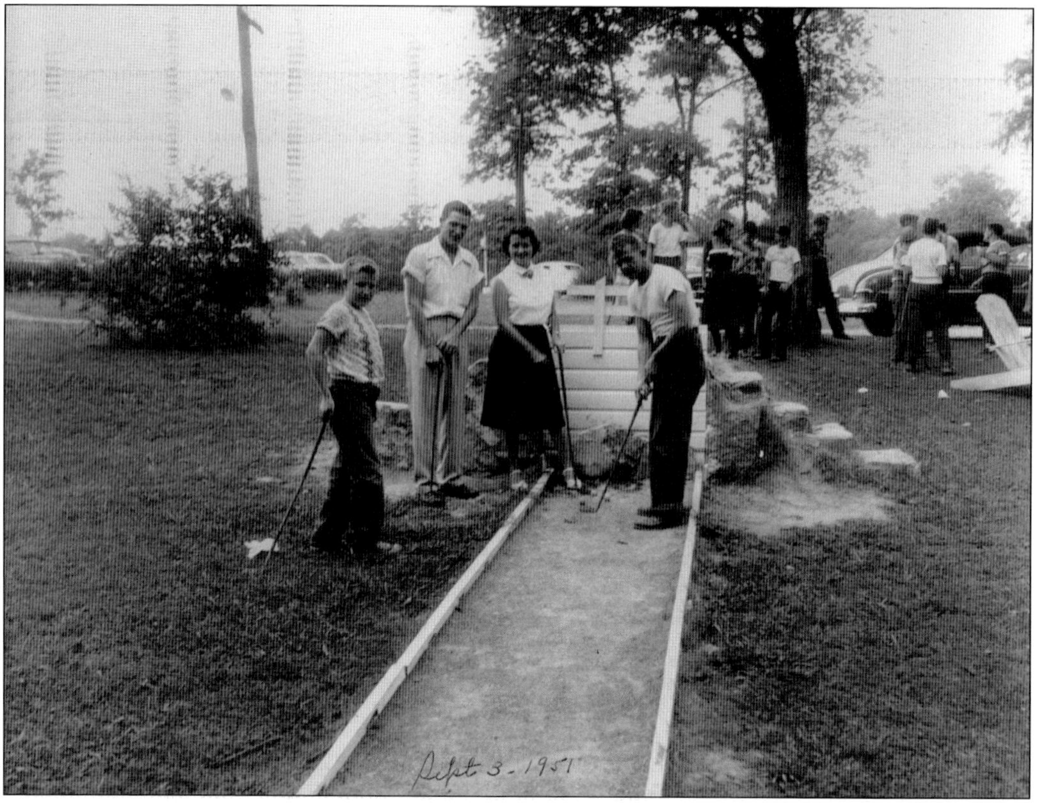

Miniature golf remained popular for all ages. It was expanded to accommodate more guests and was always mentioned in the advertisements of the time.

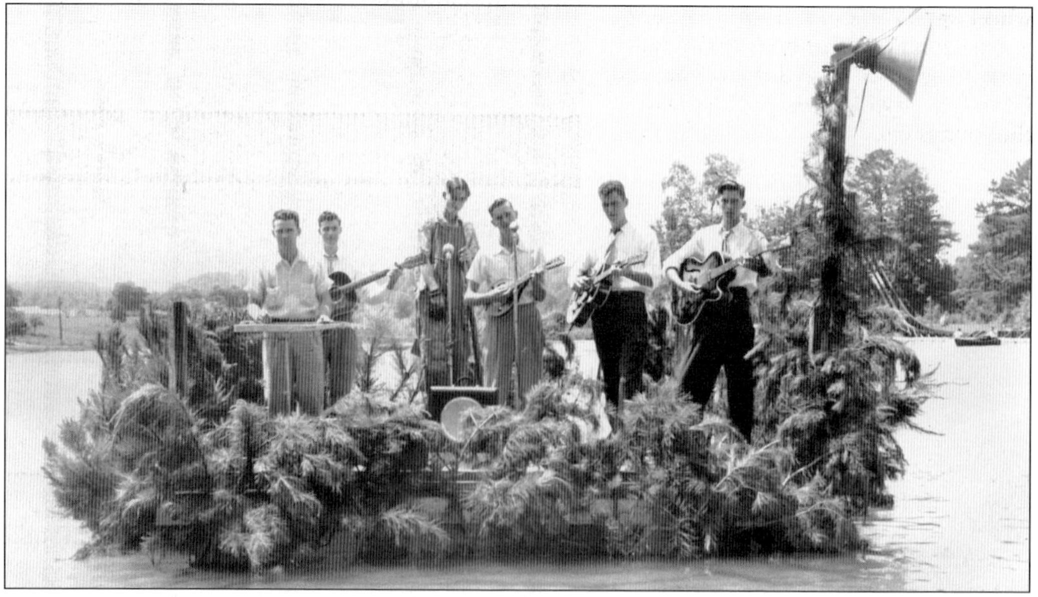

The year 1953 began the tradition of free country music shows at Lake Winnepesaukah. That year, musicians performed on a floating stage in the middle of the lake. The tradition of country artists continued for over 50 years; however, a stage was built for future shows.

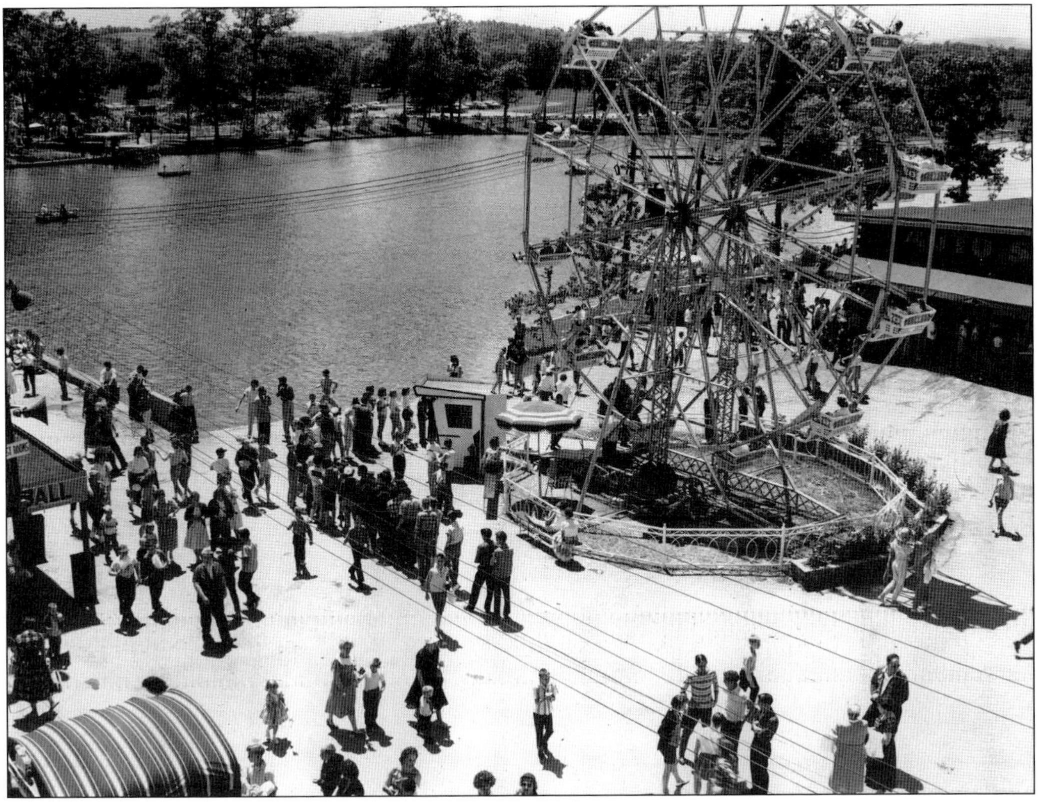

A new Ferris wheel was added in 1952, much to the delight of the guests. This wheel was taller and thus held more guests for a more thrilling view of the park. It closely mirrored the kiddie Ferris wheel, which was popular with the youngsters.

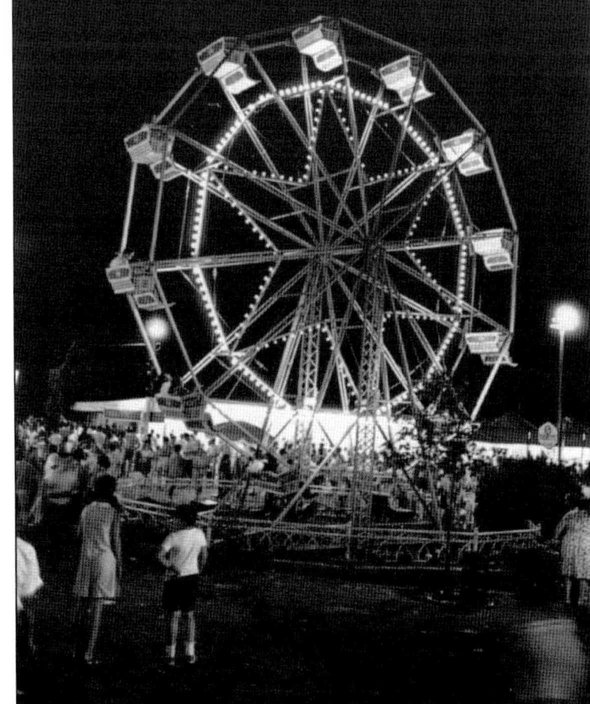

One of the features of this new Ferris wheel was the fact that it contained a neon star design that lit in the center of the wheel at night. The gate that surrounded the ride was made on-site by one of the many welders the park employed.

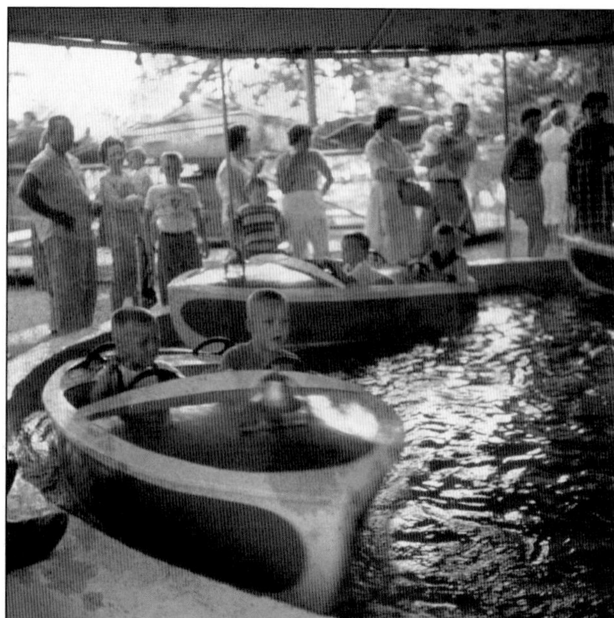

In 1952, the kiddie boats were added, and they have now been popular for generations of guests. The hum of the motor, the wake the small boats make in the water, the ability to "drive" the boat with the steering wheel, and of course, the ringing of the bell to signal "Ahoy!" has long been a delight of toddlers.

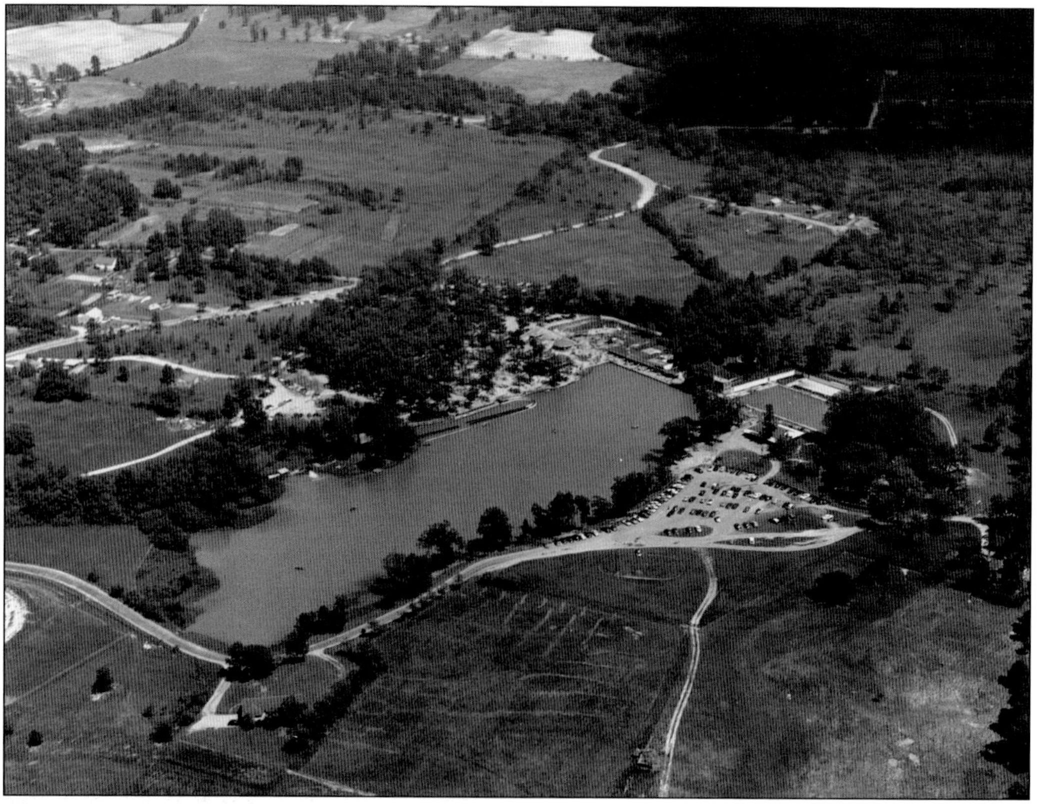

This 1953 aerial view shows the expanding property lines of the park. When possible, Minette Dixon purchased any adjacent land she could afford. Any that might contain homes, she allowed trusted employees to rent. At the time, there was a mechanic, a plumber, and a welder living on site.

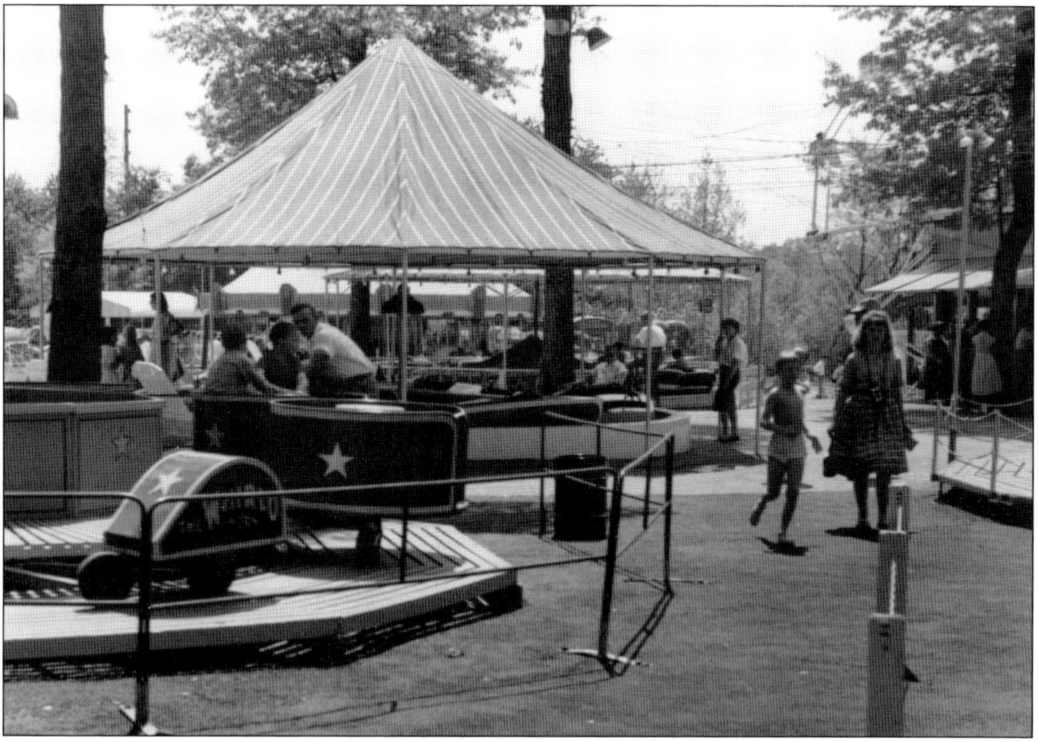

The Whirlo ride was a new kiddie ride that debuted in 1953. Also featured that year were parachute jumps into the lake from 6,000 feet, water ski shows, and hydroplaning races.

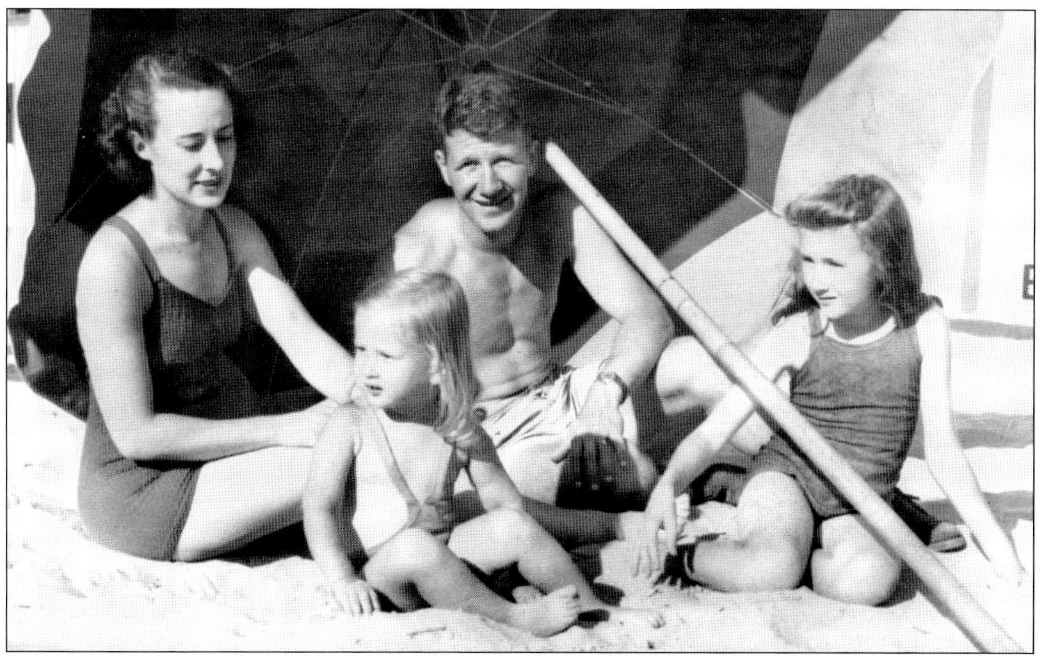

When Evelyn White was not working at the park, she enjoyed the benefits for her family. Pictured are Evelyn, daughters Tootsie and Adrienne, and husband Charlie at the sand beach beside the pool.

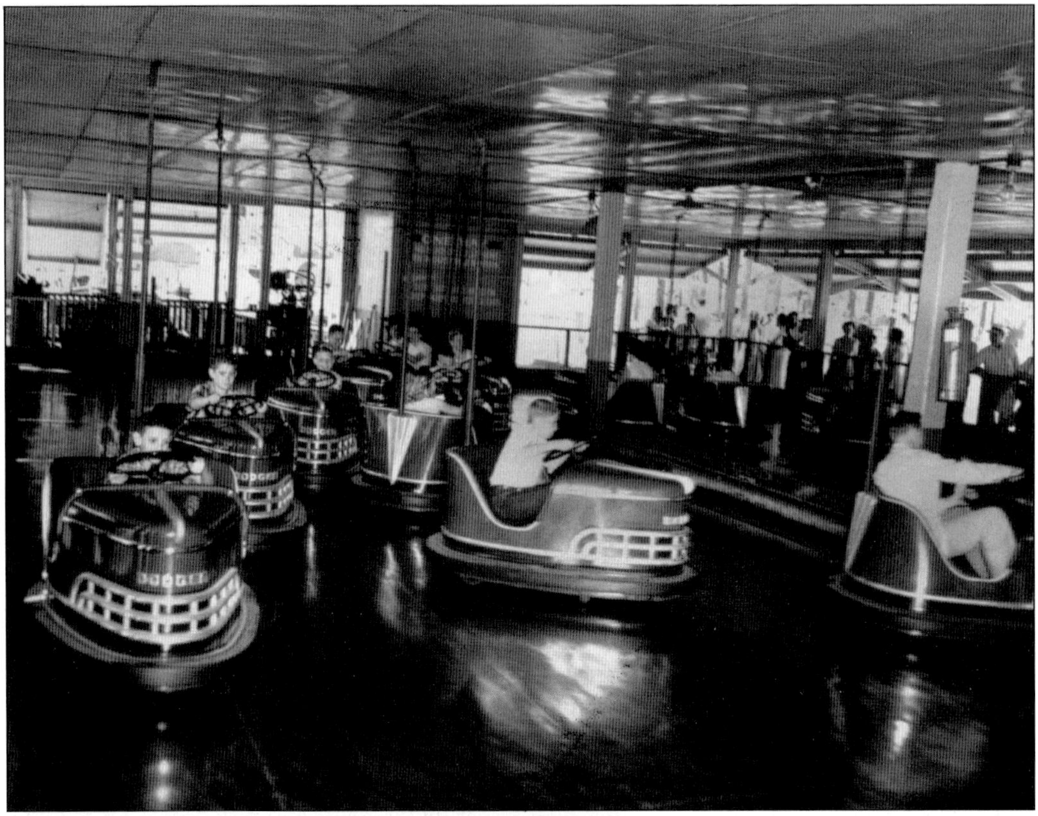

In 1953, dodgem cars, manufactured by Allan Herschell of North Tonawanda, New York, were added to the park. These became an instant favorite. Also, this year, a popular attraction was free country music shows, held on a stage floating in the middle of the lake.

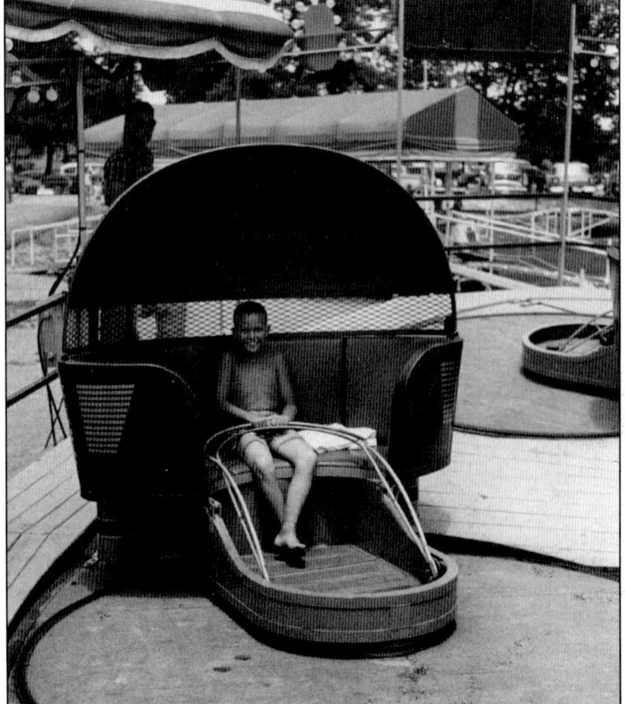

The 1955 season opened with a new Tilt-A-Whirl that was placed next to the Little Dipper, right past the "Little Royal Palm" train, and before the Ferris wheel. This proved to be a legendary ride for its undulating cars that spun while they circled the platform. A version remains in the park today.

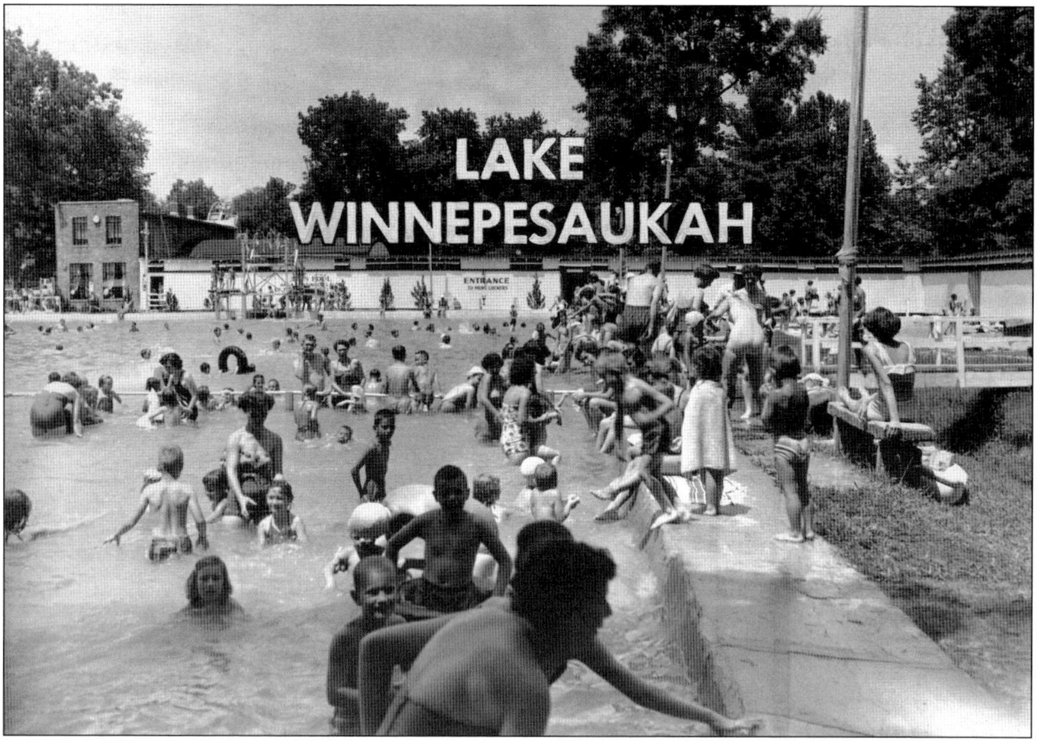

LAKE WINNEPESAUKAH

When visitors arrived for the 1956 season, they saw that the swimming pool had been completely renovated and enlarged, with a kiddie pool added for the toddlers. Spacious walkways were added around the perimeter along with a three-meter diving tower and new boards for the one-meter tower.

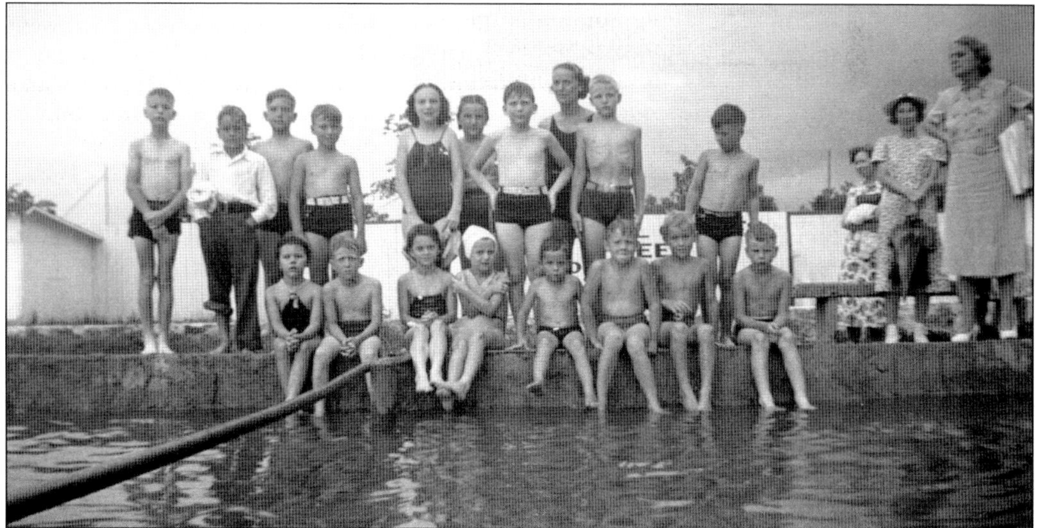

Children were offered "Bargain Student Tickets," which gave a reduction to the cost of the ever-growing number of rides in the 1950s. Many local students rode their bikes to the park. It was in this community spirit that mothers would often call and ask the park to announce over the public address system that it was time for their child to return home. The park complied, always welcoming the child back for another day of fun.

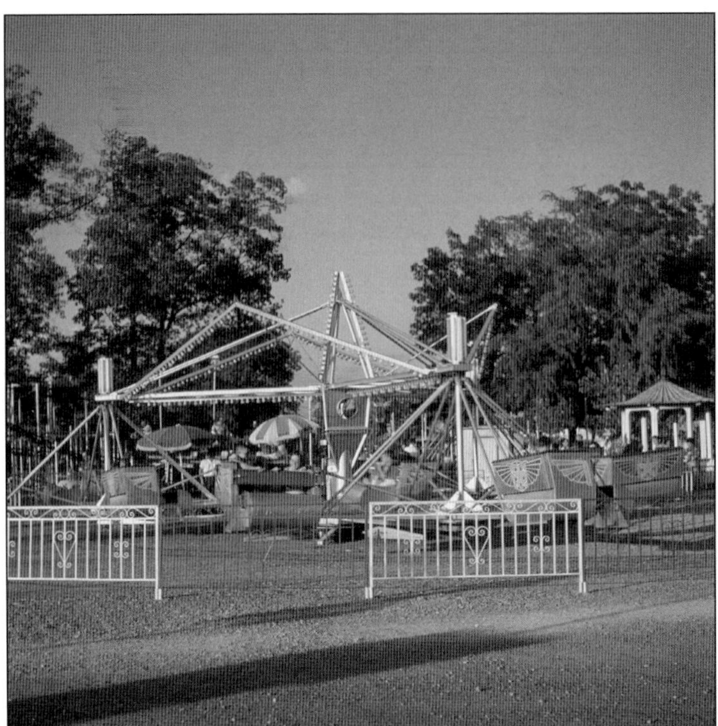

In 1956, the classic Scrambler ride was added. At this time, the park had 11 major rides, with the Scrambler becoming an instant favorite.

Also in 1956, the kiddie Sky Fighter ride was added. This ride allowed a front and back pilot, and the guns each controlled truly sounded like repetitive fire. This addition brought the total number of kiddie rides to five.

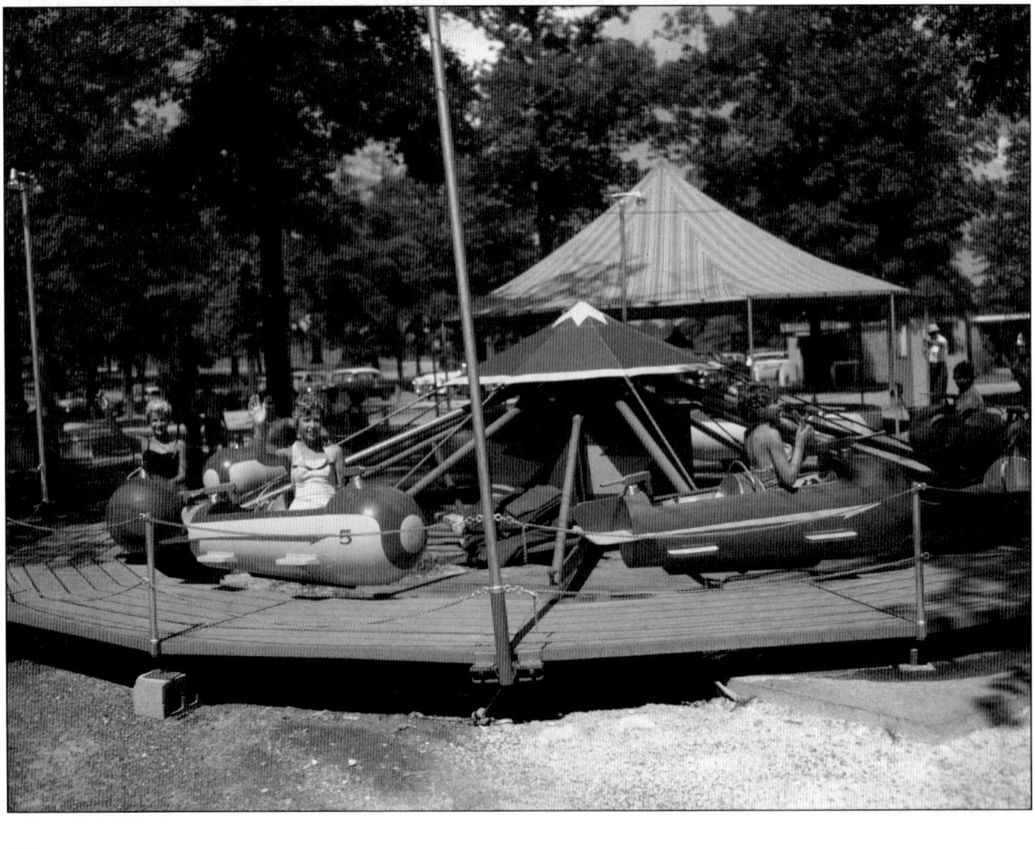

In June 1956, the *Show Boat* was introduced, and Minette Dixon's granddaughter Tootsie White christened the boat. This replica of an old-time Mississippi River steamer held 30 passengers for trips around the nine-acre lake.

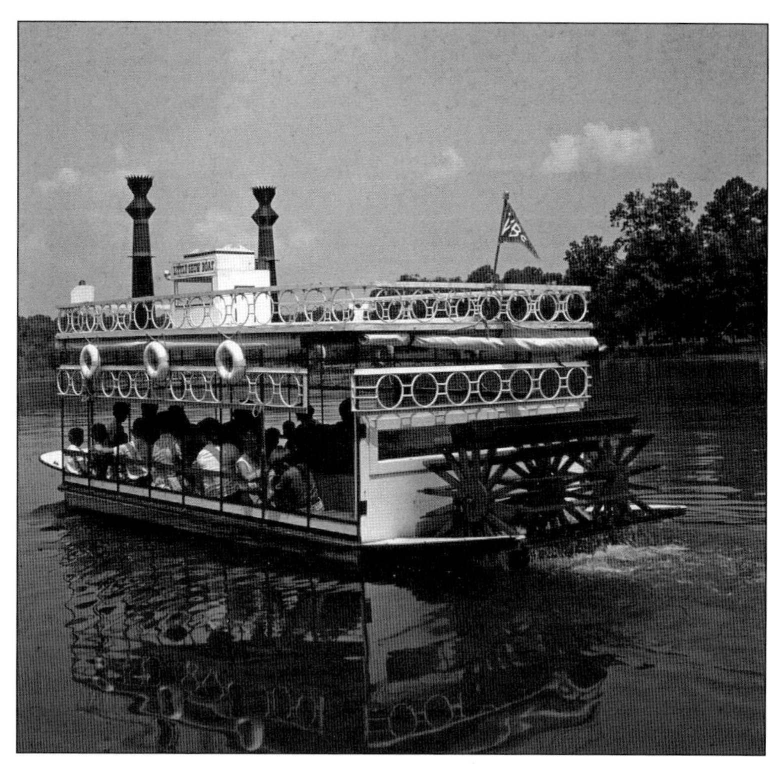

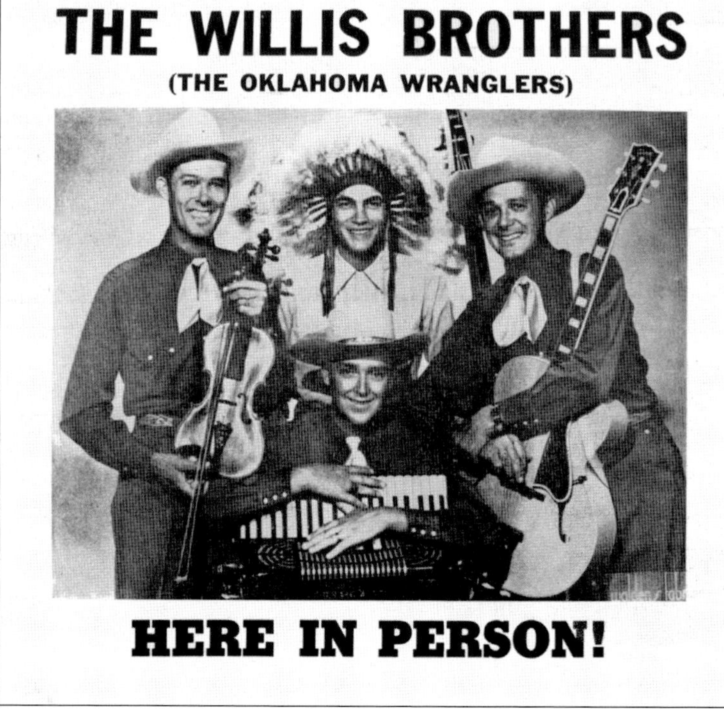

In 1956, the Willis Brothers first performed at the park. In the late 1950s, the Willis Brothers hosted a live noonday television show at the NBC affiliate in Chattanooga. Guy, Vic, and Skeeter were accompanied by Chuck Wright, who played bass in a full Indian headdress. Their top hit was "Give Me Forty Acres (To Turn This Rig Around)," which became a top 10 country hit in the United States. The park became known for offering free country music performances during this time.

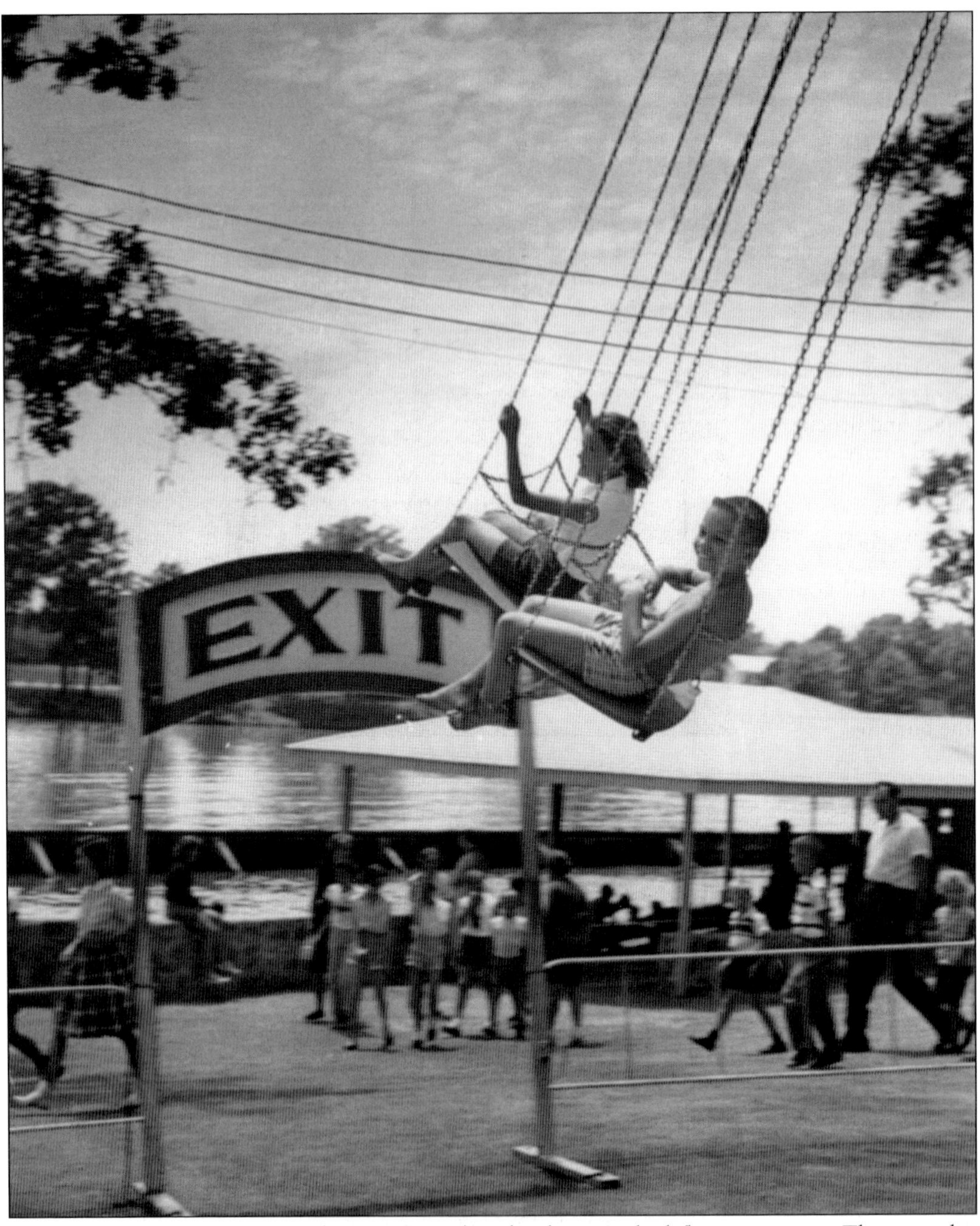

The Chairplane ride was added in 1958, and it closely mimicked flying in a seat. The year also opened with a new grass beach at the swimming pool that allowed an option from the sand beach.

The year 1958 debuted the Cake House, designed by Evelyn White especially for children's birthday parties. The pavilion is a replica of a real birthday cake, scaled to size, and boasts electric birthday candles on top. Evelyn stated she wanted the picnic tables and benches scaled to size so children could "be in a world of their own" when they celebrate their birthdays. Children from the now-named Chambliss Center for Children were invited to dedicate the building.

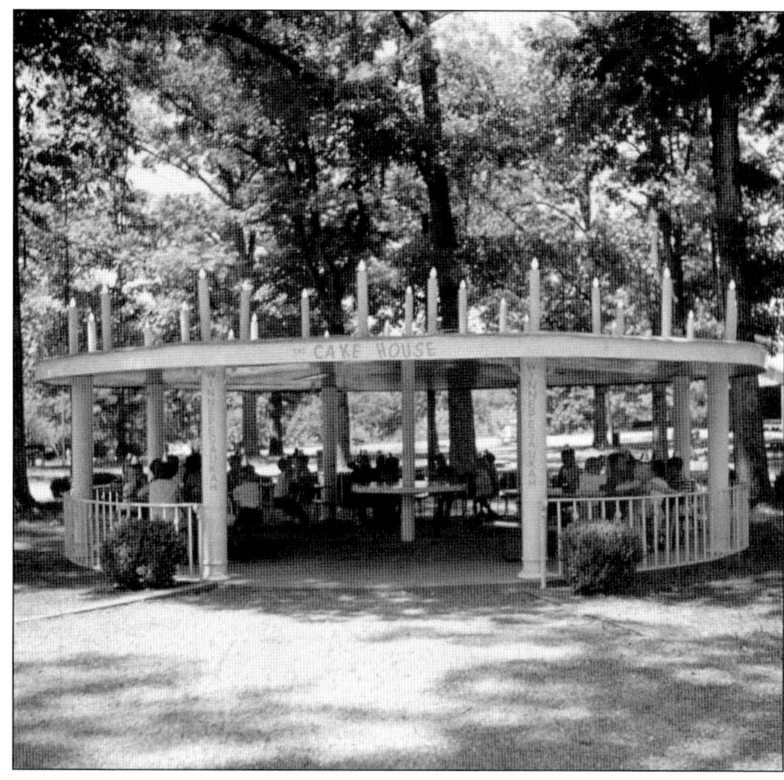

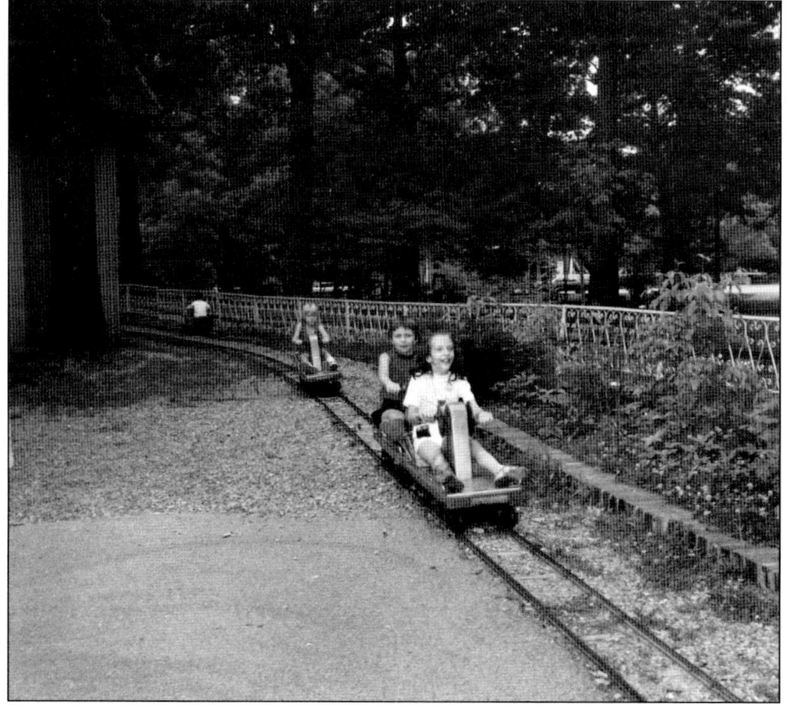

The hand cars were a favorite of young children since the day they arrived at the park in 1959. The cars operated on a small railroad-style track that was laid in a figure-eight. The cars were propelled by children turning the handles in a clockwise motion. They were removed from the park in the 1980s when the manufacturer no longer produced parts. It feels as if every baby boomer wants them back for their grandchildren.

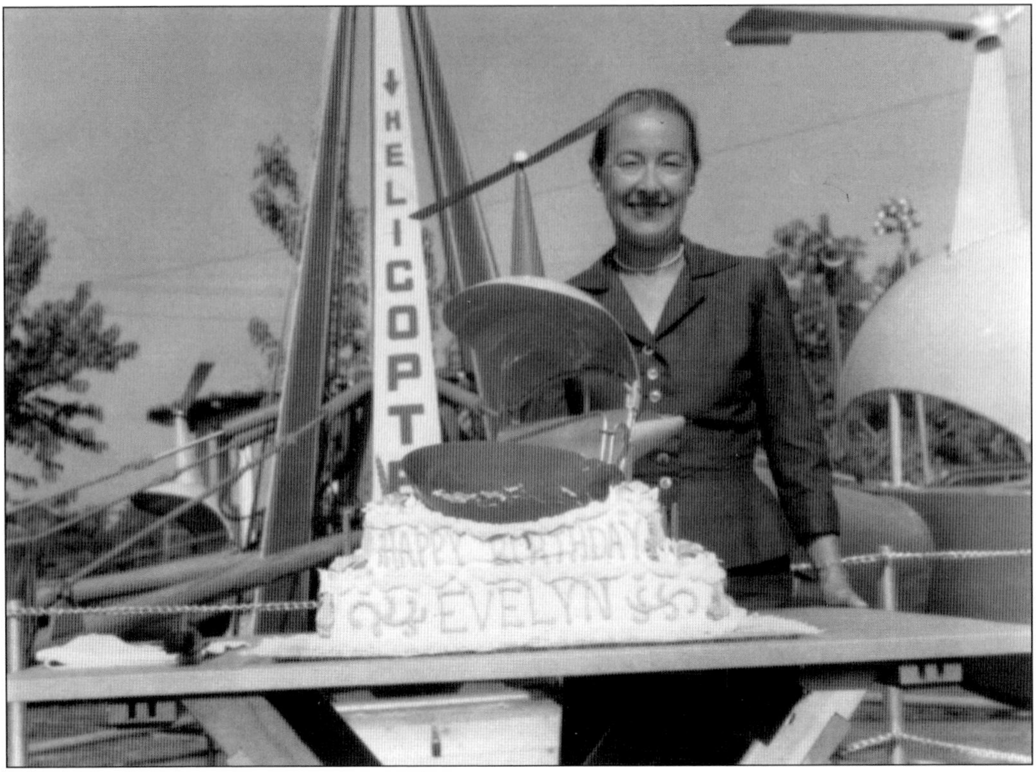

For her birthday on May 15, 1959, Evelyn White was presented with a kiddie Helicopter ride by her husband, Charlie. The surprise came complete with a cake and children ready for a spin.

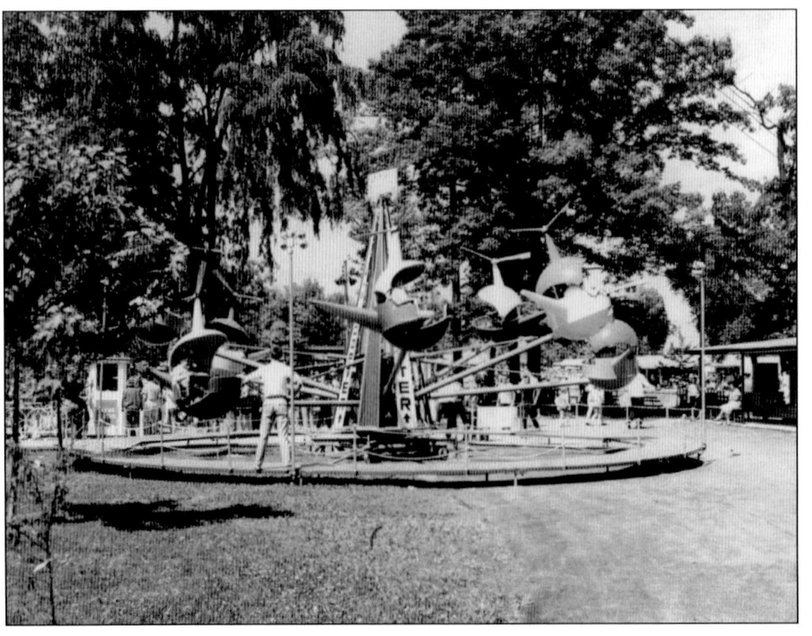

The Helicopter ride was an addition to the Kiddie Hill area of the park. Children loved not only its colorful presence, but the fact that they were the ones who made it go up or down depending on how they moved the bar.

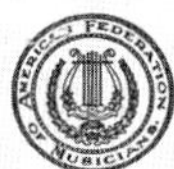

Contract Blank

AMERICAN FEDERATION OF MUSICIANS

OF THE UNITED STATES AND CANADA

(HEREIN CALLED "FEDERATION")

LOCAL NUMBER________

THIS CONTRACT for the personal services of musicians, made this 20th day of April, 1959, between the undersigned employer (hereinafter called the employer) and Four (4) (Including Leaders) musicians (hereinafter called employees) represented by the undersigned representative.

WITNESSETH, That the employer employs the personal services of the employees, as musicians severally, and the employees severally, through their representative, agree to render collectively to the employer services as musicians in the orchestra under the leadership of Porter Wagoner, according to the following terms and conditions:

Name and Address of Place of Engagement Lake Winnepesaukah Rossville, Georgia

Date(s) of employment Sunday ~~June 21st.~~ 1959 July 5th

Hours of employment 3 stage shows of 25 minutes each to be held at 2, 5, and 9 p.m.

Type of engagement (specify whether dance, stage show, banquet, etc.) Stage Show

The employer is hereby given an option to extend this agreement for a period of na weeks beyond the original term thereof. Said option can be made effective only by written notice from the employer to the employees not later than na days prior to the expiration of said original term that he claims and exercises said option.

PRICE AGREED UPON $ 225.00 (Terms and Amount)

This price includes expenses agreed to be reimbursed by the employer in accordance with the attached schedule, or a schedule to be furnished the employer on or before the date of engagement.

To be paid After engagement June 21st. 1959 (Specify When Payments Are to Be Made)

ADDITIONAL TERMS AND CONDITIONS

The employer shall at all times have complete control of the services which the employees will render under the specifications of this contract. On behalf of the employer the Leader will distribute the amount received from the employer to the employees, including himself, as indicated on the opposite side of this contract, or in place thereof on separate memorandum supplied to the employer at or before the commencement of the employment hereunder and take and turn over to the employer receipts therefor from each employee, including himself. The amount paid to the Leader includes the cost of transportation, which will be reported by the Leader to the employer. The employer hereby authorizes the Leader on his behalf to replace any employee who by illness, absence, or for any other reason does not perform any or all of the services provided for under this contract. Upon request by the Federation or the Local in whose jurisdiction the employees shall perform hereunder, the employer either shall make advance payment hereunder or shall post an appropriate bond.

The agreement of the employees to perform is subject to proven detention by sickness, accidents, or accidents to means of transportation, riots, strikes, epidemics, acts of God, or any other legitimate conditions beyond the control of the employees.

All employees covered by this agreement must be members in good standing of the Federation. However, if the employment provided for hereunder is subject to the Labor-Management Relations Act, 1947, all employees, who are members of the Federation when their employment commences hereunder, shall be continued in such employment only so long as they continue such membership in good standing. All other employees covered by this agreement, on or before the thirtieth day following the commencement of their employment, or the effective date of this agreement, whichever is later, shall become and continue to be members in good standing of the Federation. The provisions of this paragraph shall not become effective unless and until permitted by applicable law.

To the extent permitted by applicable law, nothing in this contract shall ever be construed so as to interfere with any duty owing by any employee hereunder to the Federation pursuant to its Constitution, By-Laws, Rules, Regulations and Orders.

Any employees who are parties to or affected by this contract, whose services hereunder or covered hereby, are prevented, suspended or stopped by reason of any lawful strike, ban, unfair list order or requirement of the Federation, shall be free to accept and engage in other employment of the same or similar character, or otherwise, for other employers or persons without any restraint, hindrance, penalty, obligation or liability whatever, any other provisions of this contract to the contrary notwithstanding.

The Business Representative of the Local of the Federation in whose jurisdiction the employees shall perform hereunder shall have access to the place of performance (except to private residences) for the purpose of conferring with the employees.

The performances to be rendered pursuant to this agreement are not to be recorded, reproduced, or transmitted from the place of performance, in any manner or by any means whatsoever, in the absence of a specific written agreement between the employer and the Federation relating to and permitting such recording, reproduction, or transmission.

The employer represents that there does not exist against him, in favor of any member of the Federation, any claim of any kind arising out of musical services rendered for any such employer. No member of the Federation will be required to perform any provisions of this contract or to render any services for said employer as long as any such claim is unsatisfied or unpaid, in whole or in part.

The employer in signing this contract himself, or having same signed by a representative, acknowledges his (her or their) authority to do so and hereby assumes liability for the amount stated herein.

To the extent permitted by applicable law, there are incorporated into and made part of this agreement, as though fully set forth herein, all of the By-Laws, Rules and Regulations of the Federation, and of any Local of the Federation in whose jurisdiction services are to be performed hereunder insofar as they do not conflict with those of the Federation.

Name of Employer Robert E. Norton

Street Address Rossville, Georgia

City Rossville, State Ga.

Phone

Accepted by Employer

Accepted /s/ Porter Wagoner (Orchestra Leader)

Address Box 8061 Nashville 7, Tennessee

By Don Warden (Representatives of Employees)

If this contract is made by a licensed booking agent, there must be inserted on the reverse side of the contract the name, address and telephone number of the collecting agent of the local union in whose jurisdiction the engagement is to be performed.

9-15-54 FORM B-2 Printed in U. S. A. 44

Porter Wagoner performed at Lake Winnepesaukah for the first of many times on June 21, 1959. His press release called him "one of the most likable personalities in the country western field today." Wagoner's contract at the time was $225 for three shows. Lake Winnepesaukah was the host to many top country music artists over the next decades. Archie Campbell, Bill Anderson, the Carter Family, Waylon Jennings, and Crystal Gayle are a few of those who came frequently to perform at the free outdoor performances.

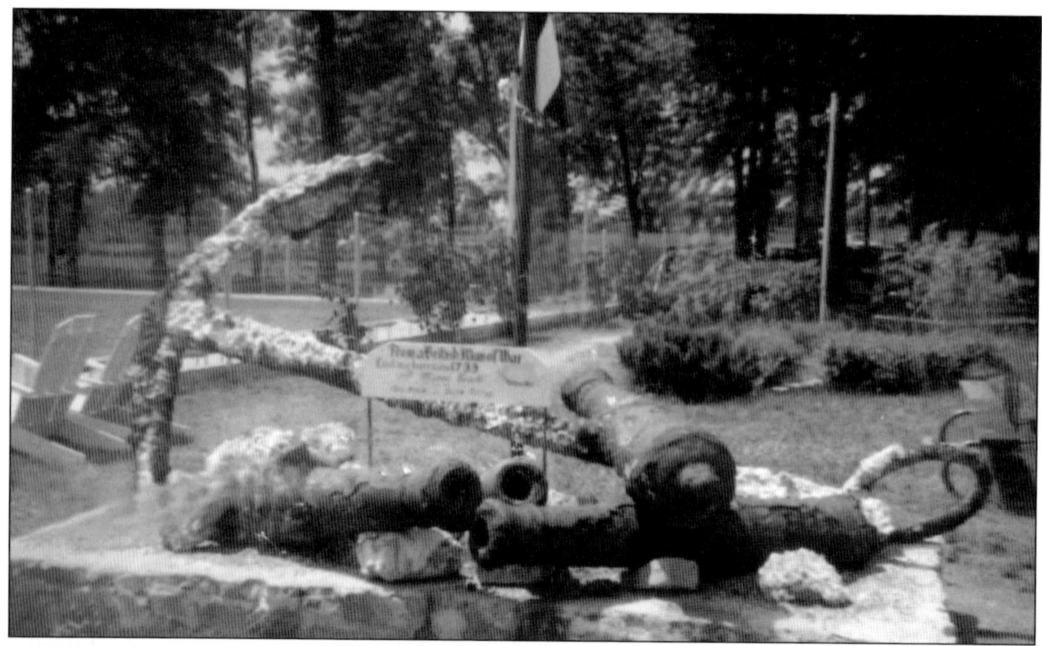

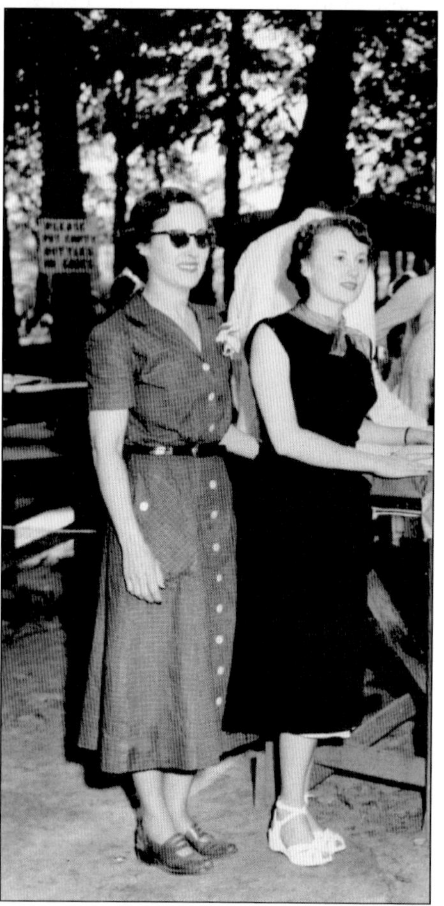

In 1959, the anchor and cannons seen here were brought to the park by Evelyn White's husband, Charlie. These were found off the coast of Miami Beach and were from the Spanish Armada. The anchor was first located to the left of the Carrousel Café and later moved to the entrance of the Cannon Ball coaster. The anchor now resides in the water park. Perhaps its addition was a foreshadowing of what was to come 64 years later.

Evelyn White and her daughter Adrienne welcome customers to the picnic grounds. All guests were given a name tag upon arrival the stated "Lake Winnepesaukah welcomes" before the name. Evelyn kept immaculate notes of all picnics from year to year that included not only the number served, but also the amount of each ingredient purchased. Provident, the Electric Power Board, and Combustion and Peerless Woolen Mills are just a few of the large picnics with over 1,000 guests that visited the park in the 1950s.

Five

The 1960s

Growing the Family and the Park

While the country was enjoying a spirit of renewed commitment to growth, as evidenced by President Kennedy's "new frontier," Lake Winnepesaukah was also expanding in both attractions and family involvement. Tootsie managed the games and gift shop, and Adrienne managed the cashiers, payroll, and daily assignments. Buddy Rhodes, Adrienne's husband, managed rides, and Butch Harless, Tootsie's husband, oversaw the kiddie area.

The Mad Mouse, a tower slide, and a Roadway car ride for children were added in 1961. The entertainment schedule featured June Carter, Porter Wagoner, the Carter Family, Bill Anderson, the Stonemans, Tex Ritter, and the Alvin and the Chipmunks show. In 1961, an event that lasted over 15 years began—the Little Miss Lake Winnepesaukah pageant debuted and was open to children under 12 years old.

In 1964, a new section of the park called Pioneerland opened. It depicted the Old West and guests traveled on a train named "1864 Iron Horse," which was a replica of the famous Civil War train the *General*. Outposts, farmlands, water towers, and an Old West shoot-out were all part of the thrill of the journey. The Iron Horse also puffed its way through train robberies and Wild West action. This year also marked the final year of the pool operating for swimming. It reopened with electric boats driven by customers added to the pool. Paddleboats were on the lake, and a new sky ride, the Astro Lift, was added. The Antique Car ride was the next attraction for 1966.

During the winter of 1966, construction of the biggest and most exciting ride in the park's history took place. After six years of planning, the Cannon Ball Roller Coaster opened. Designed and built by the Philadelphia Toboggan Company, the coaster is constructed of 200,000 board feet of specially treated long-leaf yellow pine along a special U-shaped track. The coaster is a half-mile-long ride that propels customers over a 70-foot incline and nine other hills, reaching speeds up to 50 miles an hour.

In late 1967, Evelyn White learned that there was an antique carousel for sale at Lakewood Park in Atlanta, built by the Philadelphia Toboggan Company and hand-carved in 1916 by Swiss and Italian artists. A lover of art and antiques, she knew she wanted it to be the next acquisition. A new building in the swimming pool was erected to house the ornately carved horses, chariots, and calliope music.

The 1968 season opened with three additional new rides: the Spider, the Trabant, and the Kiddie Sports Cars. In 1969, the Castle, designed by Bill Tracy, debuted. In 1969, Buddy and Adrienne Rhodes left Lake Winnepesaukah. Buddy purchased an oil and gas distributorship, and Adrienne did the books for the company. They continued to live at the park until 1978.

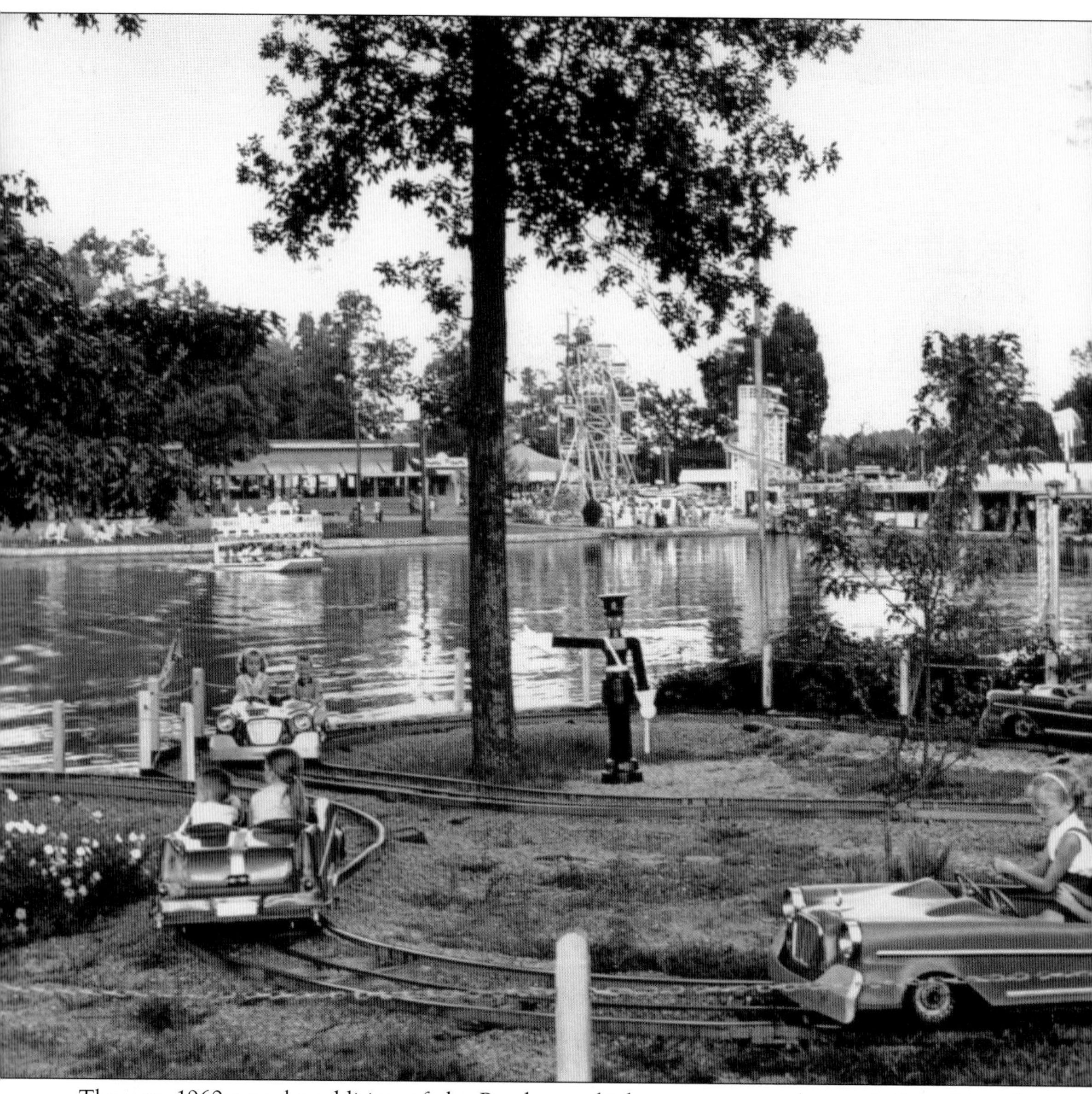

The year 1960 saw the addition of the Roadway, which were motorized cars children "drove" around a curving track by the lake. Free entertainment in 1953 included double parachute jumps over the lake, an aerialist performing while suspended 140 feet over the lake, and fireworks.

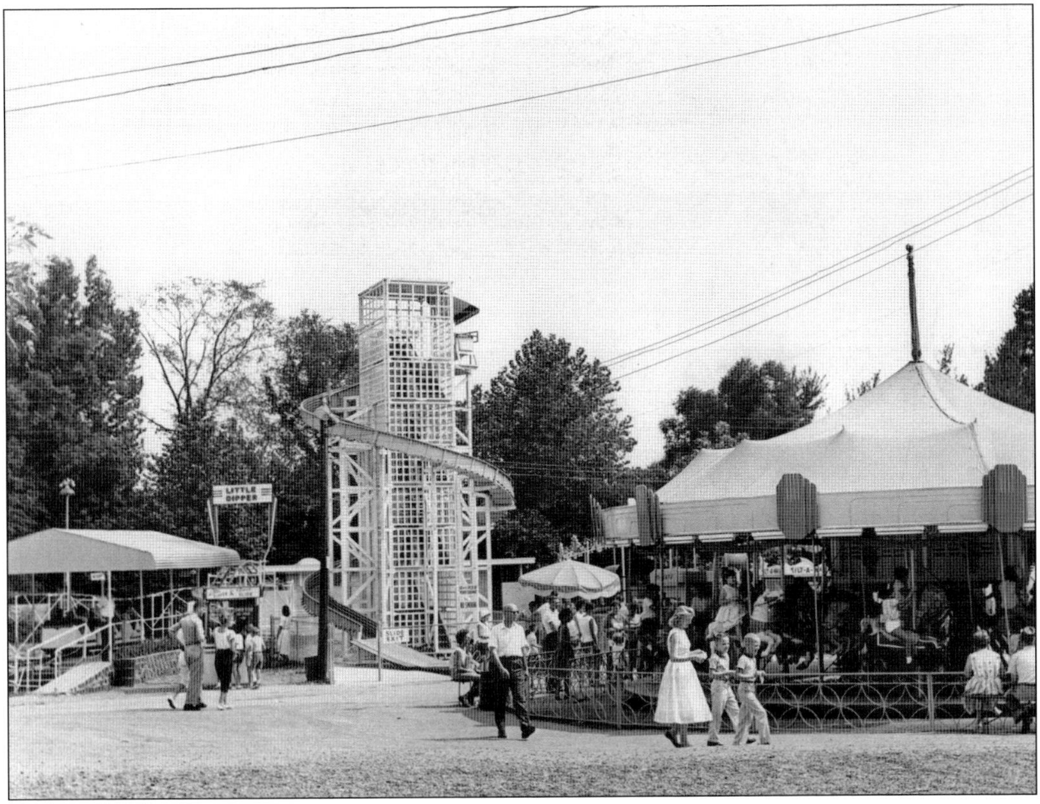

A tower slide was added in 1960. This was placed between the Little Dipper and the Tilt-A-Whirl. This proved to be popular with all ages; guests walked up the stairs to enter the platform and then slid down circular levels of fun.

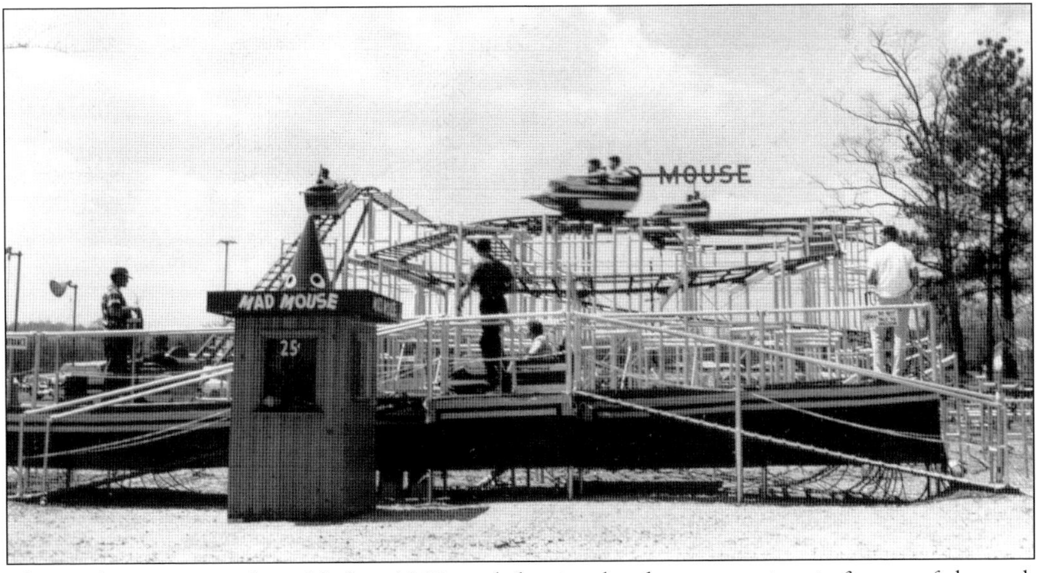

The Mad Mouse was also added in 1960, and the sign has become an iconic fixture of the park since. The ride slowly took guests up 50 feet, with sharp turns and unexpected dips that covered three levels of thrills.

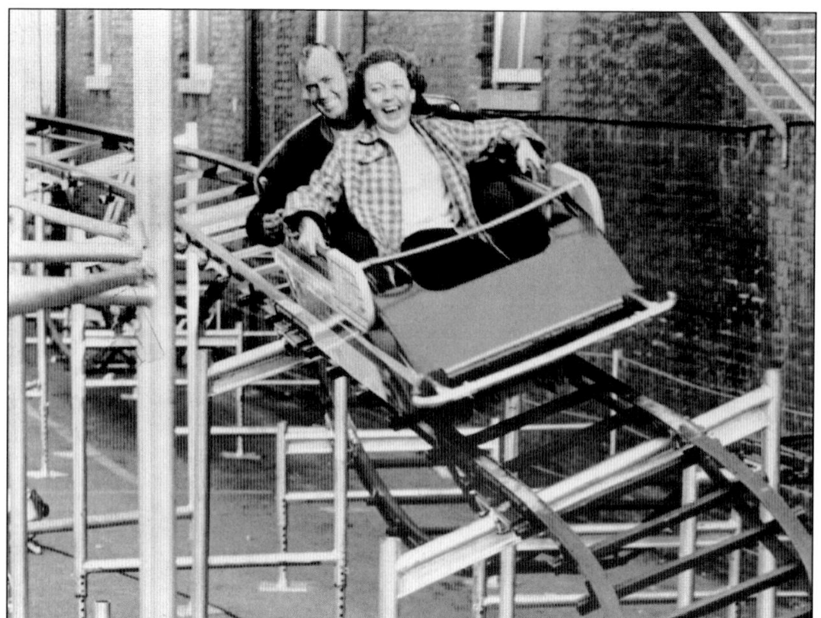

The thrill of the Mad Mouse was the feeling that the car would go off the rails into the lake beside the ride, as the turns were quite abrupt and in no way rounded. In the 40-plus years the ride was operable, there were no instances of the cars derailing; however, the sensation led to numerous "tall tales" of wet adventures.

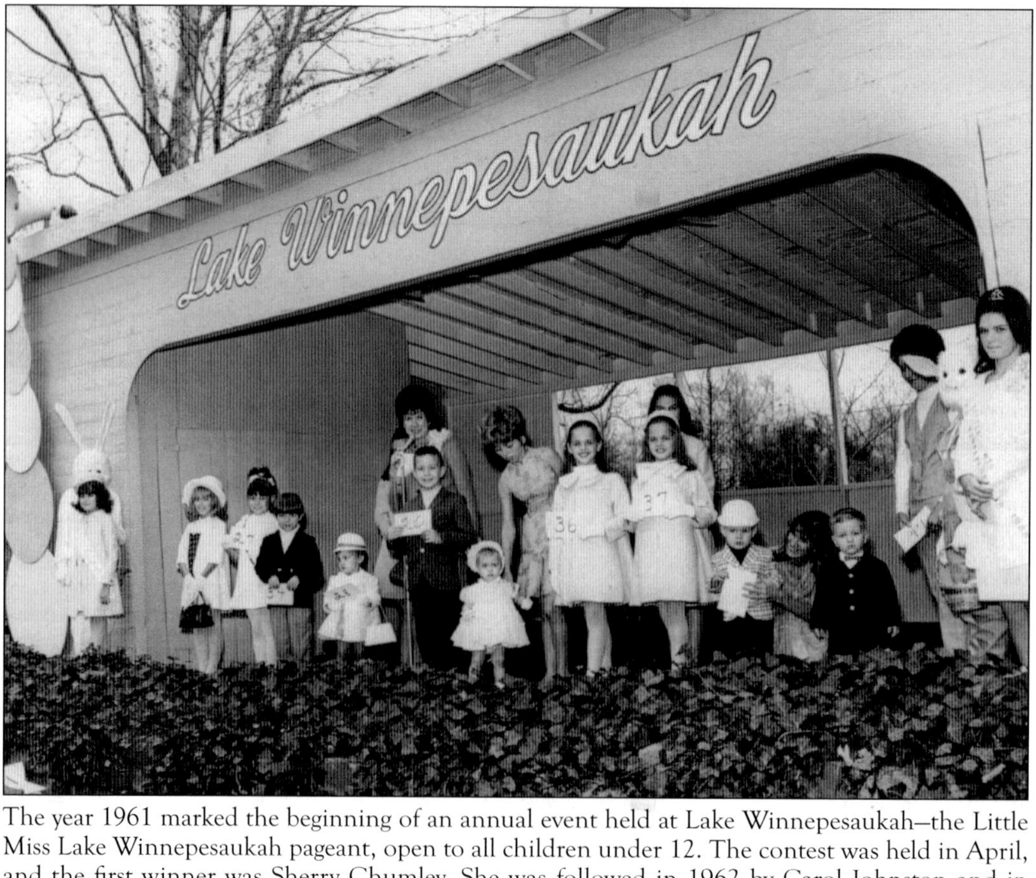

The year 1961 marked the beginning of an annual event held at Lake Winnepesaukah—the Little Miss Lake Winnepesaukah pageant, open to all children under 12. The contest was held in April, and the first winner was Sherry Chumley. She was followed in 1962 by Carol Johnston and in 1963 by Cheryl Reed.

The Paratrooper, an amusement park classic, was added to the park in 1961. It was originally placed across from the Boat Chute, as seen in this photograph.

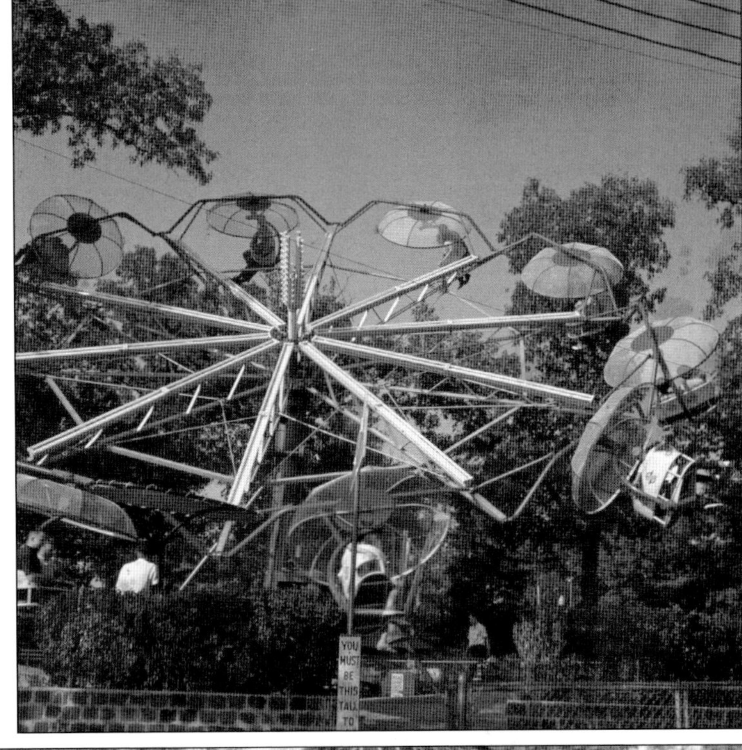

The Jolly Caterpillar was added in 1961. This was a kiddie ride with a cover that mysteriously appeared from the side and left children wondering if they would emerge from the caterpillar as a butterfly.

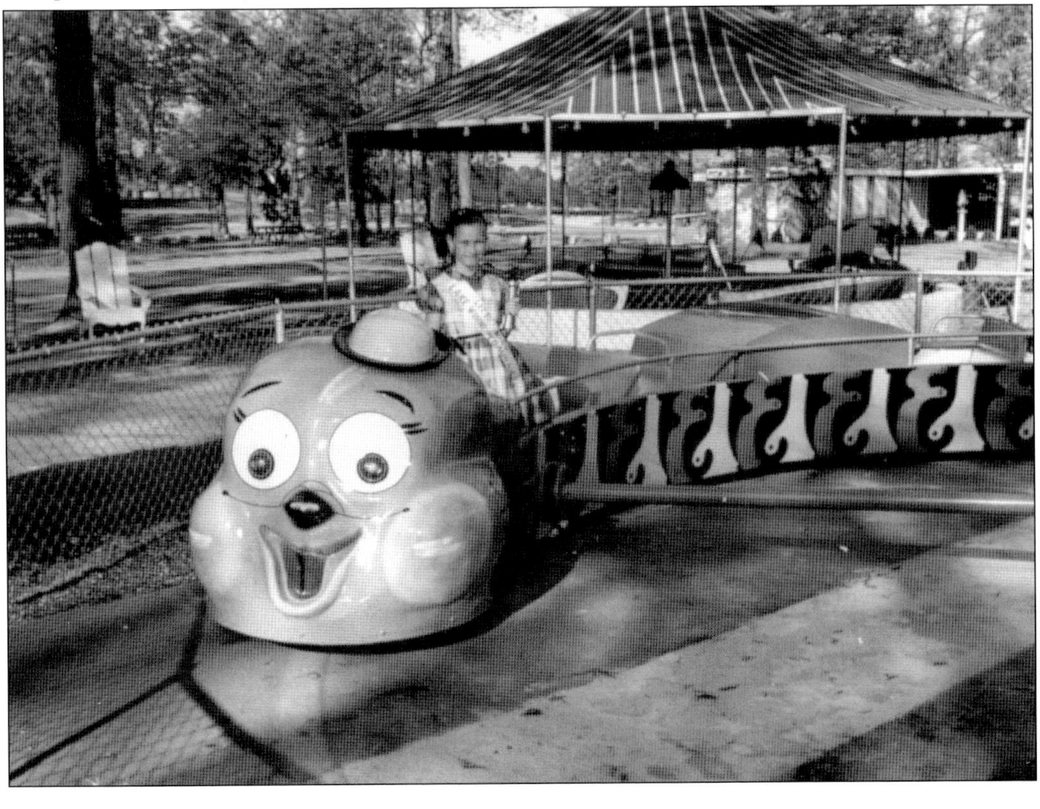

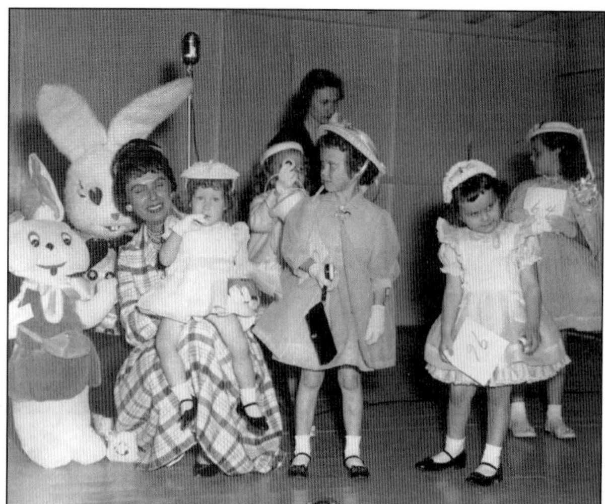

The year 1963 began the season with an Easter parade. This had become a tradition in the park that children and adults all relished. Entertainment for the season included Mother Maybelle & the Carter Sisters and Lonzo and Oscar.

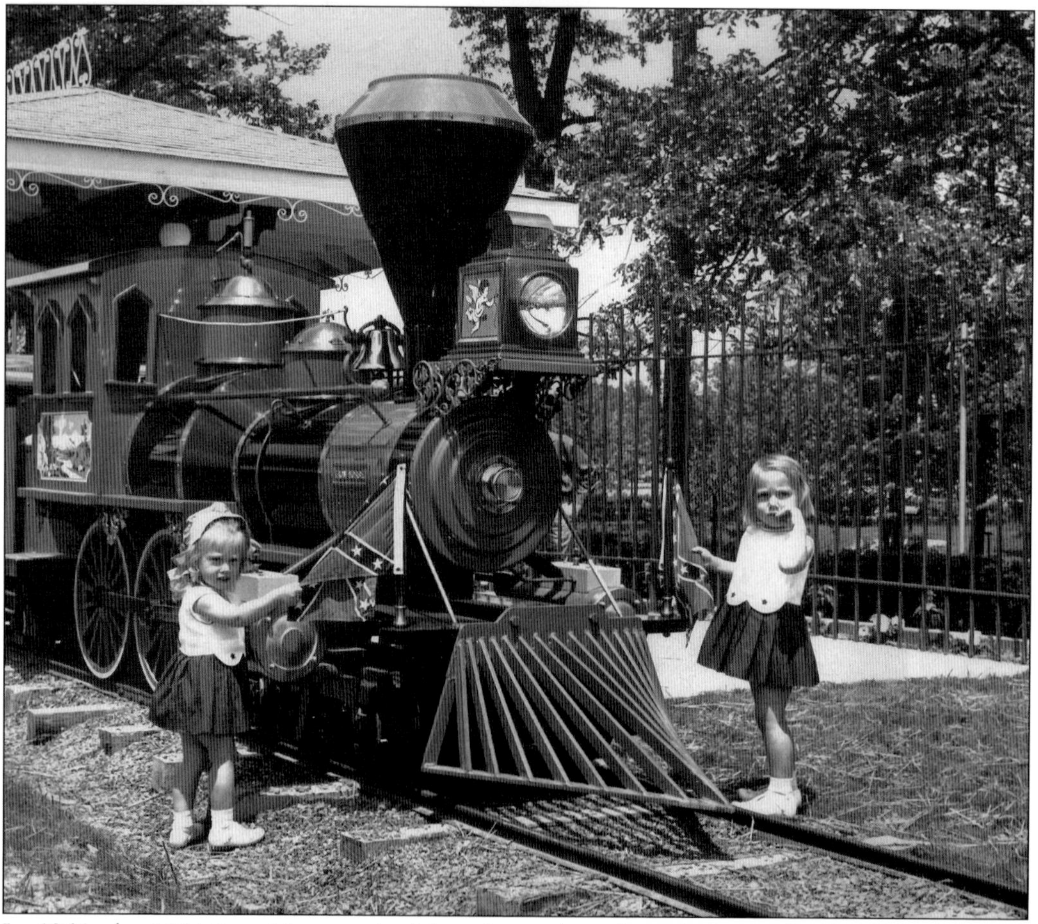

In 1964, the 1864 Iron Horse train debuted, traveling through Pioneerland. The train was a replica of a Civil War train, the *General*, complete with billowing smoke, the sound of steam, the shriek of whistles, and the clanging of bells. Pictured are Tootsie White Harless's children Kelly (left) and Evelyn (right), great-granddaughters of the founders.

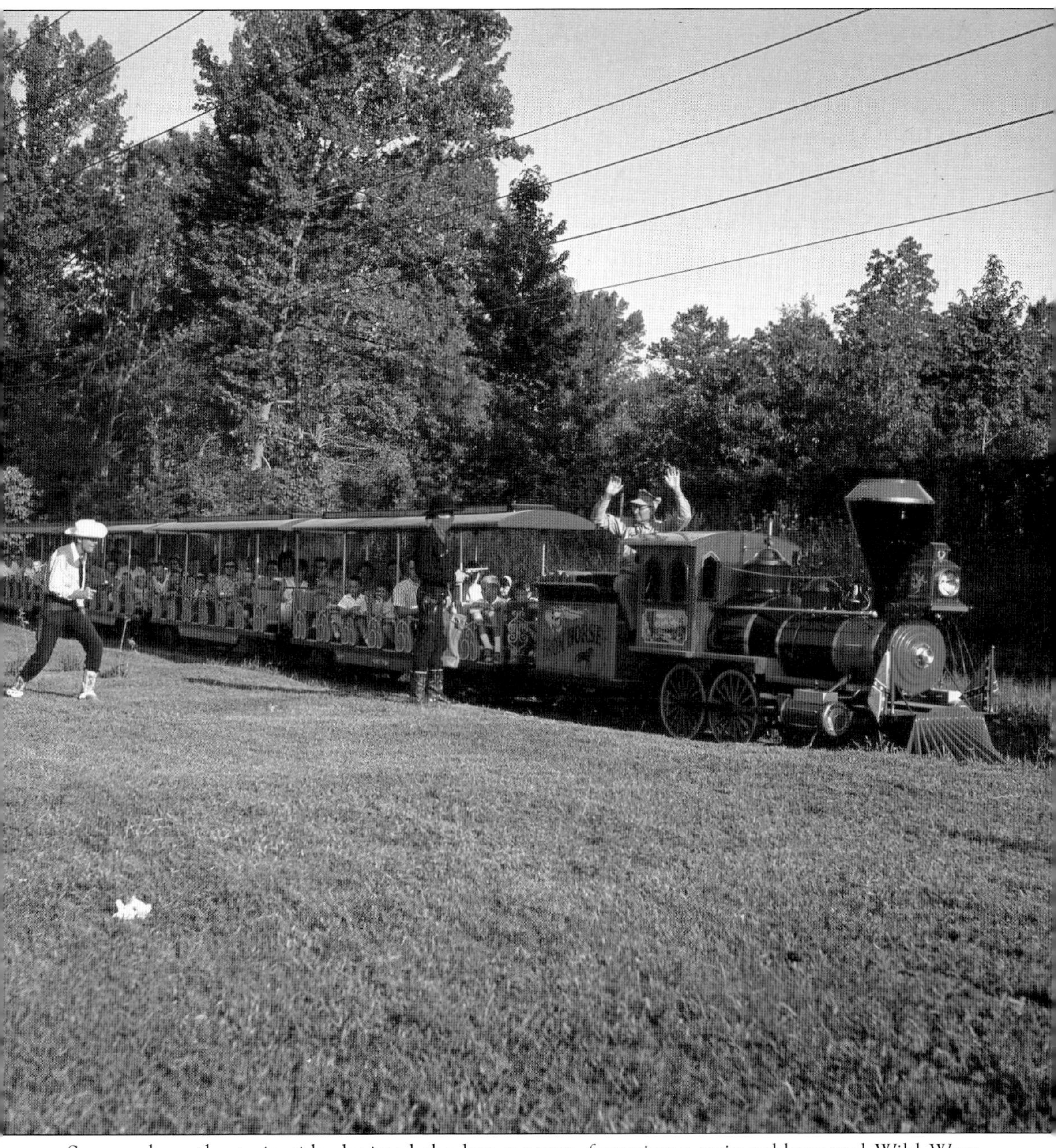

Scenes along the train ride depicted the last century, featuring a train robbery and Wild West action. There were cattle and outpost stations to complete the scenery as well as a barn with chickens and donkeys.

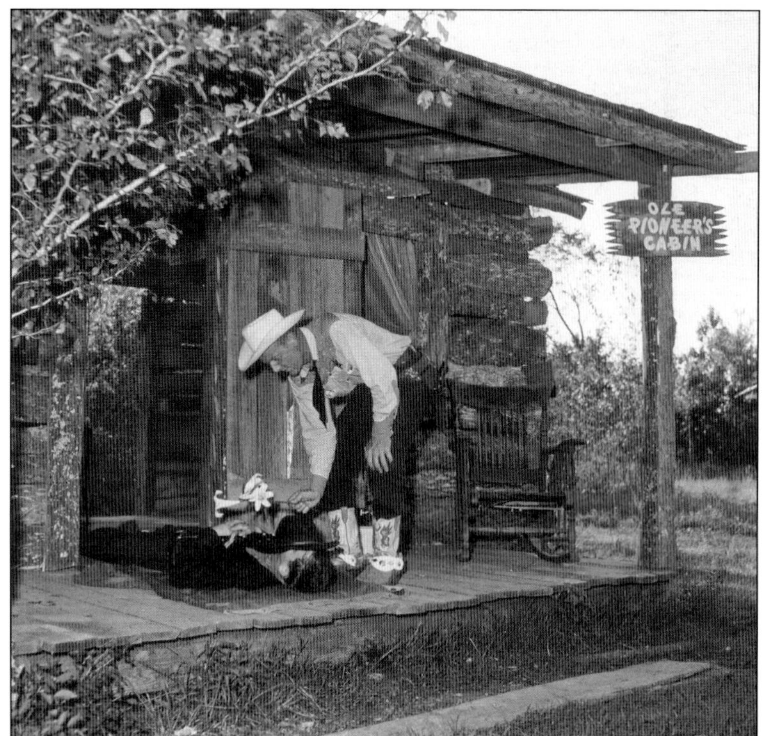

The sheriff always got the bad guy in Pioneerland, and the train robber was laid to rest in peace. The various barnyard animals roamed freely in the area and often interacted with guests.

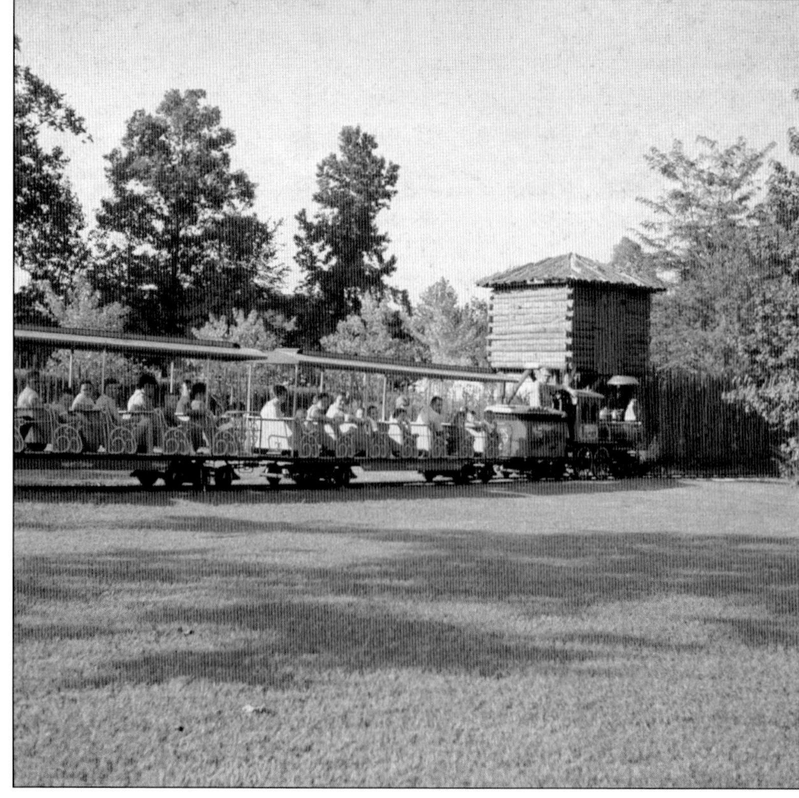

The conductor of the train always made sure there were no enemies hiding in the outposts and took careful care to guard the passengers around the bends. All customers returned safely to the station.

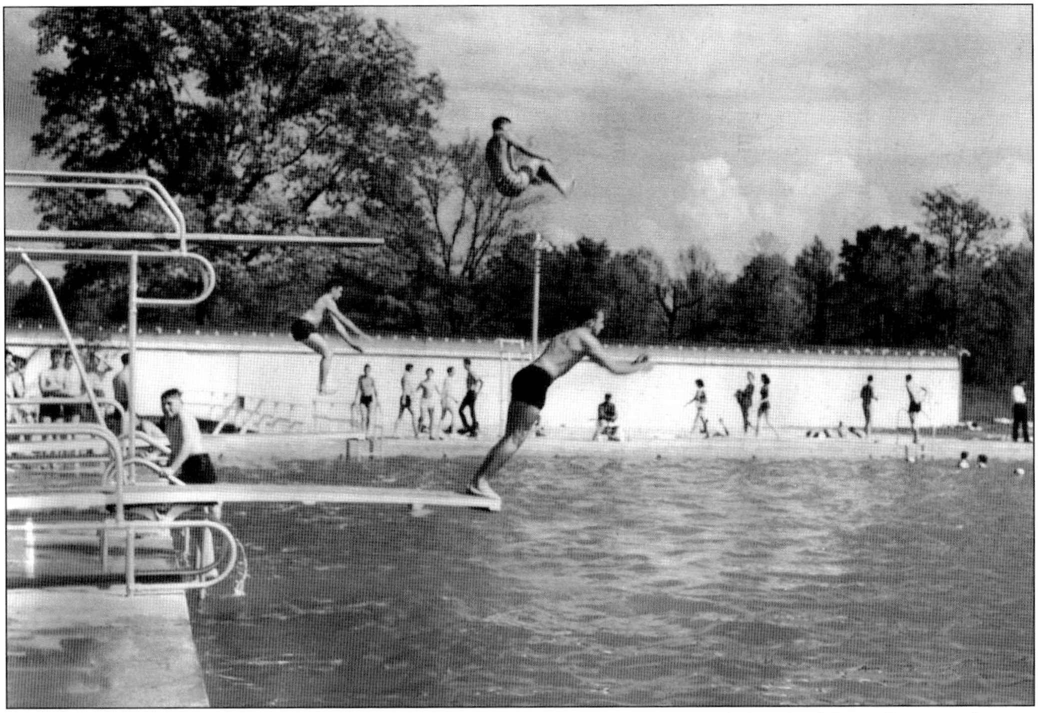

The year 1964 was the final year for swimming in the 38-year-old pool that had been host to dozens of Mid-South and AAU swim meets and hundreds of area children learning to swim. More fun was in store for the area, as customers soon learned.

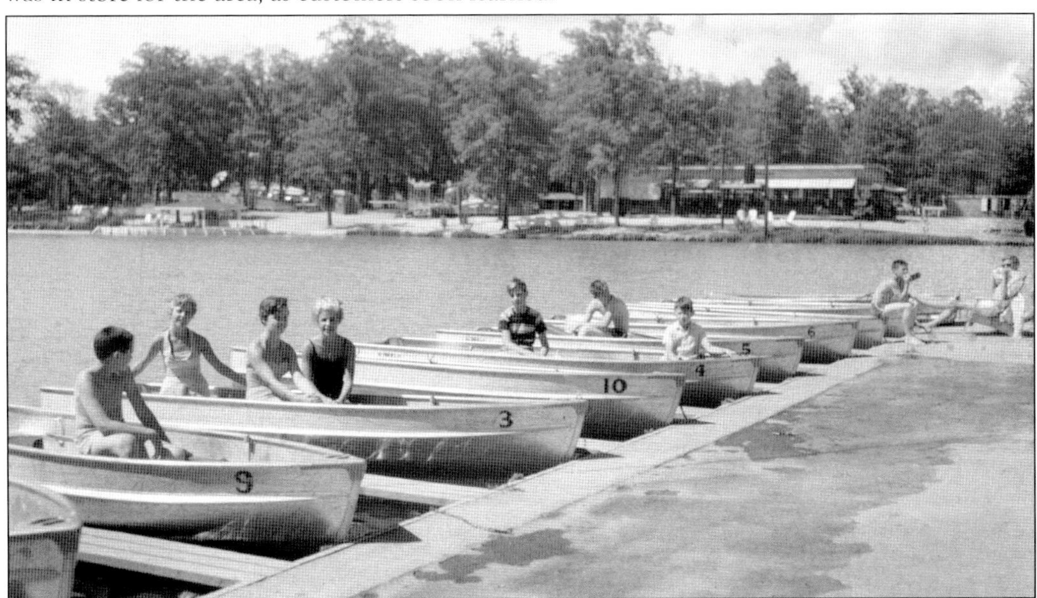

Boating remained a popular activity on the lake. Rowboats, canoes, and paddleboats were available for guests at different stations. A lifeguard was always on duty to ensure safety. All the boats were numbered, and in the event one was too close to the shore or rides, the lifeguard blew a whistle and reprimanded the number of the boat over a megaphone. Typically, the only issue was young boys deciding to repurpose the paddles for splashing!

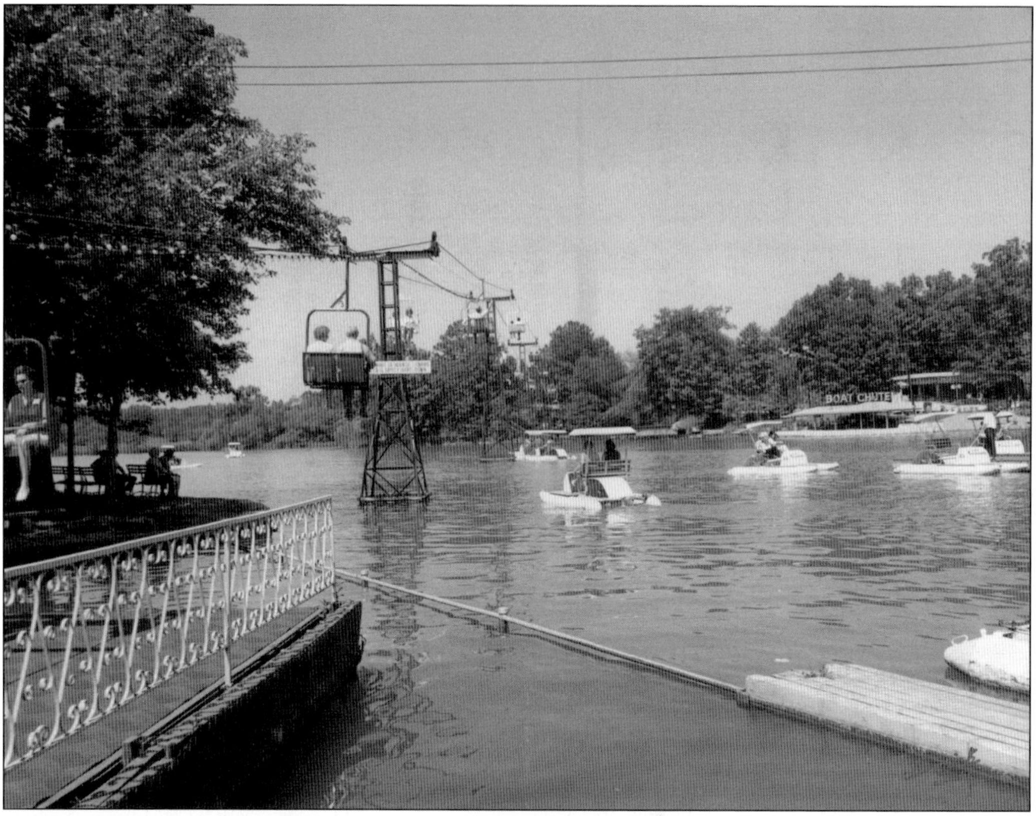

A new Skyride across the lake was added in 1965: the Astro Lift. It offered a bird's-eye view of the lake, and some customers marveled at seeing the famous carp from the sky.

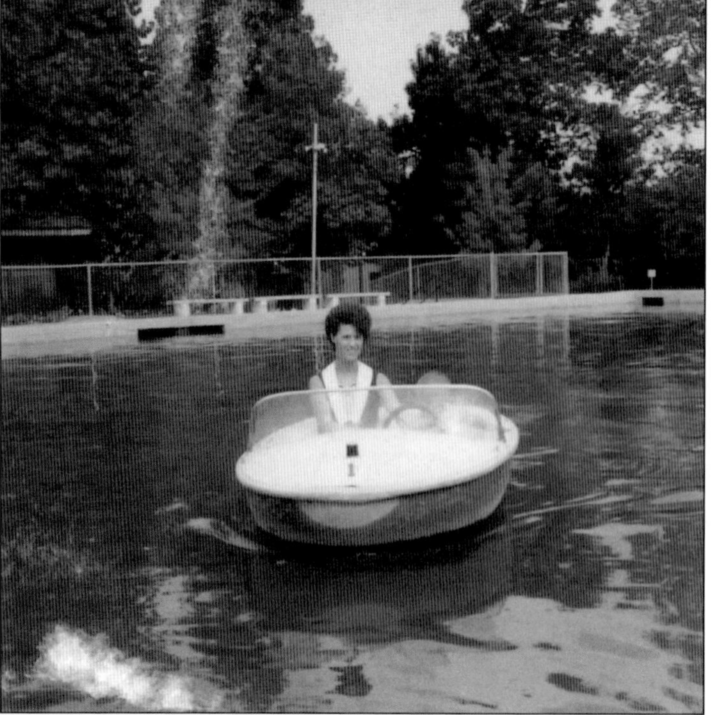

In 1965, new electric boats were the attraction in the swimming pool. Riders could steer and dock the boats themselves. This was the next step for the children from the kiddie boats that were attached to a central spoke.

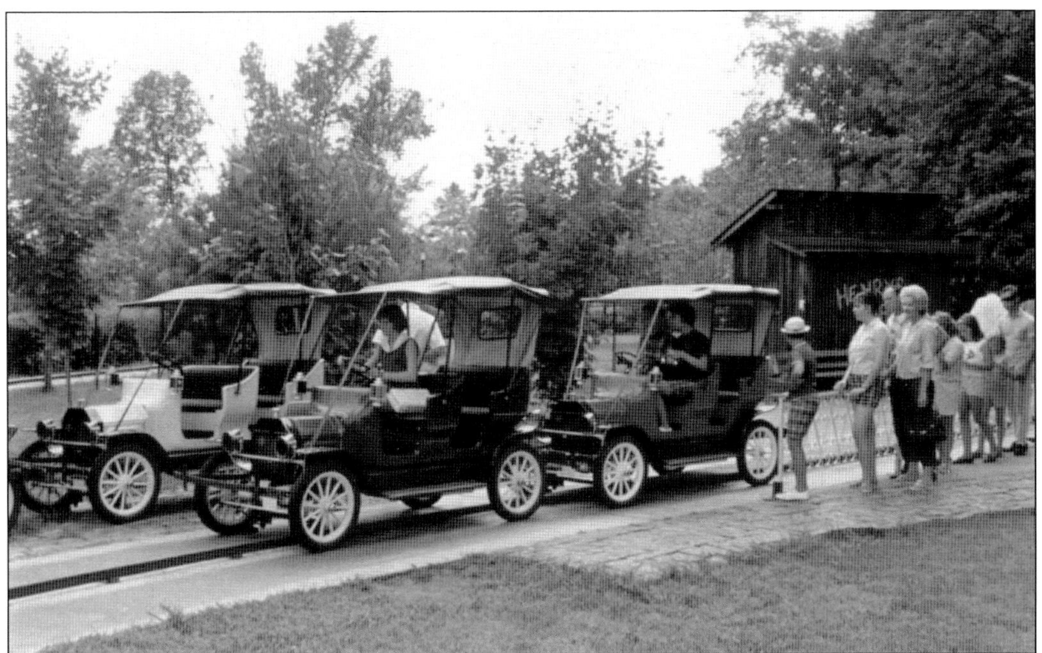

In 1966, guests tall enough to reach a floor pedal would motor around a winding roadway and back into the days of horseless carriages and raccoon coats. The colorful reproductions of the old-time touring cars were complete with all the interesting accessories of the era.

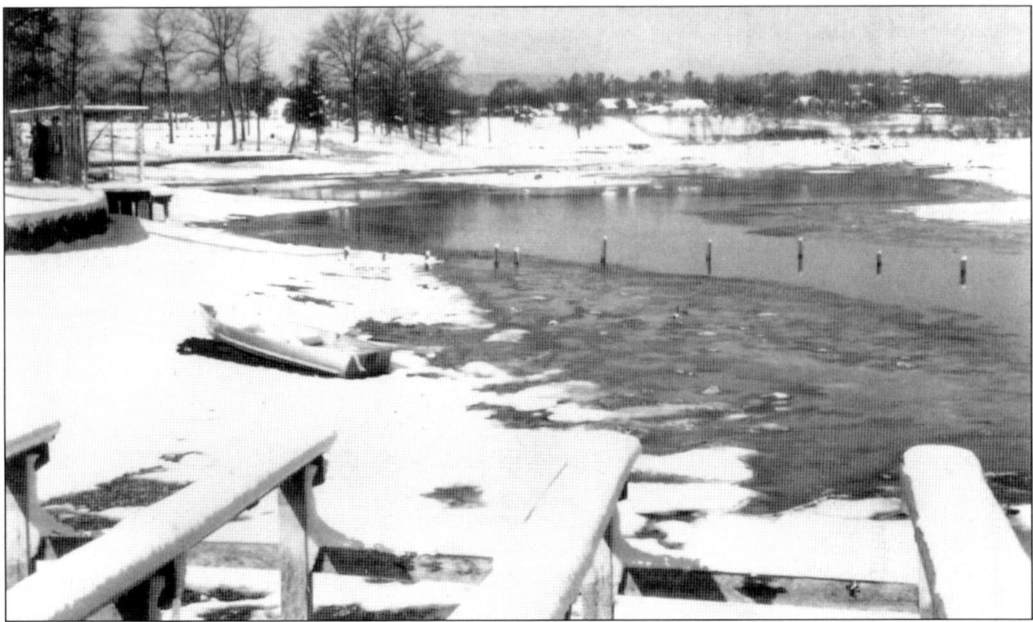

This picture was taken after a snowstorm of eight inches in February 1960. People often ask what happens to the water in the winter months. Historically, the lake is drained by raising a gate, and the water flows into Black Creek. Enough water remains in the lake for the carp to survive. This is done for two reasons: to allow the algae to die off and to inspect and perform construction on any of the structures in the lake. The poles protruding from the lake bed at the time are remnants of cypress wood used to designate the swimming section in 1925.

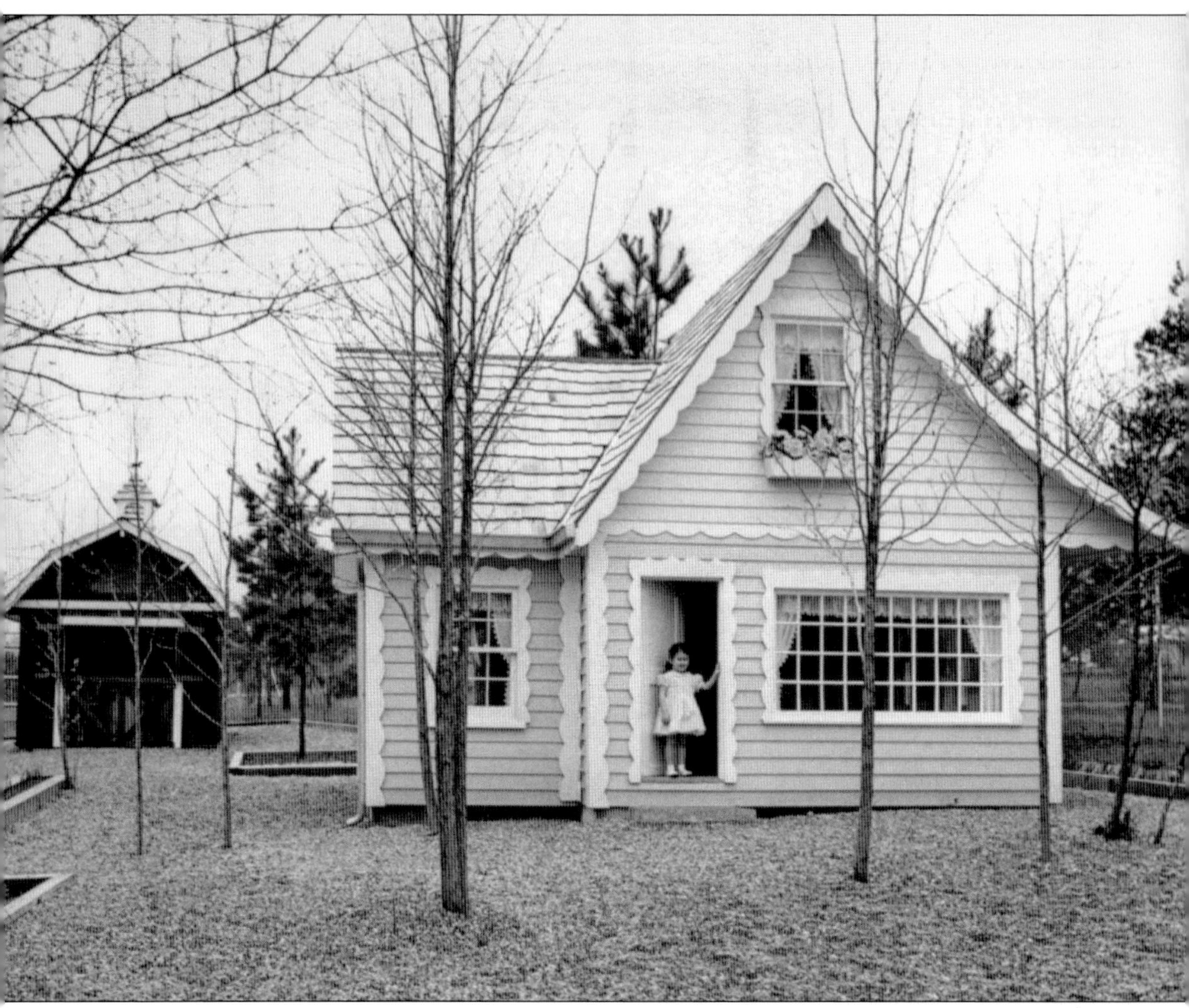

In the winter of 1966, Evelyn White had a miniature house erected near Pioneerland. She called it "the dollhouse," as it was perfectly proportioned for small children. Pictured is her granddaughter Talley, who, as a two year old, found it enchanting. Guest could look in the windows at all the miniature Victorian antiques Evelyn enjoyed collecting.

Lake Winnepesaukah became known for showcasing country music stars in the 1960s and 1970s. Shows were typically held on Sundays at 2:00 p.m., 5:00 p.m., and 9:00 p.m. and were free. The shady grove where the stage was located was the place to spend a summer afternoon.

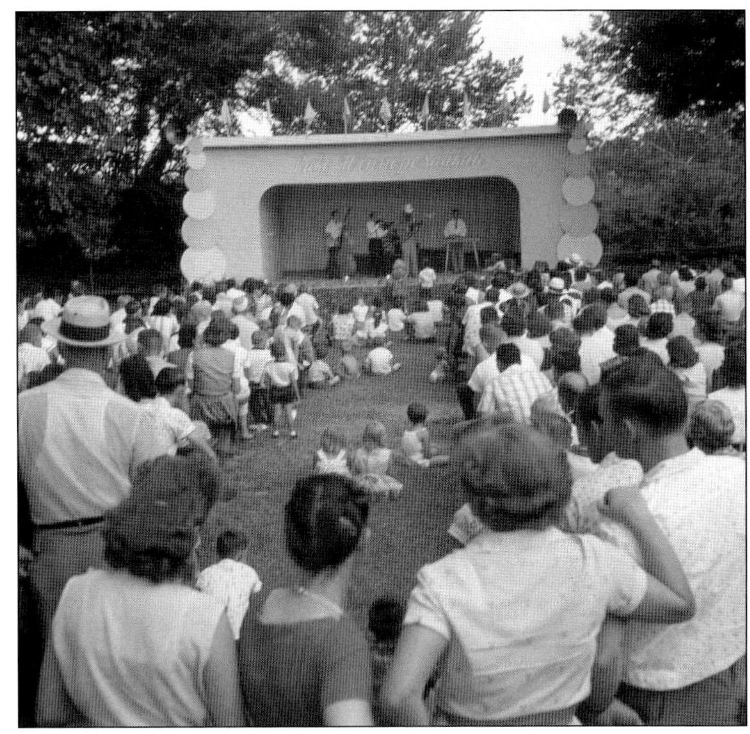

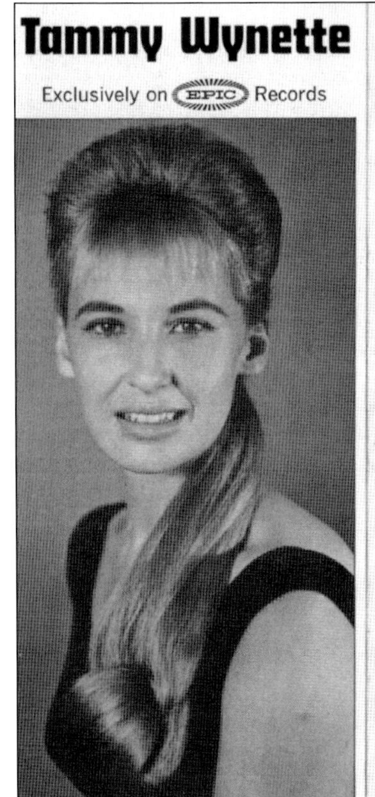

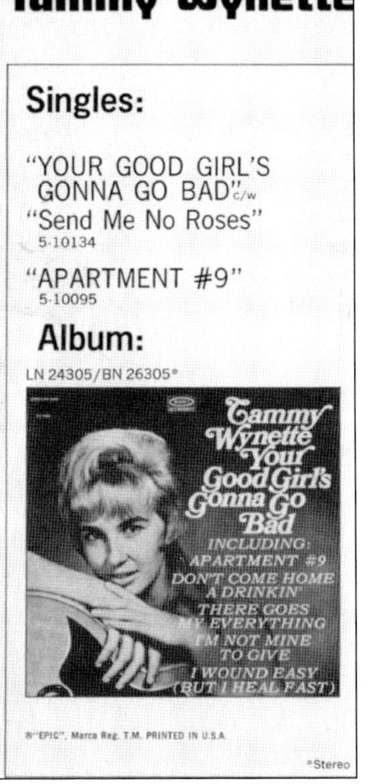

Names such as the Stonemans, Bill Anderson, Loretta Lynn, Crystal Gayle, Waylon Jennings, Jeannie C. Riley, Porter Wagoner, and Tim T. Hall all performed free shows at Lake Winnepesaukah. This picture is an advertisement for Tammy Wynette's performance.

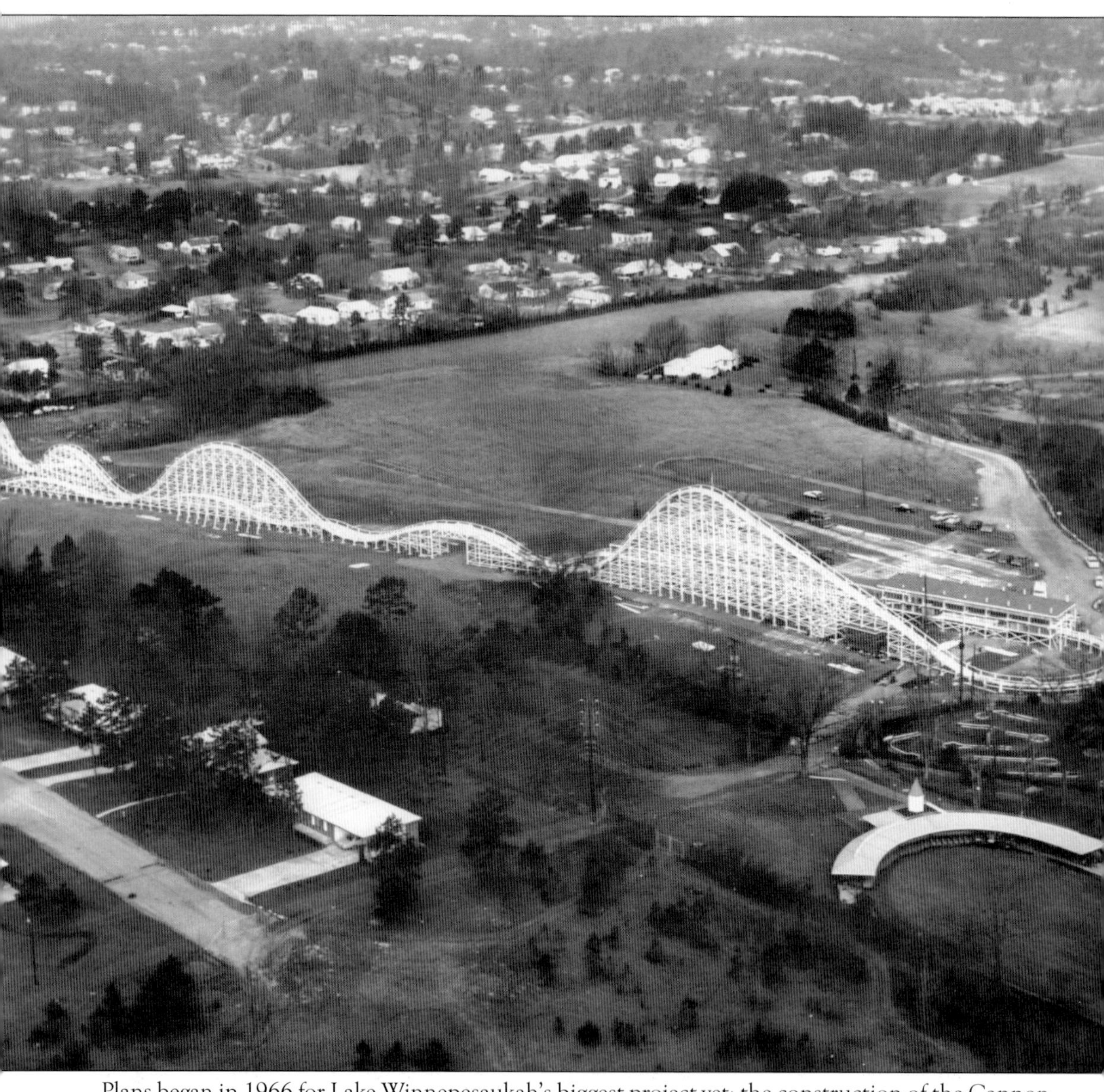

Plans began in 1966 for Lake Winnepesaukah's biggest project yet: the construction of the Cannon Ball Roller Coaster. The structure holds 25 tons of steel track. Special lumber as well as special paint was used. When completed, the structure contained 200,000 board feet of specially treated yellow-leaf pine and approximately 60,000 nuts, bolts, and washers.

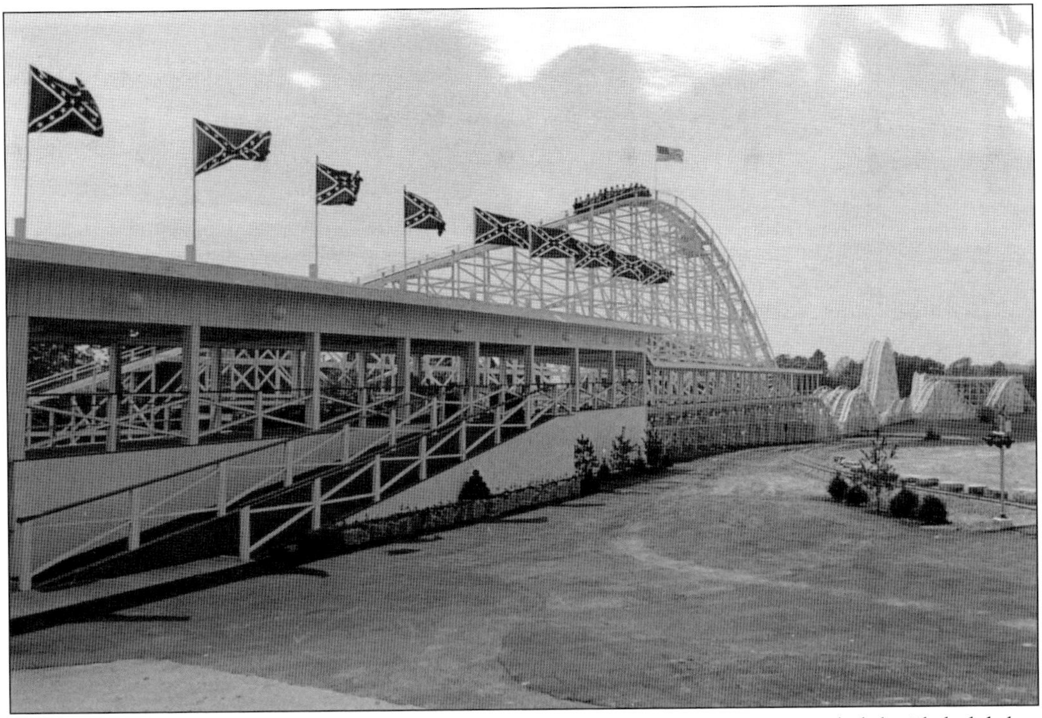

The Cannon Ball was designed and engineered especially for Lake Winnepesaukah by Philadelphia Toboggan. At the time it was built, it was the fastest and largest ride in the tristate area. Over 1,000 gallons of white paint and 40,000 nuts, bolts, and washers, along with 600 cubes of concrete, were part of the construction.

Each day of operation, a man is required to walk the track of the entire Cannon Ball structure on a safety check. From the top of the half-mile-long giant, riders are propelled over a 70-foot incline. There are nine other hills on the breathtaking ride, which has been commended by coaster enthusiasts for the "airtime" it offers.

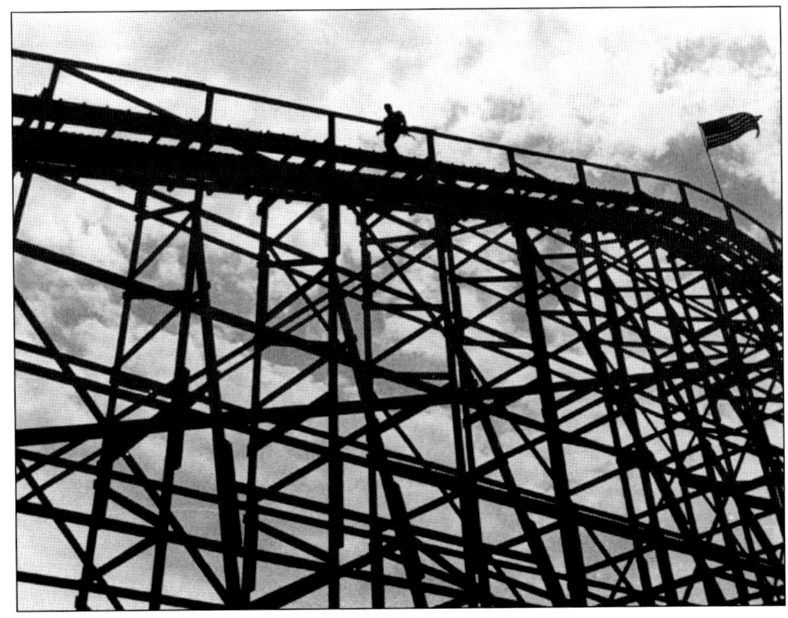

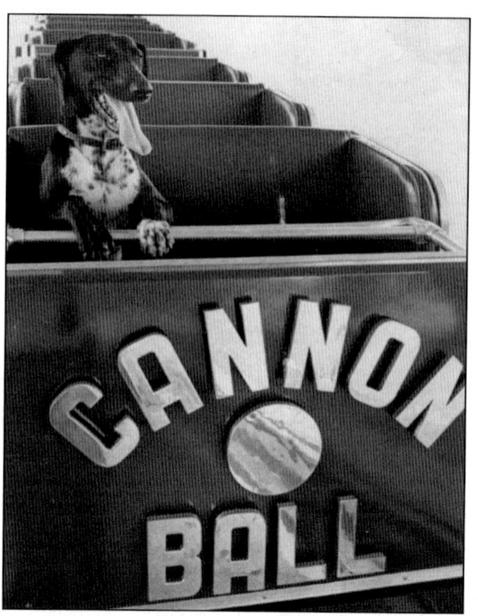

While the coaster was being built, there was a stray dog who faithfully watched the workmen. When the ride was tested, he followed the cars around the half-mile track, keeping up every pace until it returned to the station. When the ride opened, Cannon Ball the dog chased the coaster train every inch of the half-mile track, always returning to the starting point at the same time as the fast-moving cars. Tom T. Hall, an artist who performed at Lake Winnie, was so enthralled with the dog, he wrote a song about him: "Chattanooga Dog."

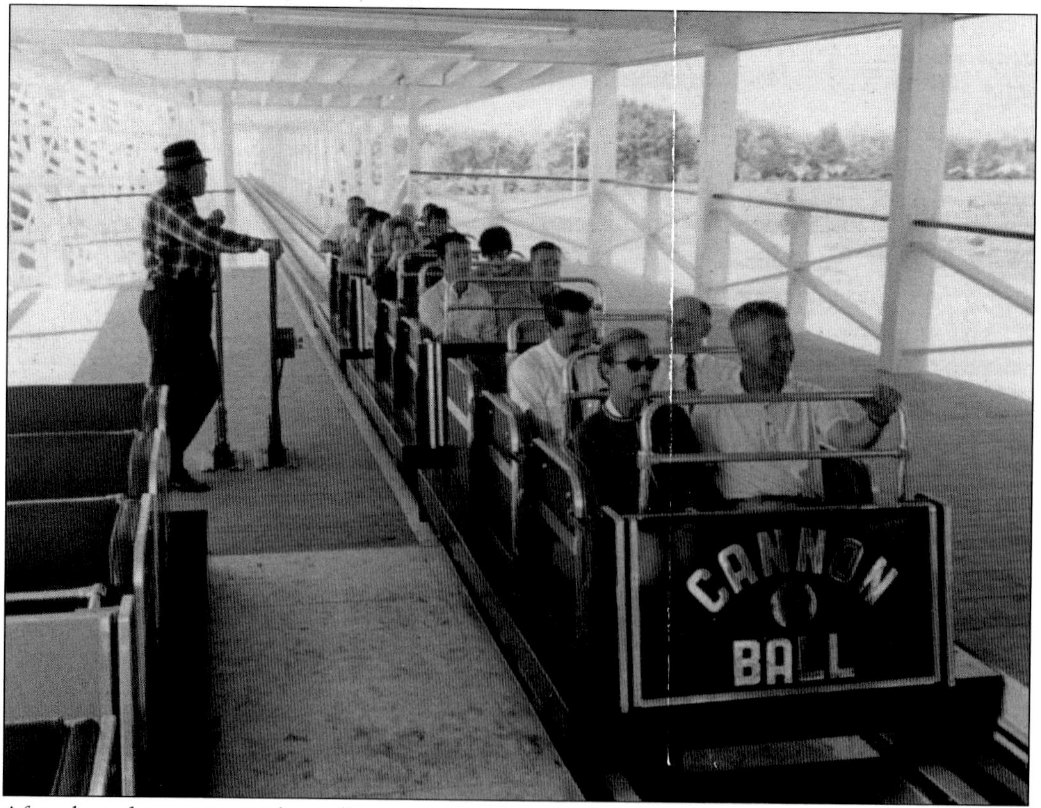

After the safety testing with sandbags was complete, Evelyn and Charlie White took the first ride. The trains are propelled to the top of the 70-foot first hill by a 75-horsepower, 440-volt electric motor pulling a chain that engages at the bottom of the train and pulls it to the 200-foot incline to the top of the hill and down a 45-degree plunge. All further motion of the train is furnished by the car's momentum.

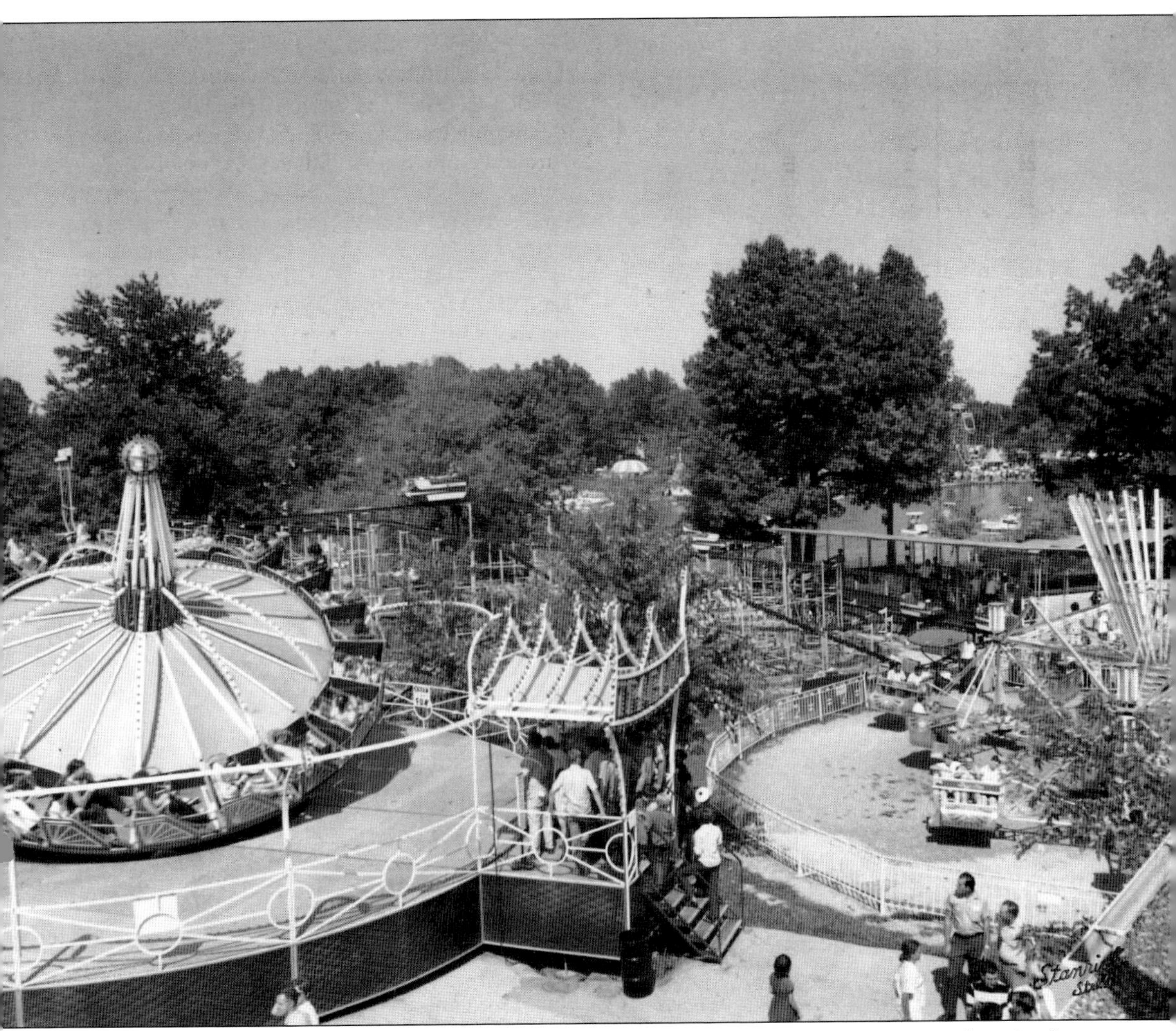

The Trabant debuted in 1968 across from the Cannon Ball Roller Coaster. It was a favorite for those who liked a rollicking good time. It was constantly changing motion, swiveling and tilting in all directions. A galaxy of light, brilliant colors, and multi-action combined to make it a favorite for thrill-seekers.

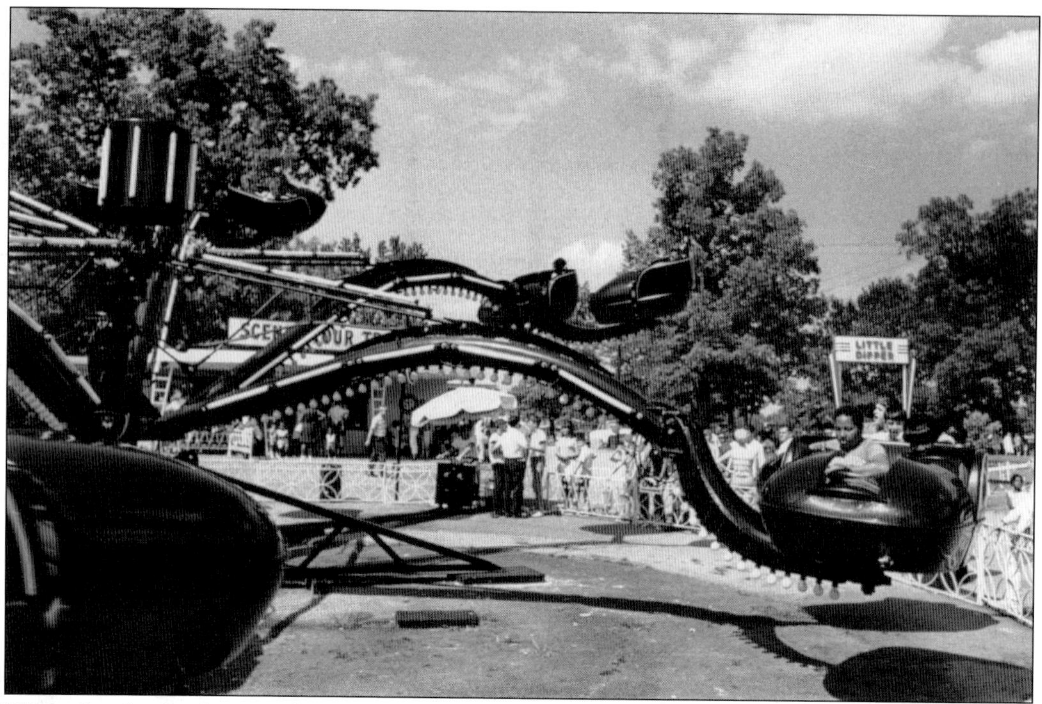

This ride, the Spider, was located behind the Ferris wheel when it first arrived on the scene in 1968. Its six long black arms individually rotated and moved up and down while the individual tubs spun, weaving a web of fun.

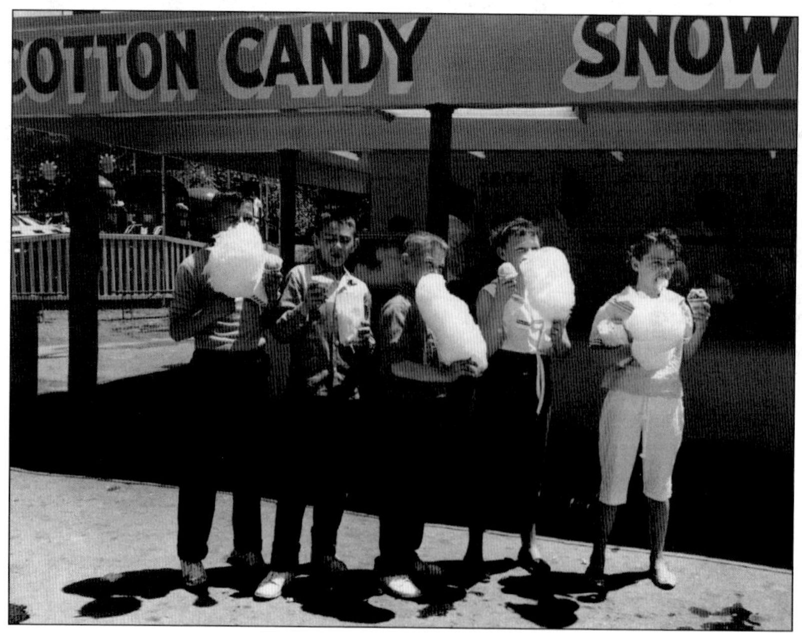

No trip to Lake Winnie was ever complete without the advertised specialties: snow cones, popcorn, and cotton candy. It was the 1960s that brought student discount cards, and schoolchildren (and many adults) could not resist a sugary treat.

Overall, Evelyn White was ecstatic to learn of a 1916 hand-carved carousel for sale in Atlanta. The 1916 hand-carved carousel was created by Alan Herschell and is No. 56 of his company's carving legacy. It is hand-painted by Swiss and Italian artists and includes 68 horses and two chariots.

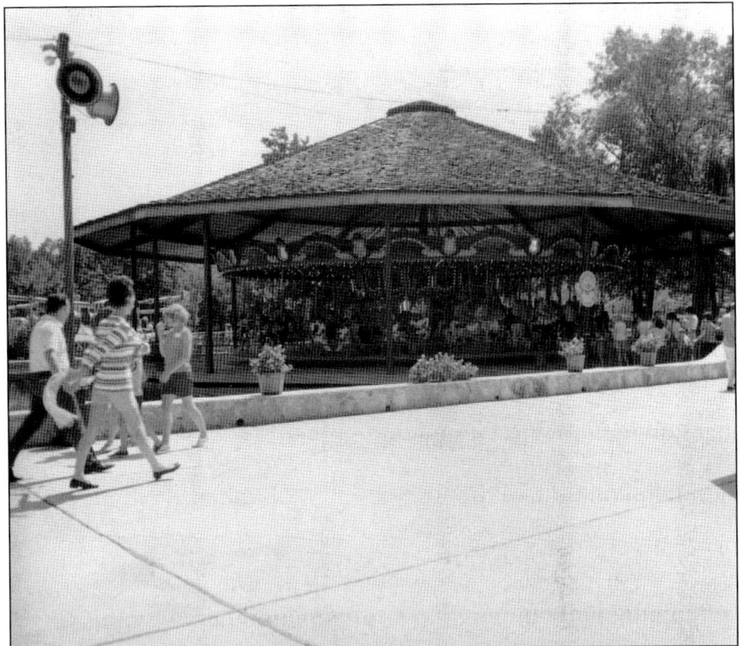

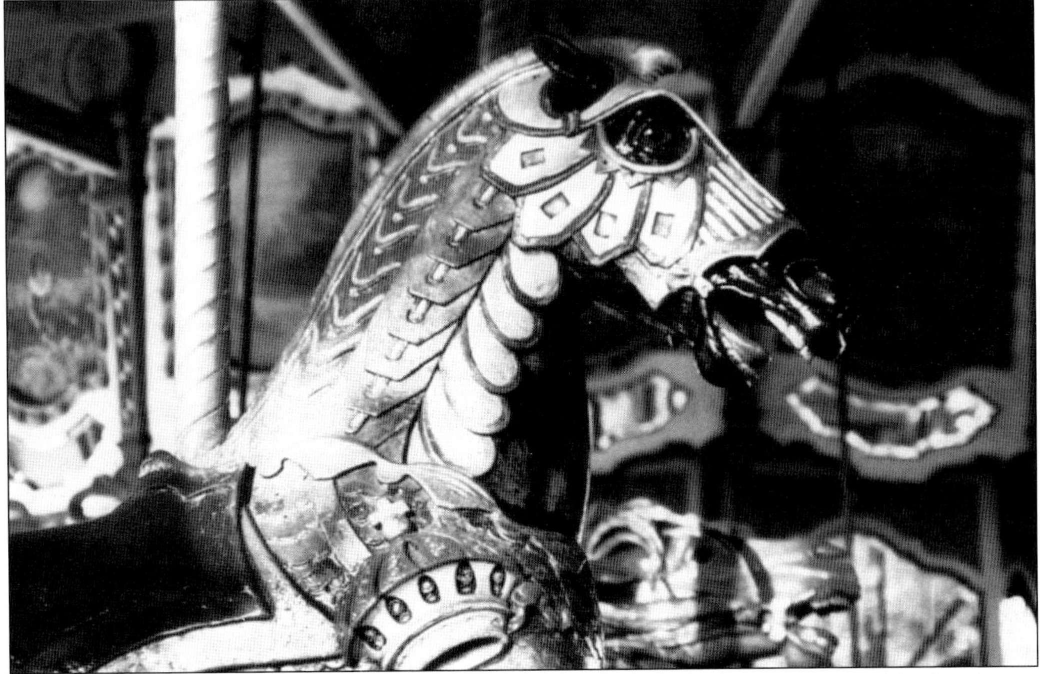

No two of the 68 horses are alike. They each have their own distinct features and looks. One is carved with a bearskin rug on his flanks, and another has a barrel tucked behind the saddle. One has a cherub's face carved in the bridle, and yet another gallant steed is carved ready for battle clad with armor, while one features a quiver of arrows. The horses are four abreast and graduate in size, with the largest horses on the outside and horses decreasing in size on the next two rows, while the ponies are on the innermost ring. There are very few of the Philadelphia Toboggan carousels remaining intact today.

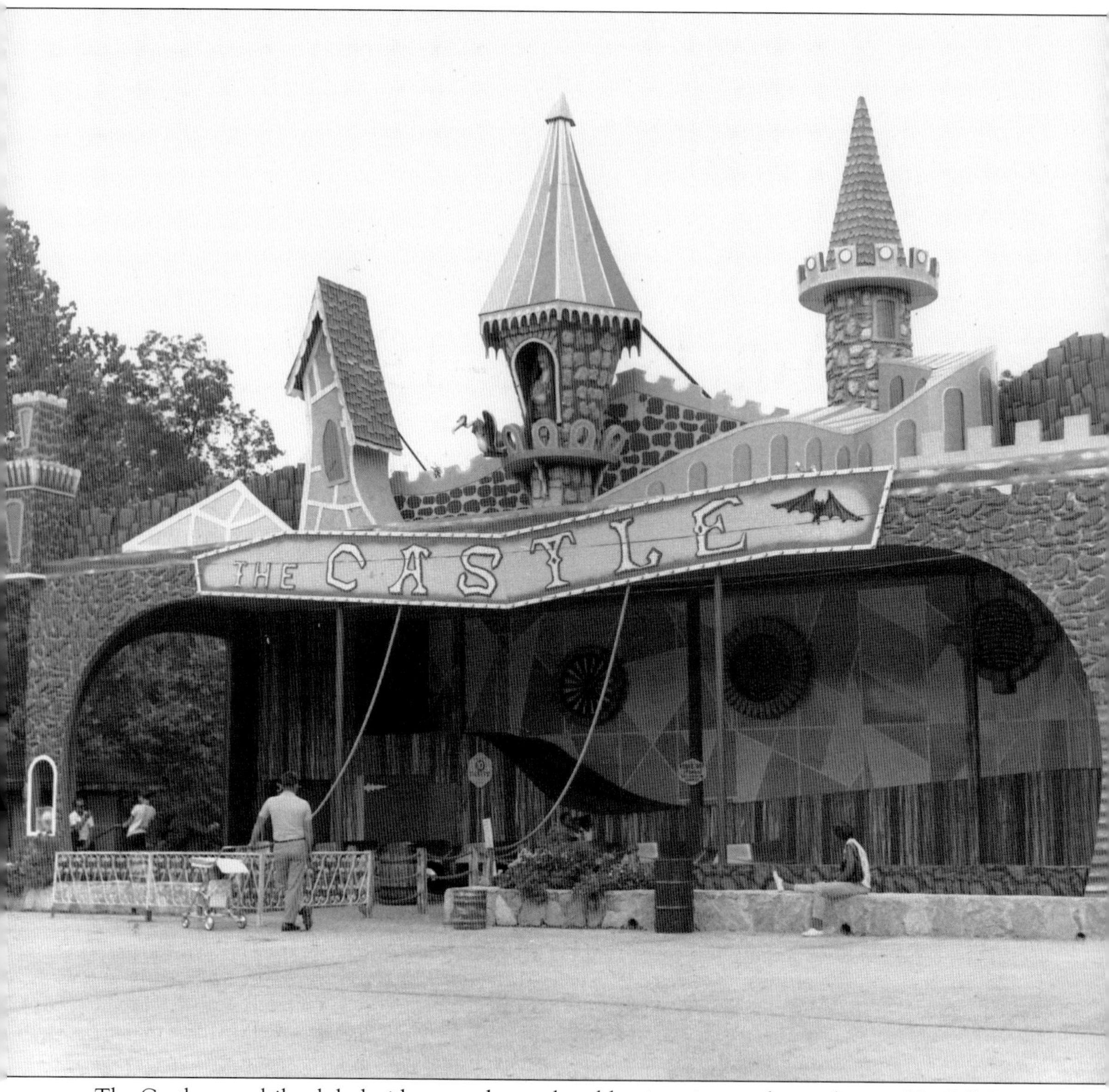

The Castle, a multilevel dark ride erected over the old swimming pool, was designed by Bill Tracy, who described the park's new addition as "the finest project I've ever done." It was unveiled in 1969. The sensational 4,875-square-foot fiberglass and plywood structure with its winding track "incorporates everything I've ever dreamed of," the imaginative designer declared. A drawbridge leads to the entrance, which is surrounded by water. The psychedelic lighting, endless illusions, and tricky scenes along the way lead to a climactic exit.

Six

The 1970s–1997

Under New Management

The 1970s were a tumultuous time in America, both for the rights of minorities and protests against the Vietnam War. This seemed to be mirrored in changes taking place at Lake Winnepesaukah. The year 1971 started smoothly. A new ride, the Indy 500, was introduced, and many top-name acts, including Crystal Gayle, the Leamon Sisters, Loretta Lynn, and Waylon Jennings, performed. In 1974, at age 63, Evelyn White was ready to retire, and she announced the beloved park would close. She canceled the insurance on the Cannon Ball Roller Coaster and let it be known the park would not reopen. The twists and turns of the rides seemed evident in some next events. In 1975, Tootsie and Butch Harless, Evelyn's daughter and son-in-law, respectively, rented the north side of the park and opened Kiddie Winnie, an area for kiddie rides only. This remained in effect for two years. In 1977, Evelyn entered into a 20-year lease with Funtown Inc., a carnival operation run by J.D. Floyd. The family still owned the land and the memories, but day-to-day operations were released to Funtown. The pictures in this chapter represent the various rides the Floyds brought on during this period.

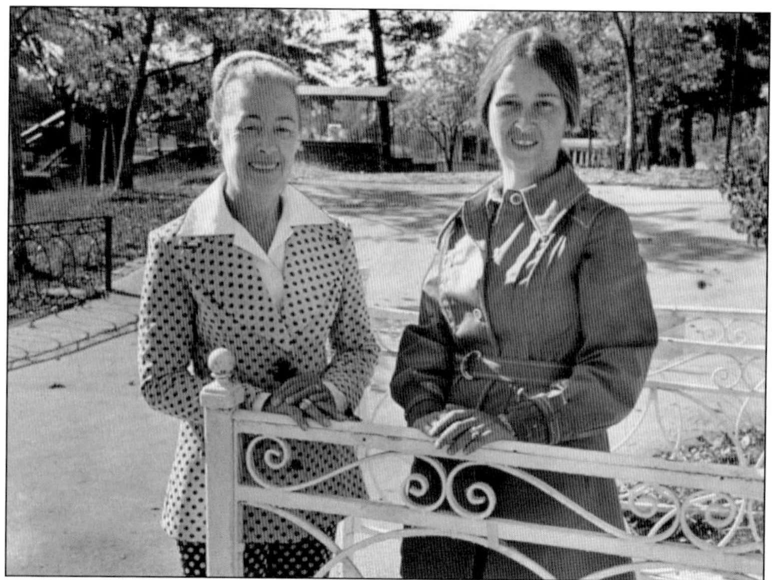

Evelyn White (left) and Tootsie Harless (right) opened the park in 1970, committed to maintaining the same standards of affordable family fun that customers had come to expect. Tootsie's focus was the gift shop and games; her husband, Butch, managed the rides; and Evelyn continued to oversee the food department.

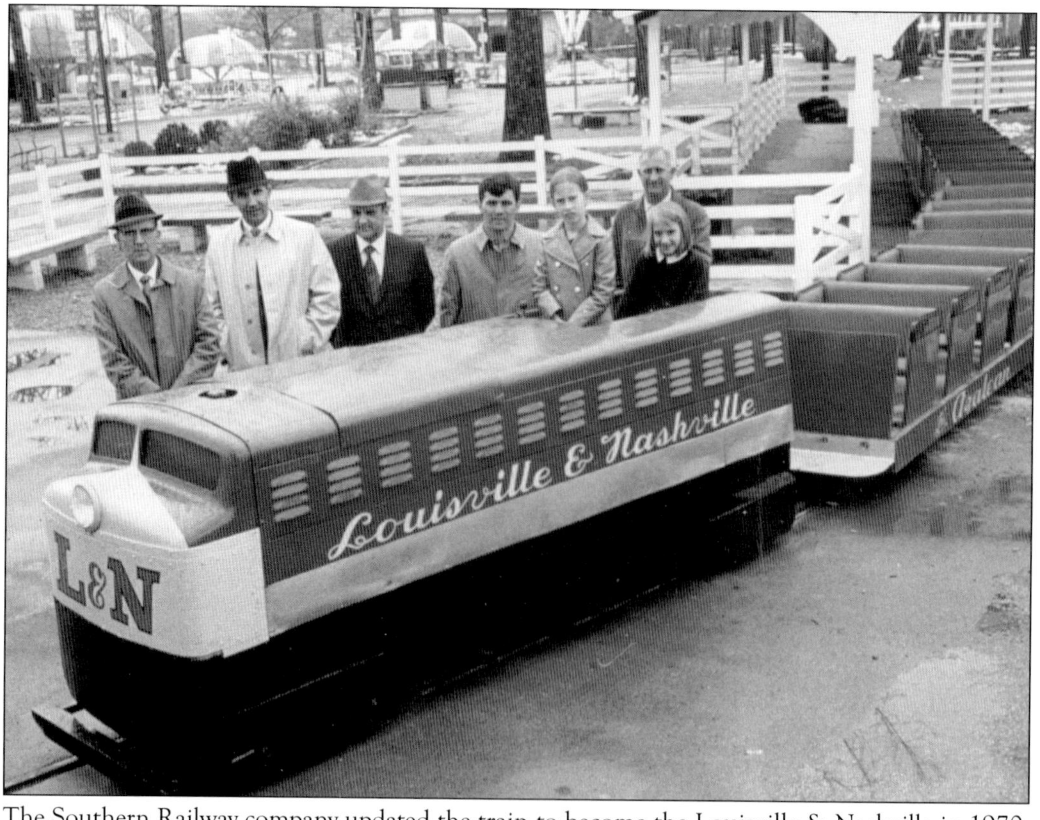

The Southern Railway company updated the train to become the Louisville & Nashville in 1970. Pictured are, from left to right, three representatives from Southern Railway, Butch (Tootsie's husband), Kelly and Evelyn Harless, and Leonard Guinn (food manager). The train continued to be a favorite at the park. The 1.1-mile track provided a good overview of the layout of the park.

The 1970 season kicked off on May 1, unveiling exciting new updates to two beloved attractions. The park proudly introduced refreshed versions of the Tilt-A-Whirl and Scrambler flat rides, promising guests an exhilarating experience like never before.

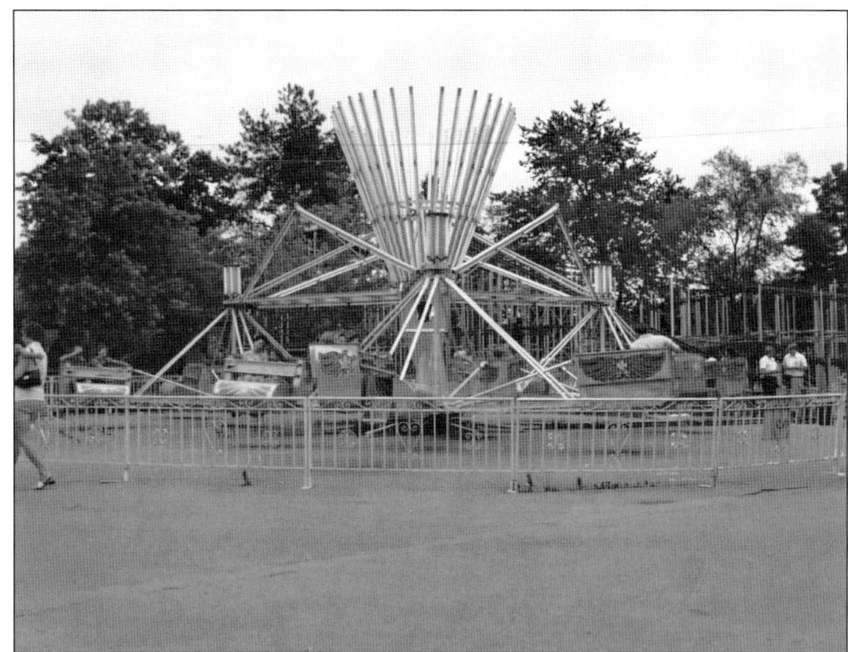

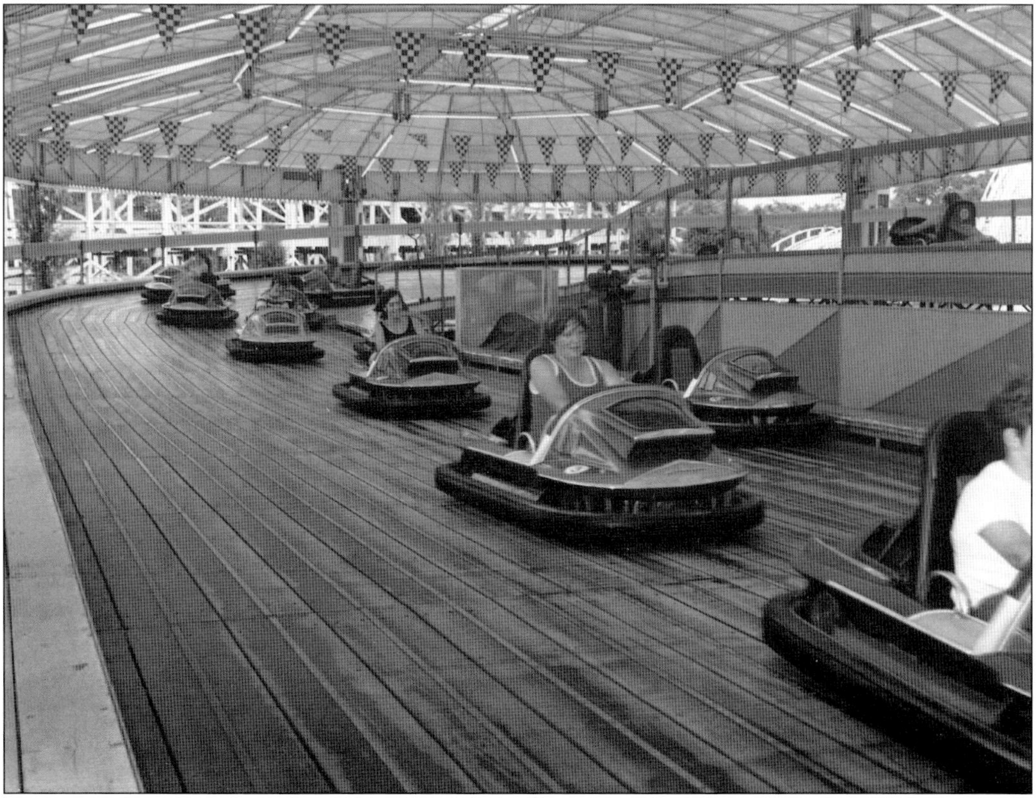

Also in 1970 came the addition of the Indy 500, an Italian bumper car ride with a brilliantly illuminated pavilion. The ride seemed to harken back to the races held at Lake Winnie 45 years prior.

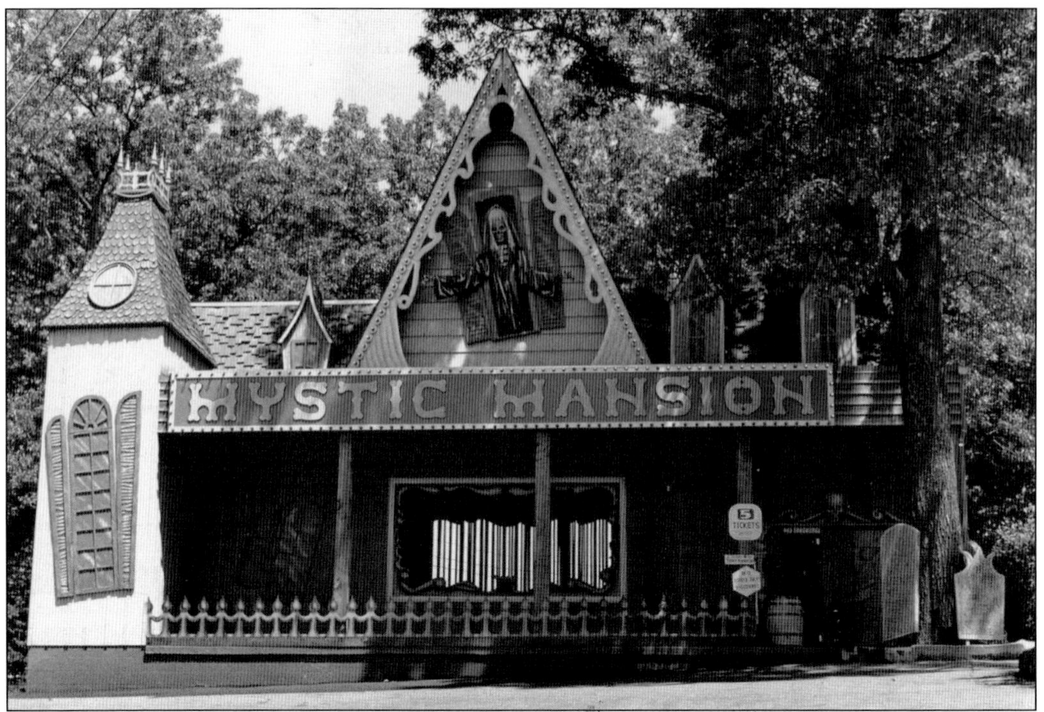

The Mystic Mansion was introduced to Lake Winnie in 1971, captivating guests with its immersive walk-through experience. Visitors were delighted by the eerie Chamber of Horrors and the enchanting Mystery Room, where water defied gravity and ran uphill, adding an unforgettable twist to their adventure.

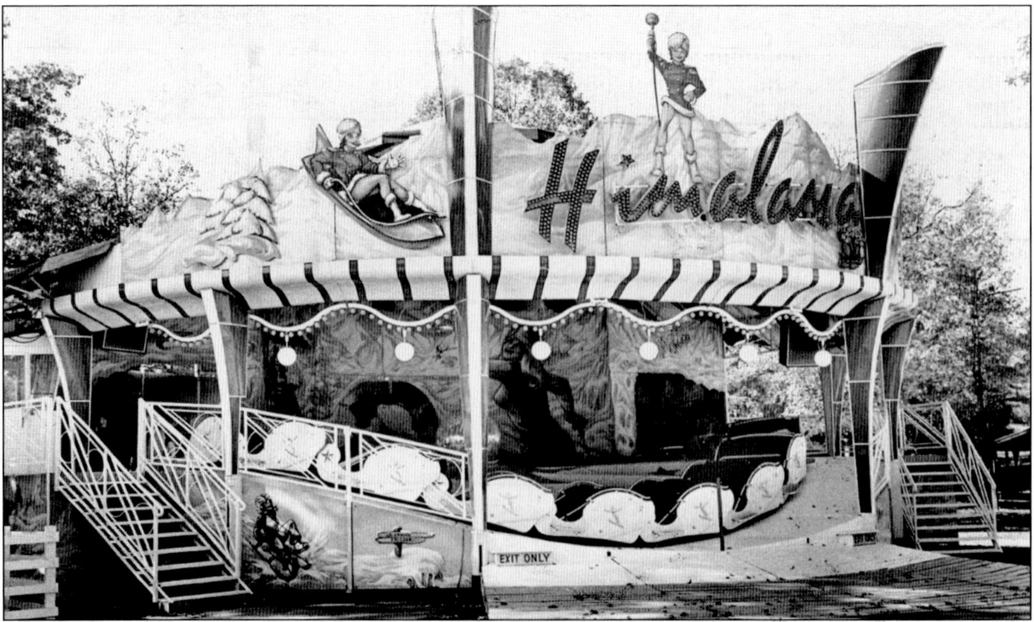

The Himalaya ride was added in the 1970s. The ride cars were connected in a circle and rotated on a track with alternating sloped and flat sections. Moving both backward and forward, it was a family thrill ride that was not for the weak of heart!

The Labyrinthe walk-through fun house was an enchanting maze of mirrors and glass. As one navigates this whimsical space, the reflective surfaces create fascinating illusions, revealing glimpses of pathways one might explore.

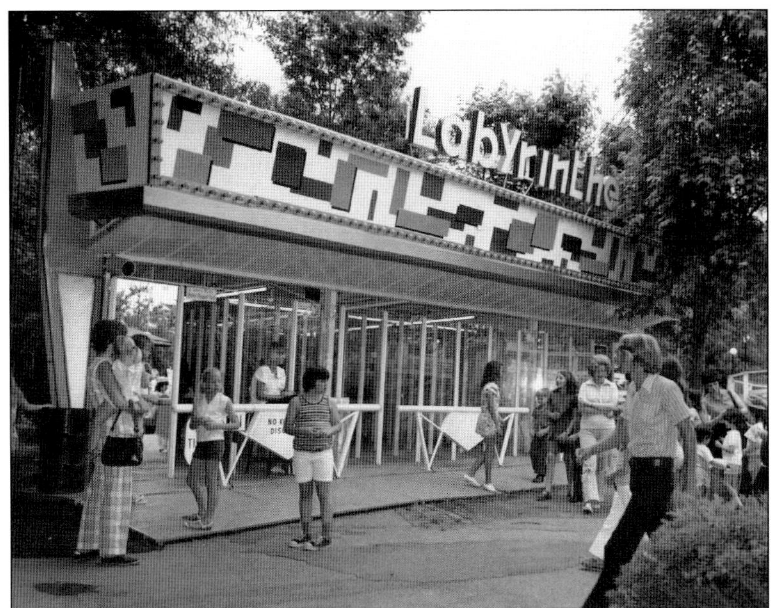

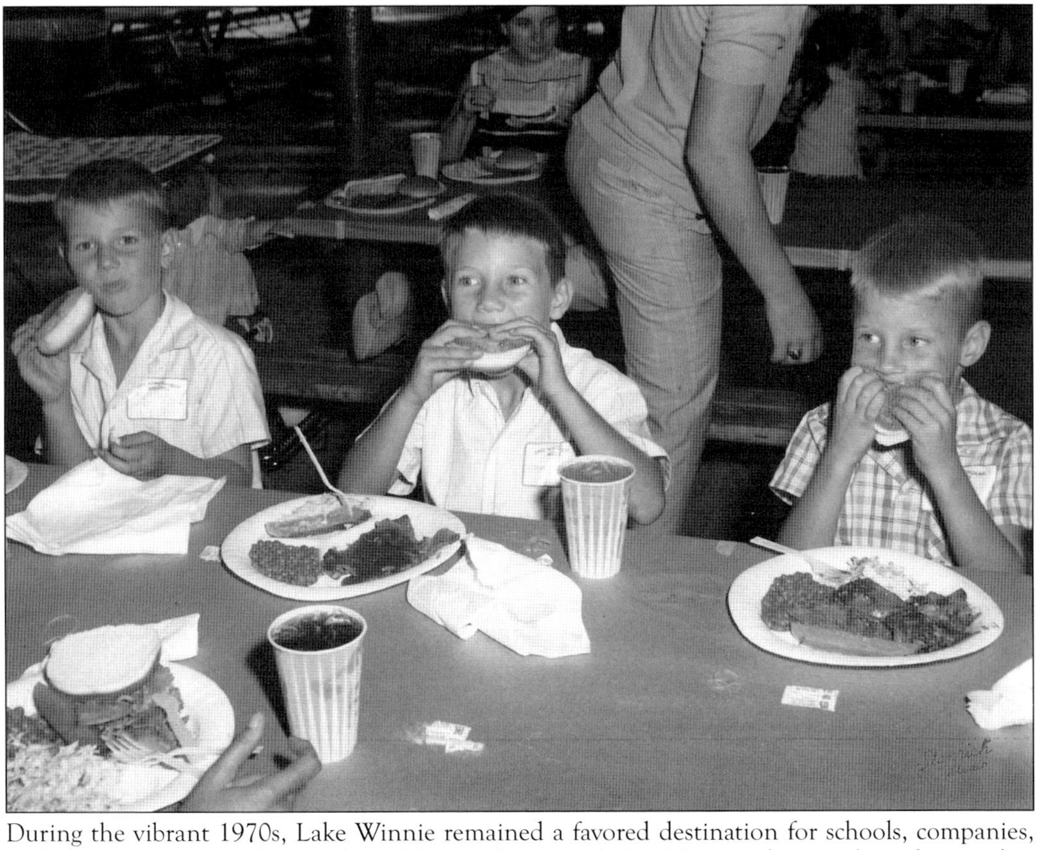

During the vibrant 1970s, Lake Winnie remained a favored destination for schools, companies, and church groups seeking a day of fun and camaraderie. These gatherings brought together friends and families, all eager to enjoy a thrilling array of rides, indulge in delicious food, and revel in lively entertainment.

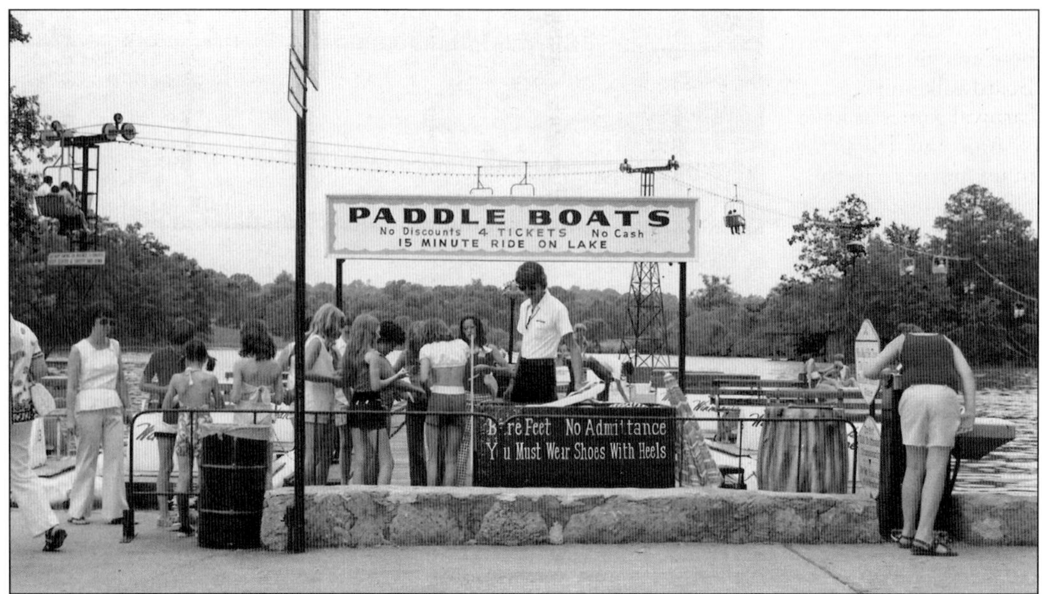

The paddleboats enjoyed continued popularity in the 1970s. In this photograph, one can see a ride operator assisting guests as they load and unload on the boat dock, eagerly preparing for their boating adventure on the shimmering water.

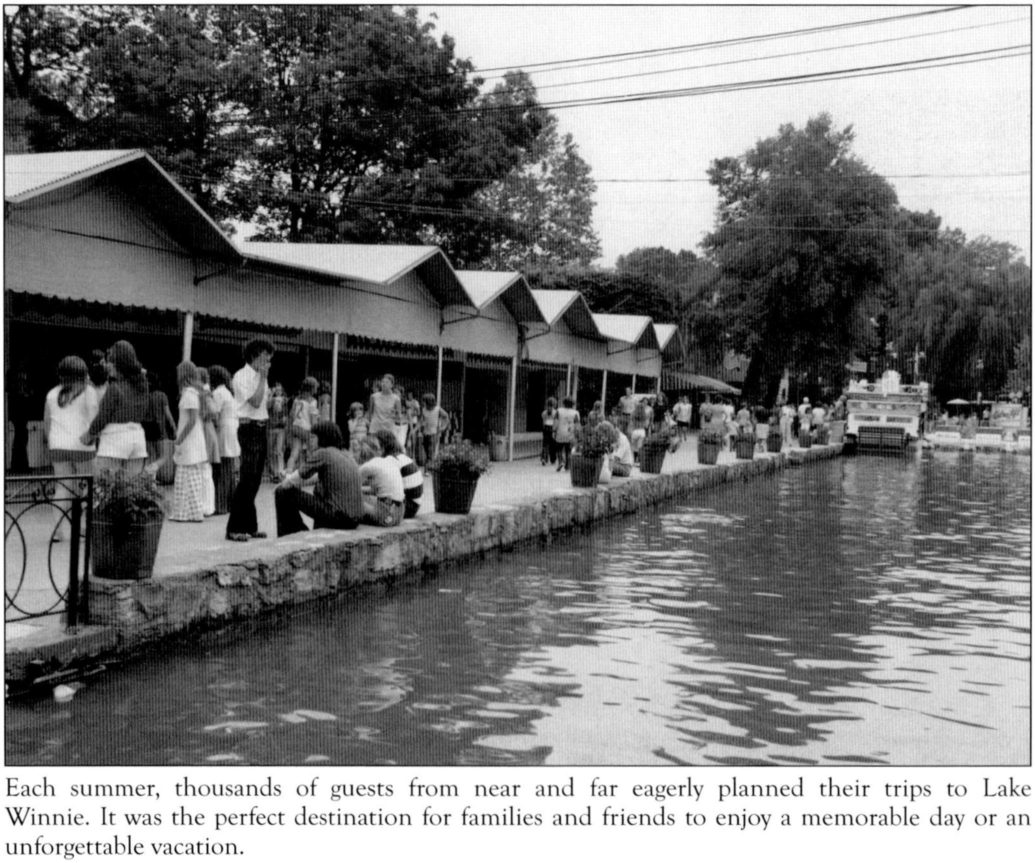

Each summer, thousands of guests from near and far eagerly planned their trips to Lake Winnie. It was the perfect destination for families and friends to enjoy a memorable day or an unforgettable vacation.

Families are seen here enjoying the Boardwalk and carnival games at Lake Winnie and delighting in ice cream from the Show Boat, which was originally used for scenic boat tours on Lake Winnepesaukah.

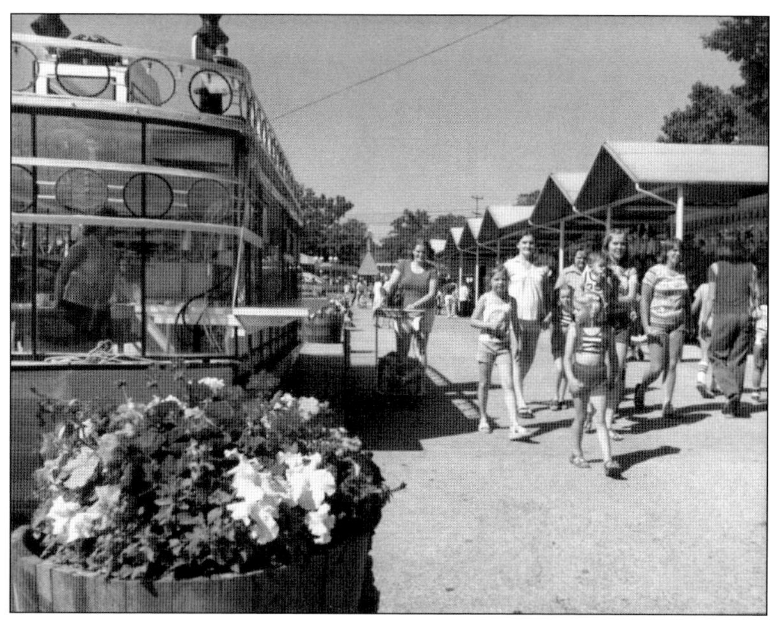

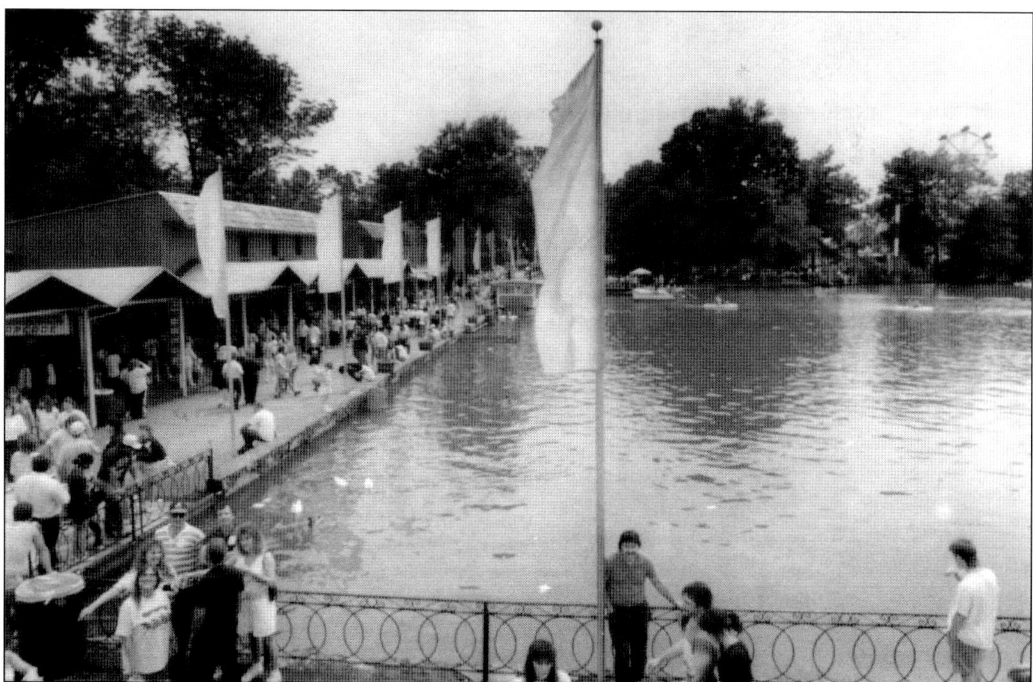

Lake Winnie opened for the 1980 season on April 5, offering visitors continued memorable experiences while remaining firmly rooted in the family's rich heritage. Pictured here is a view from the Ferris wheel.

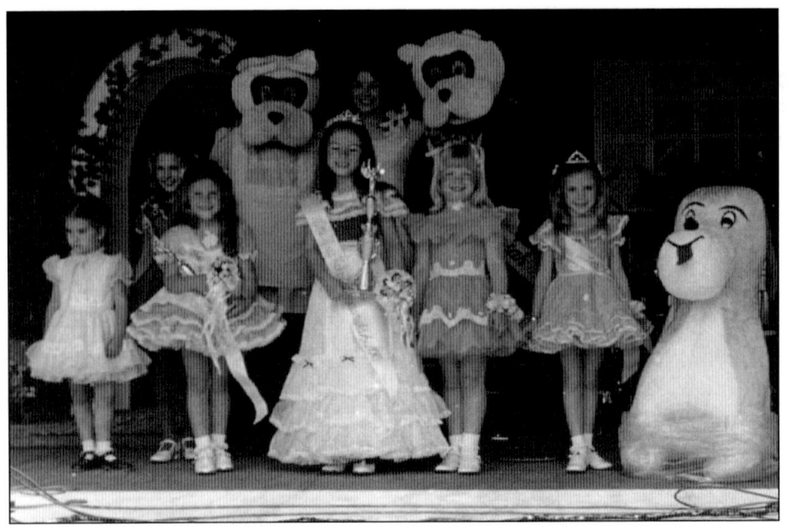

Pictured is the crowning ceremony for the Little Miss Lake Winnepesaukah Pageant in 1980, a delightful celebration of charm and talent that captured the hearts of all in attendance. The pageant showcased the hopes and dreams of its contestants, leaving everyone inspired and filled with memories to cherish.

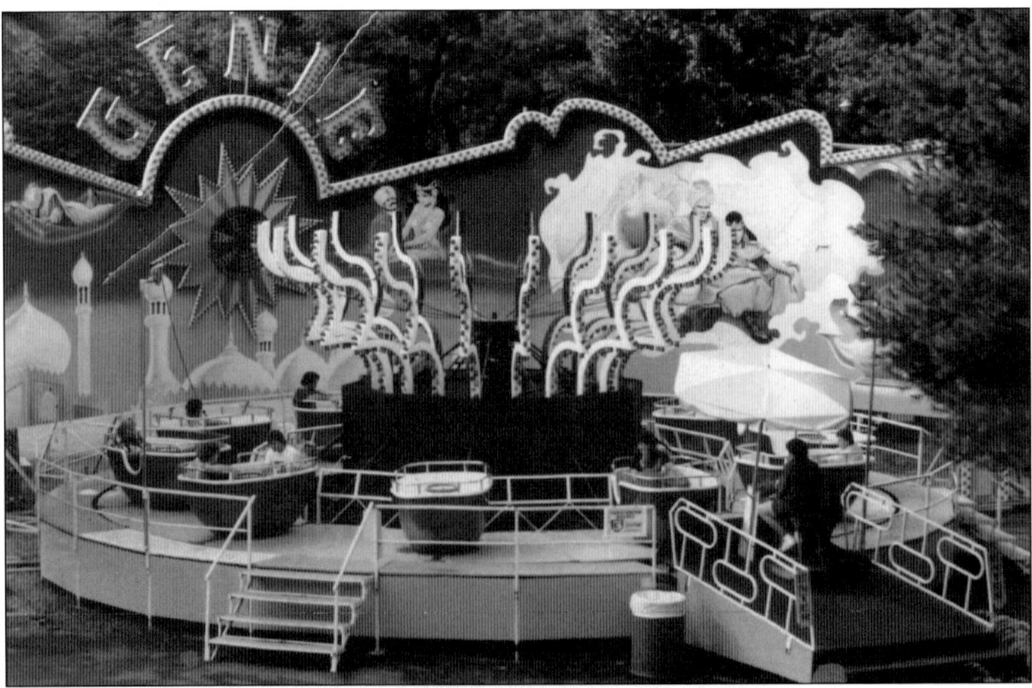

The original Genie ride, seen here at Lake Winnie in 1982, brought a captivating new twist to the classic Teacups ride. This enchanting attraction offered guests a whimsical experience, combining delightful spinning with a magical theme that transported riders into a world of fun and imagination.

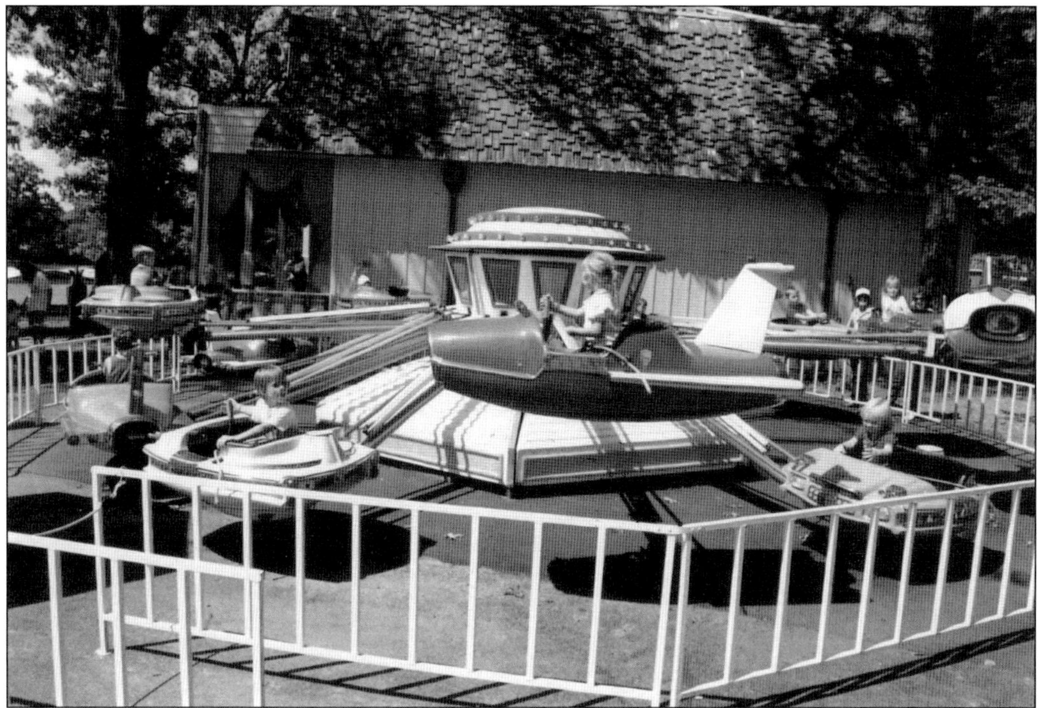

Parents watch from nearby while children are having a blast as they take a spin on the exhilarating Spaceship ride at Kiddie Hill. With a gentle start, the ride lifts off, and the kids are soon soaring through a series of delightful twists and turns.

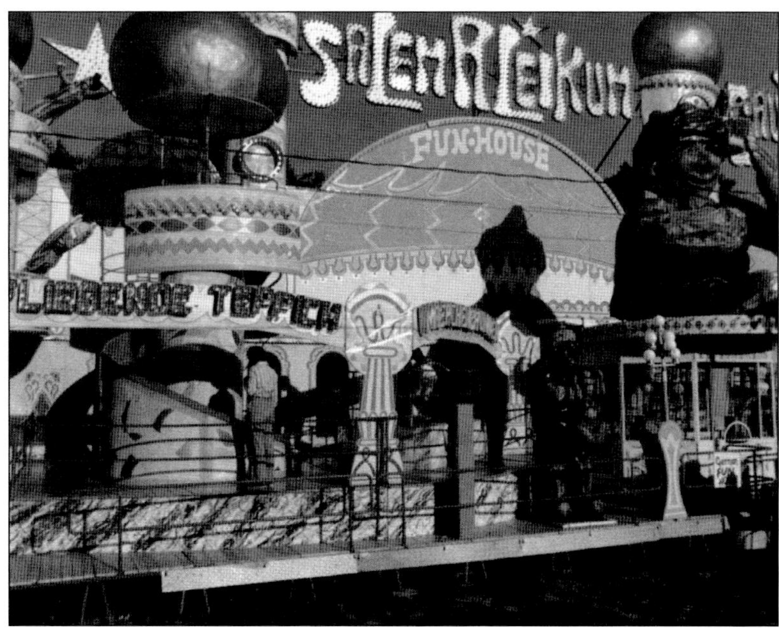

A brand-new temporary fun house called Aladdin's Lamp was introduced for the 1982 season, adding an exciting attraction that promised laughter and adventure for guests of all ages. This whimsical addition invited visitors to explore its intriguing mazes and playful surprises.

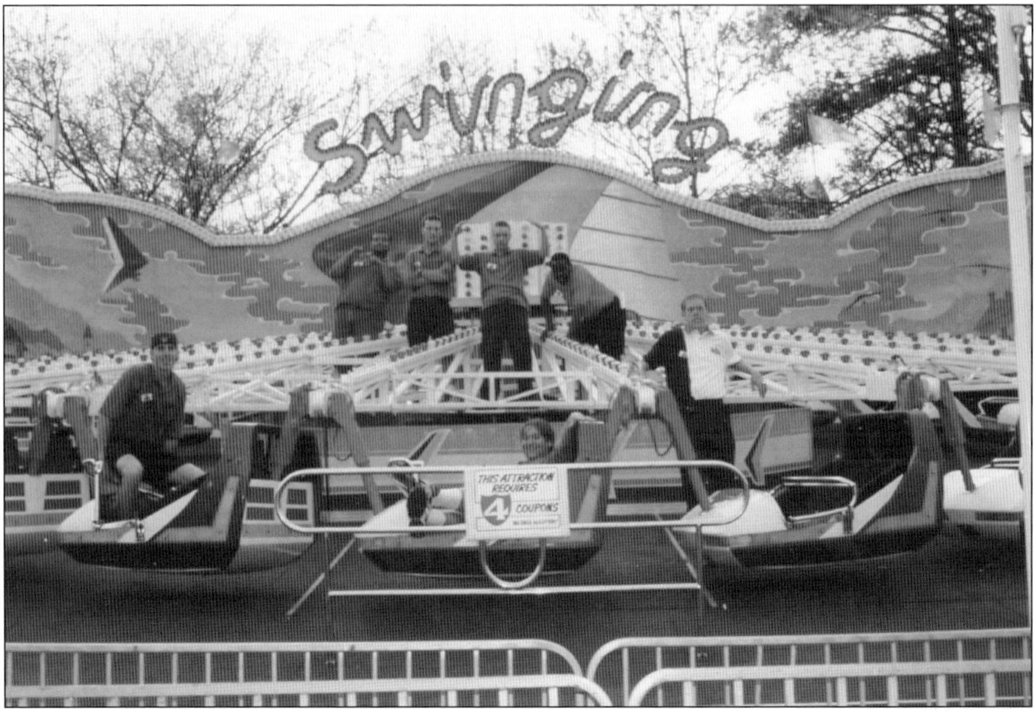

The ride operators of the Swinging flat ride are captured here, posing for a photograph before warmly welcoming guests to the park on a sunny summer day. Swinging was a popular centrifuge ride in the early 1990s.

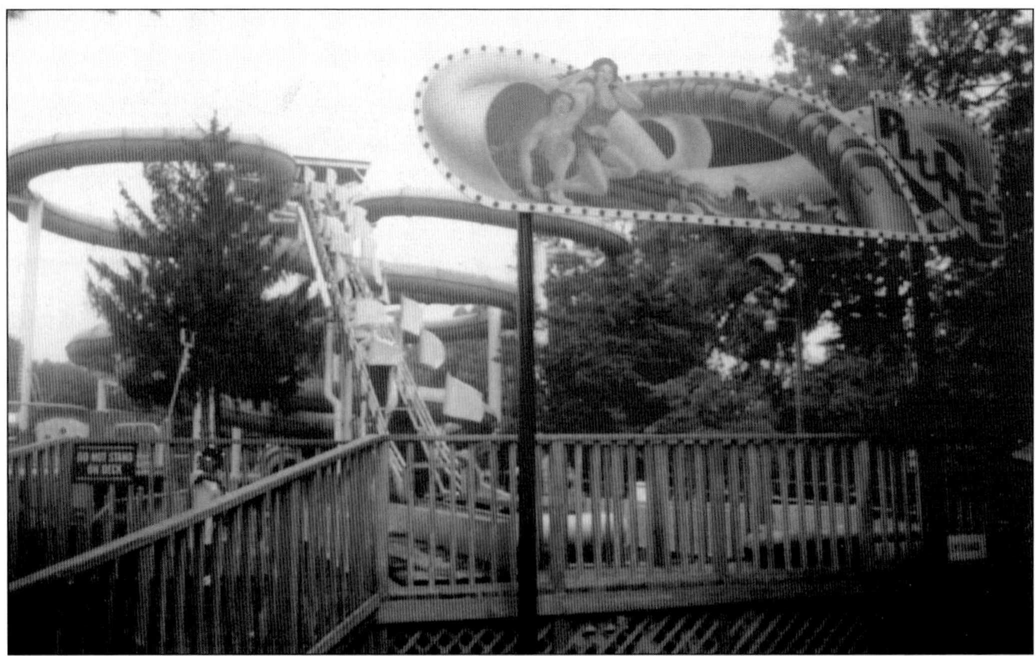

The Pipeline Plunge was added in the 1995 season. The second water ride added to Lake Winnie, it offered guests an exhilarating adventure. Riders climb a 52-foot tower then board rafts and dive into dark, twisting tunnels, culminating in a thrilling splashdown at the bottom of the slide.

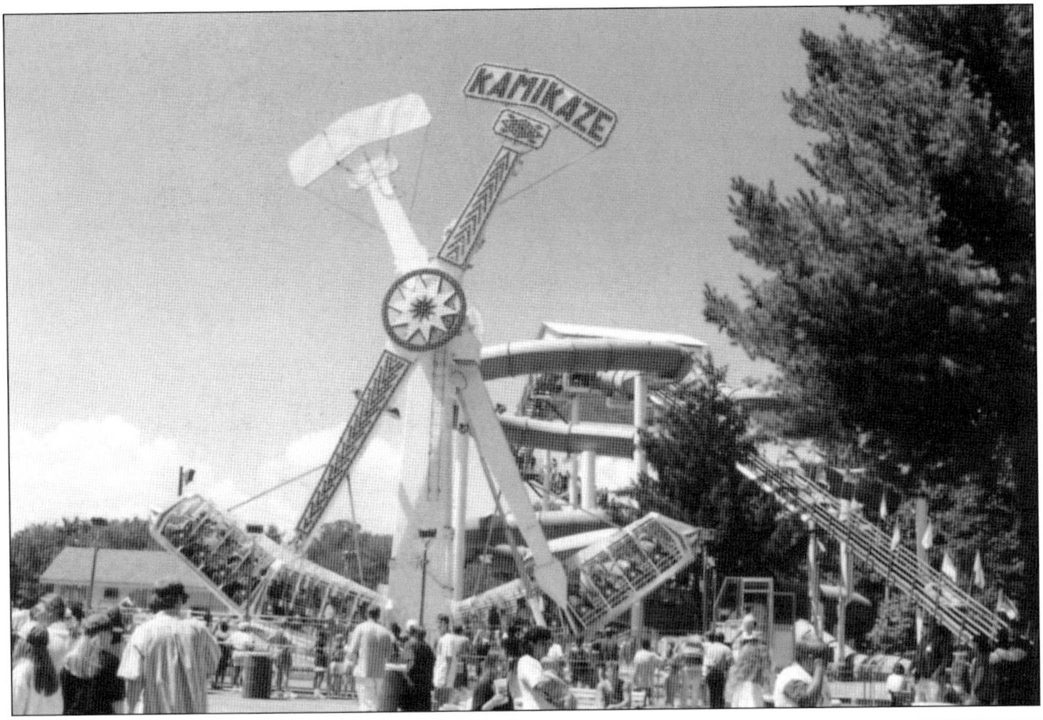

The Kamikaze was one of the park's most thrilling new additions in the 1990s. This exhilarating ride features a pendulum that swings back and forth in a sweeping motion, spinning guests upside down for an unforgettable experience.

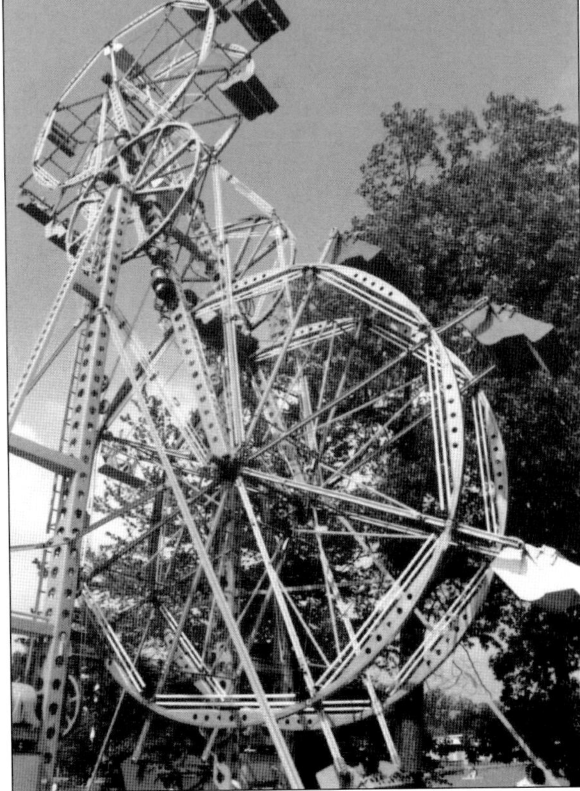

The double Ferris wheel provided riders with an exhilarating twist on the traditional Ferris wheel experience. This stunning attraction allowed guests to enjoy breathtaking views while spinning in tandem, creating a thrilling adventure that added a fresh dimension to a beloved classic.

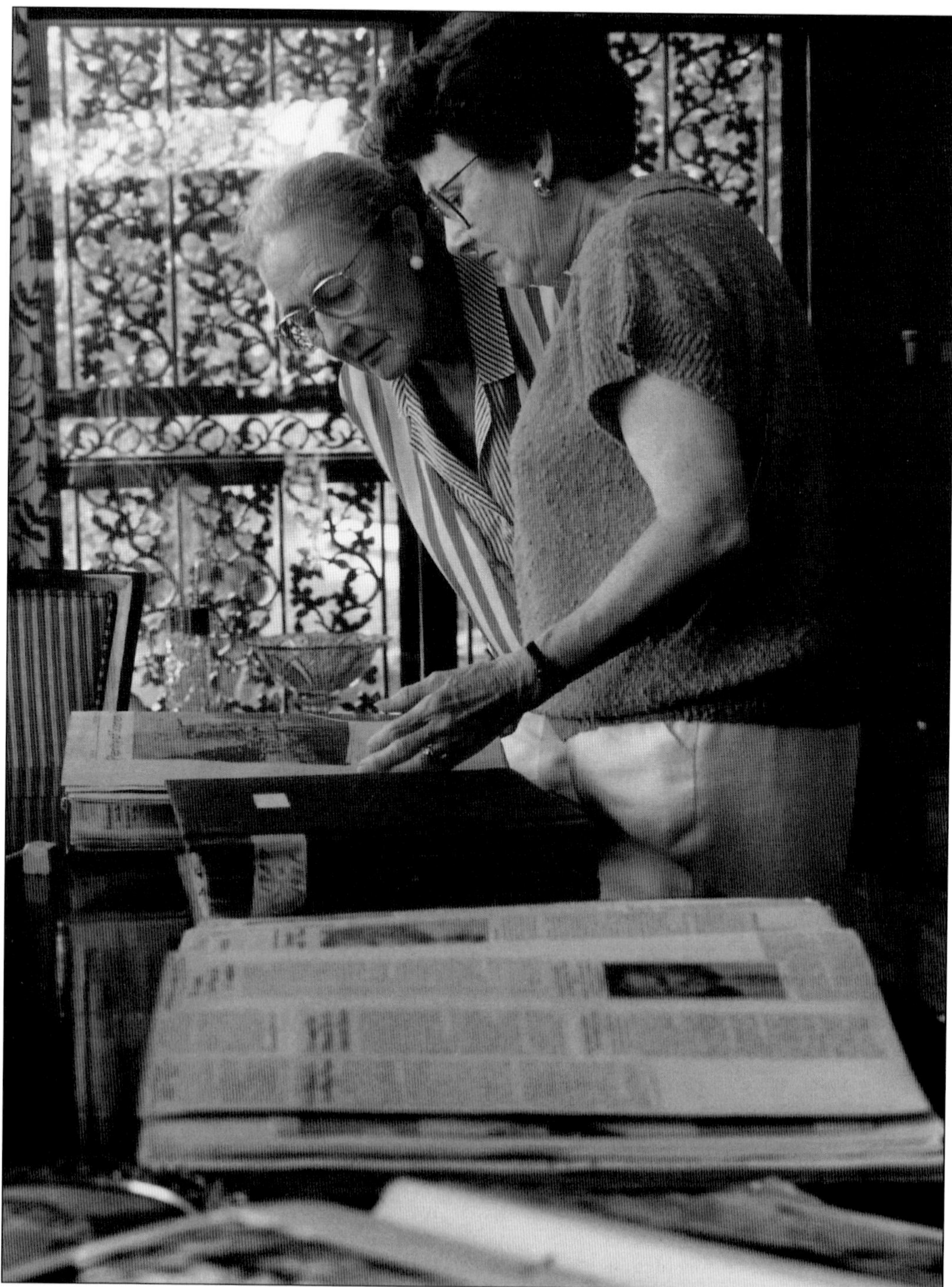

In 1998, the original Rhodes family returned to take the helm of Lake Winnie, embarking on a transformative journey to revitalize the brand. This effort involved substantial upgrades to infrastructure, meticulous maintenance, and comprehensive staff training. The revitalization included the introduction of a fresh logo, updated marketing materials, and an innovative advertising campaign, all aimed at reinvigorating Lake Winnie's legacy.

Seven

1998–2009

The Family Returns

Having been totally involved in every decision and every acquisition for many years, Evelyn White, Adrienne Rhodes, and Tootsie Harless were becoming more disenchanted with the way the park was looking and operating. They thought that the business principles they strongly believed in were not being maintained to their satisfaction. Two months before opening in 1998, they decided to come back in and actively manage the park. They were fortunate to have many of the "old school" managers available to help. There was much painting, repairing, and resurfacing to be done, but with such a brief time frame, no new rides were brought in; rather, the focus was on training new employees and getting the park ready to open. Adrienne's daughter Talley joined the staff to work in public relations and advertising, and Tootsie's son Charlie worked on the maintenance team. The following year, Adrienne's daughter Tennyson joined to lead group sales, and Tootsie's daughter Evelyn worked with the catering and food areas. New rides were added for 1999, including the balloon ride and the Frog Hopper. Wanting to harken back to the "good old days," two models of the Eyerly Fly-O-Plane ride that first debuted in 1947 were purchased in order for the park's maintenance team to then construct one working ride. Other rides added during the decade include the Conestoga; Free Whale; Wave Swinger; Wild Lightening; a new Ferris wheel; OH-Zone!; the Run Around Playground; and Chill Down Kid Town, an internal test for the demand for a potential water park in the future.

Structurally, there was much work to be done. The dam area was dug up and replaced, and the food stand next to the Ferris wheel was replaced with a new two-story one, built with a specially designed Coke bottle proudly atop. The arcade became a gift shop, with the 1940s pine floors remaining, while a new ticket booth at the front was constructed along with a new restroom building in the picnic grounds. Stable and tall lighting was added, as were freezers and ovens and fencing necessary for the changing world.

Perhaps most important was the focus on the customers and the way of doing business. Calendars for the season were made and kept, marketing was done to attract corporate customers and the pricing was published, safety standards were posted on all rides, and employees were specially trained. Maintenance and cleanliness were the primary focus. As one bus driver said when he walked in the gate in 1998, "Yes, the family is back!"

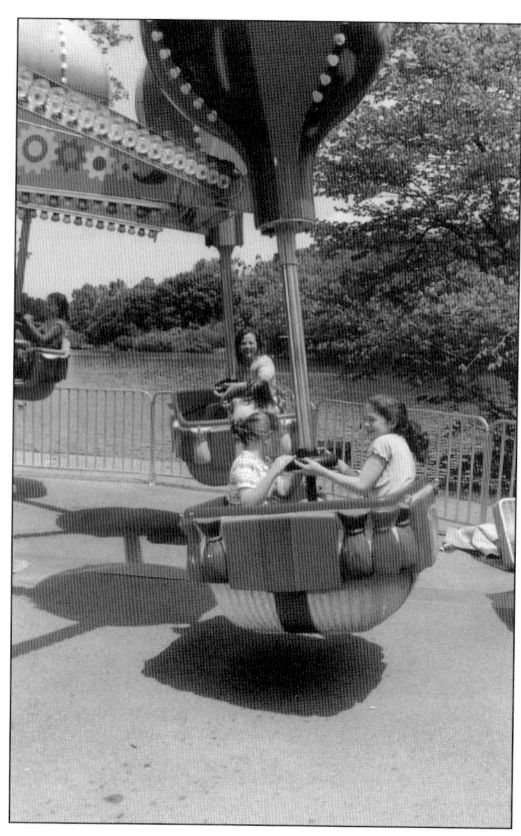

The 1999 season introduced an array of exciting new rides for children and families, including the delightful Frog Hopper, the Zamperla Balloon Ride, and the whimsical Free Whale. These attractions added a fresh sense of adventure to the park, ensuring that young visitors and their families could create lasting memories together. The Frog Hopper, built by S&S Worldwide, takes children up a 25-foot-tall tower, bouncing all the way back down.

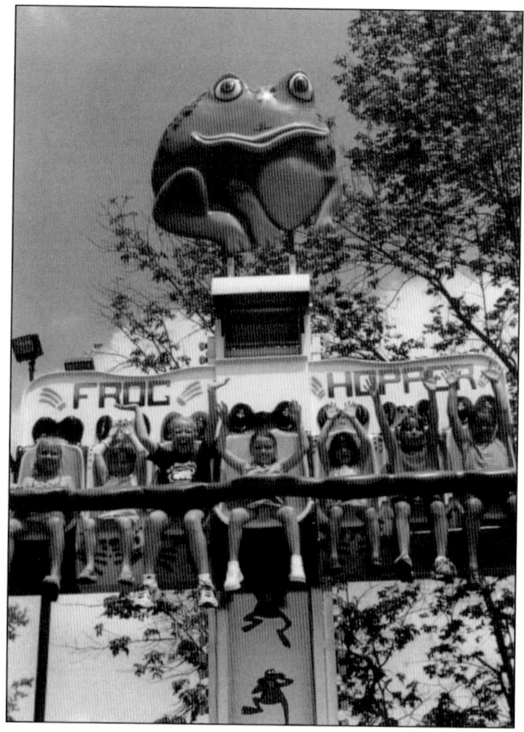

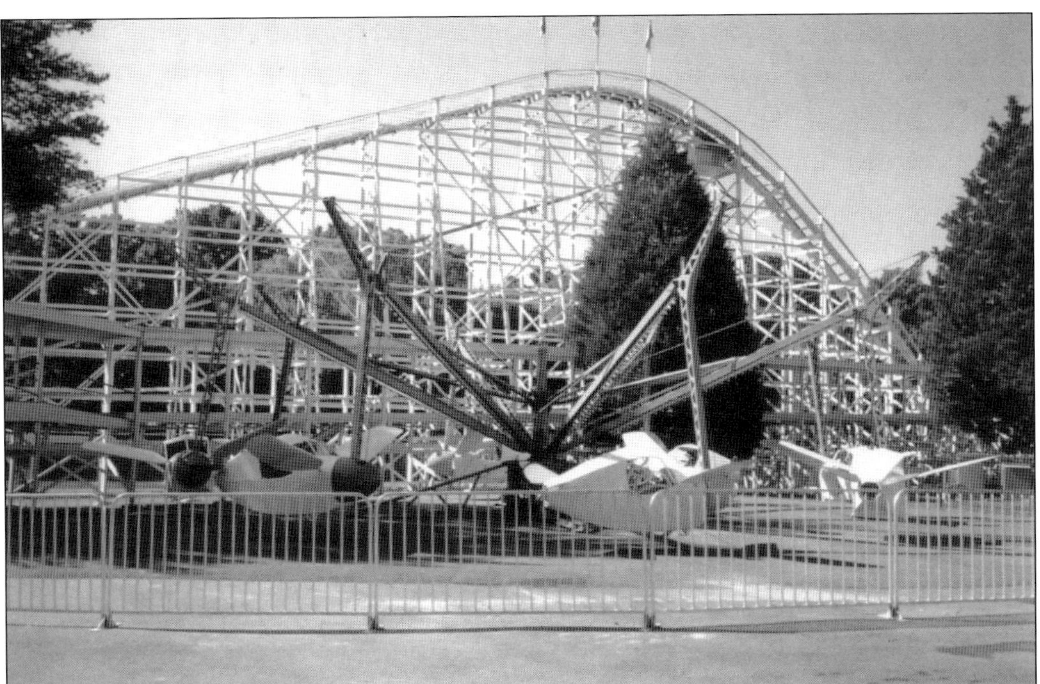

The Fly-O-Plane was manufactured by Eyerly Aircraft Company in Oregon. These planes were originally designed to train pilots during World War II. The park purchased two nonoperating rides, and the maintenance team worked diligently to combine parts and create one functioning ride, which operated in the 1999 season.

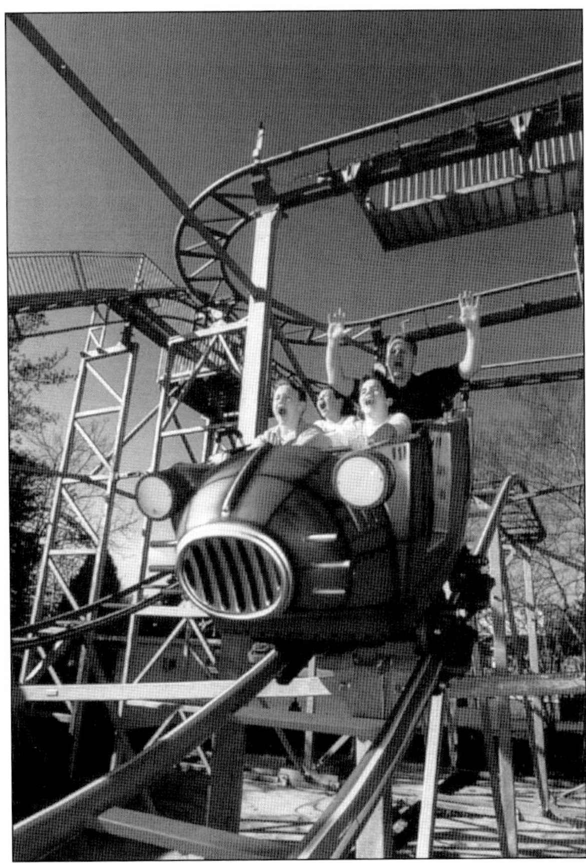

The Wild Lightning coaster by L&T Systems was opened during the 2001 season. It was the second wild mouse coaster at the park. A wild mouse is a type of roller coaster consisting of single cars traversing a tight-winding track with an emphasis on sharp, unbanked turns. The upper portion of the track featured multiple 180-degree turns, known as flat turns, that produced high lateral g-forces.

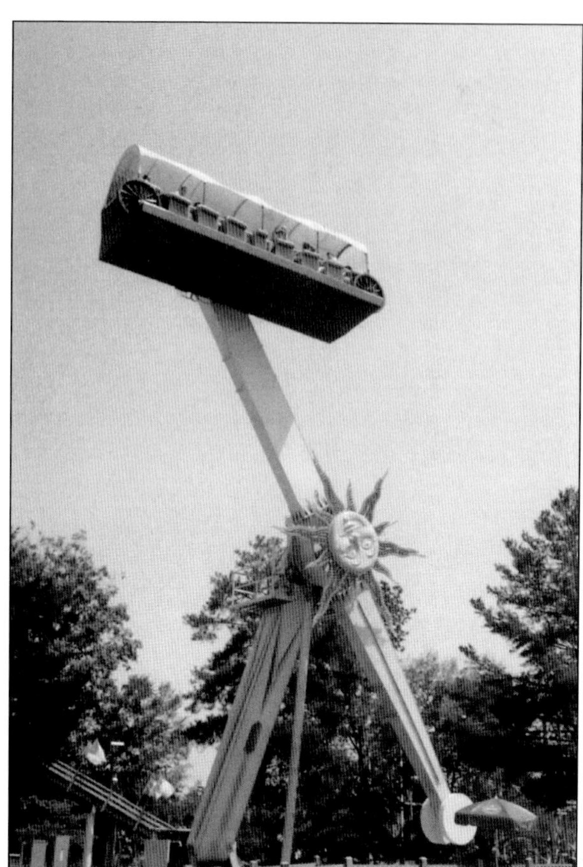

The Conestoga, introduced in 2002, is a HUSS Rainbow flat ride that originally delighted guests at Hersheypark in Pennsylvania. This attraction appeals to riders of all ages, providing a thrilling experience with its wide orbiting sensation. Guests are treated to alternating speeds, as the ride gracefully spins both clockwise and counterclockwise, ensuring an exhilarating journey filled with excitement and joy.

A significant enhancement to Lake Winnie in 2003 was the introduction of a brand-new entrance gate. This striking addition not only elevated the park's aesthetic appeal, but also welcomed guests with a fresh sense of excitement and anticipation as they stepped into a world of fun and adventure.

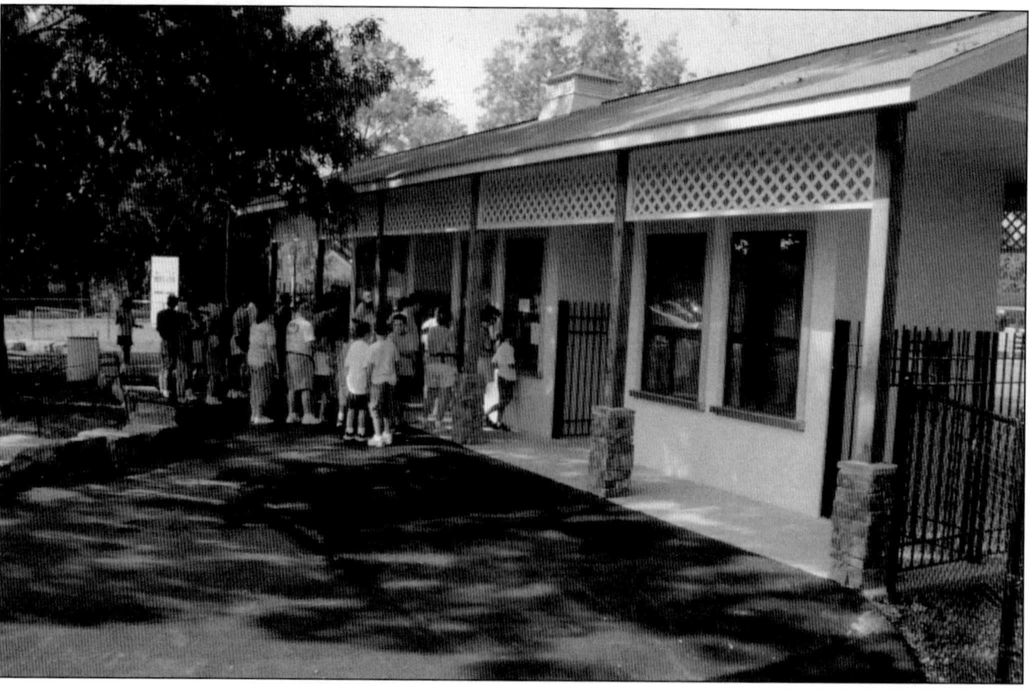

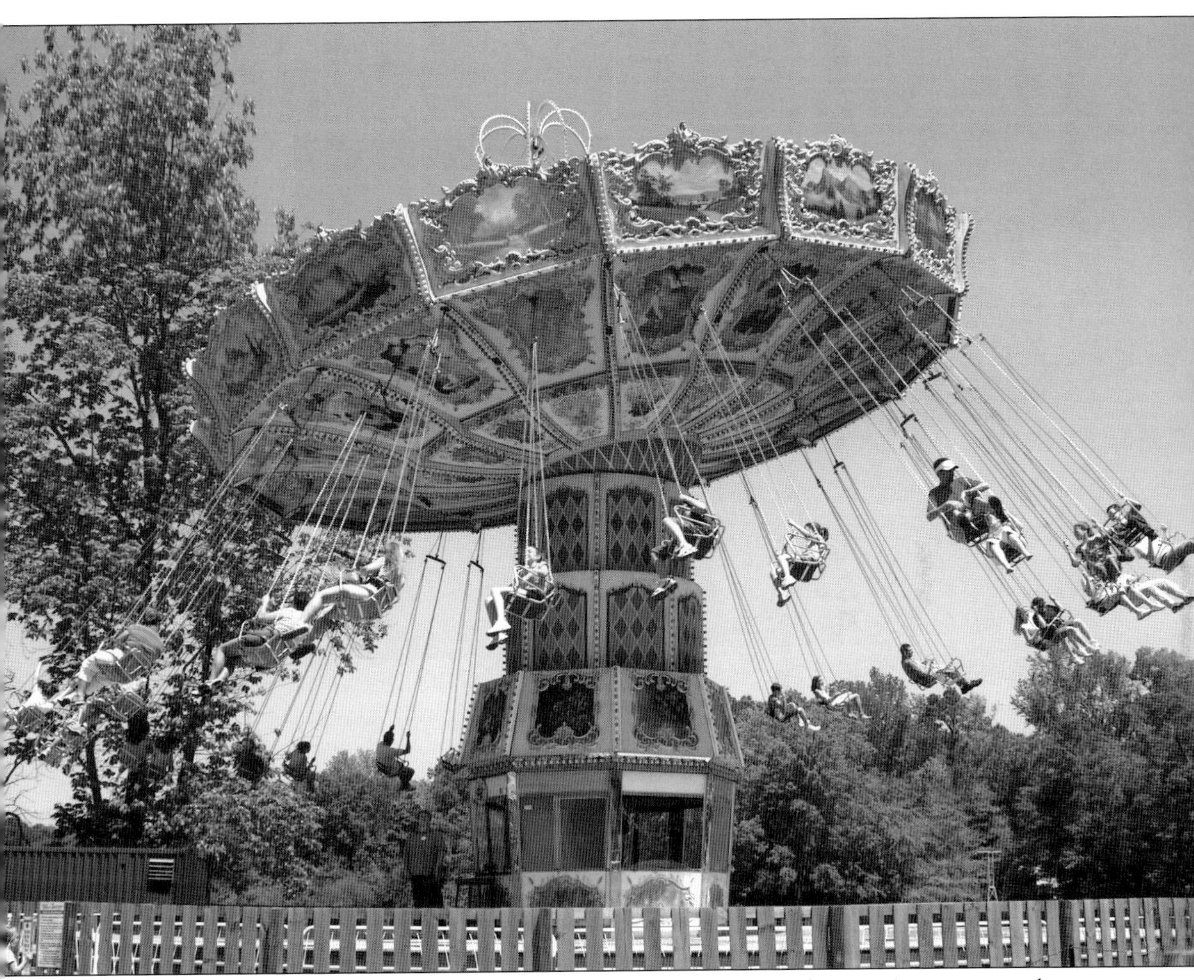

A brand-new Wave Swinger ride made its exciting debut during the 2005 season, marking a delightful return to the park. This charming attraction invites guests to soar through the air, creating a joyful atmosphere filled with laughter and exhilaration. The Wave Swinger quickly became a beloved addition, captivating riders of all ages with its thrilling swings.

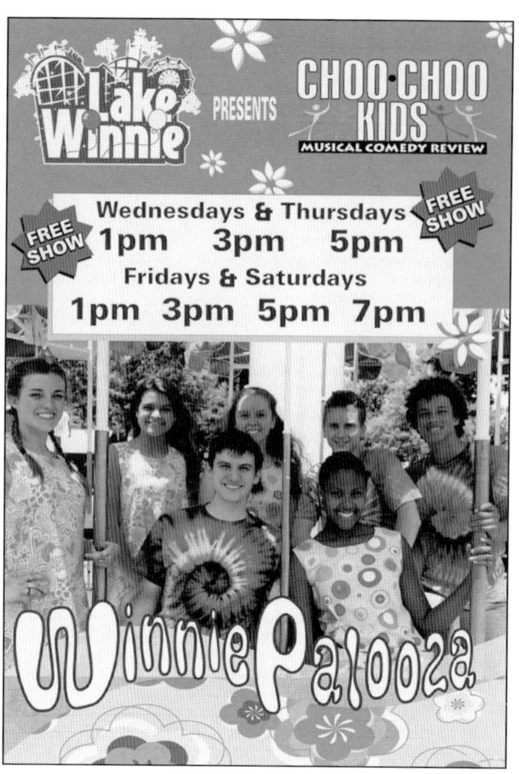

The Choo Choo Kids entertained guests in the Jukebox Junction area (formerly Pioneerland) with original theater productions written by Alan Ledford and choreographed by Lindsay Fussell. All were students at the Center for Creative Arts, and their singing, dancing, and acting talents were apparent to all the guests. Shows were offered three times a day, and guests seemed to always report that their energy and enthusiasm were contagious.

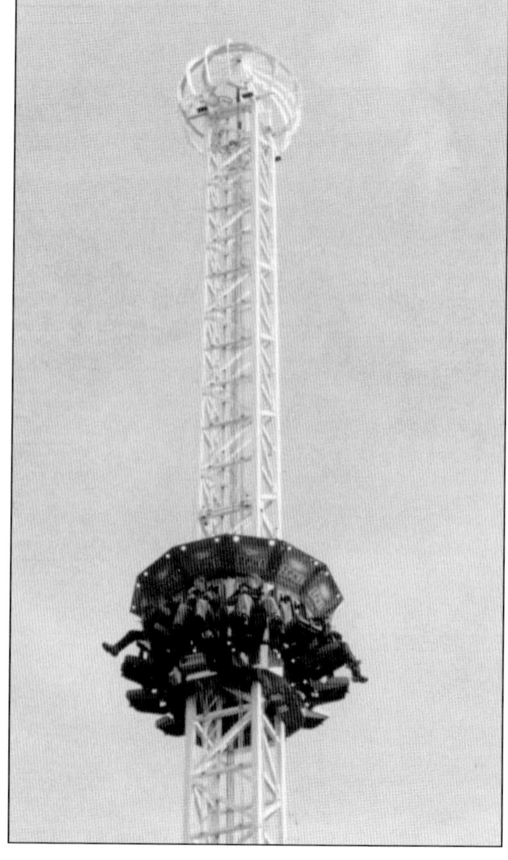

The OH-Zone!, introduced in 2006, is an exhilarating ARM Rides drop tower. This towering attraction plunges riders a staggering 14 stories straight down. As one ascends to the top, anticipation builds, and the breathtaking views stretch out before them. Then, in a heartbeat, they are hurtling downward at speeds of up to 50 miles per hour, feeling the rush of adrenaline surge through their body.

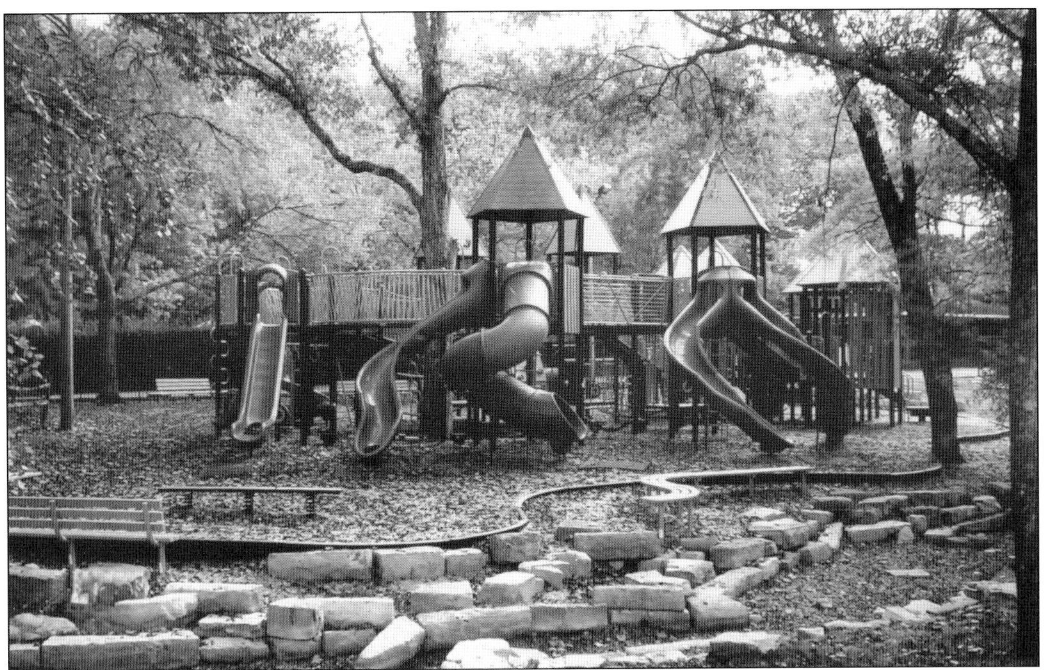

The Runaround Playground, introduced in 2008, is a vibrant and engaging play area designed for children. Manufactured by Playcore, it offers a dynamic and fun environment for young adventurers to explore and enjoy.

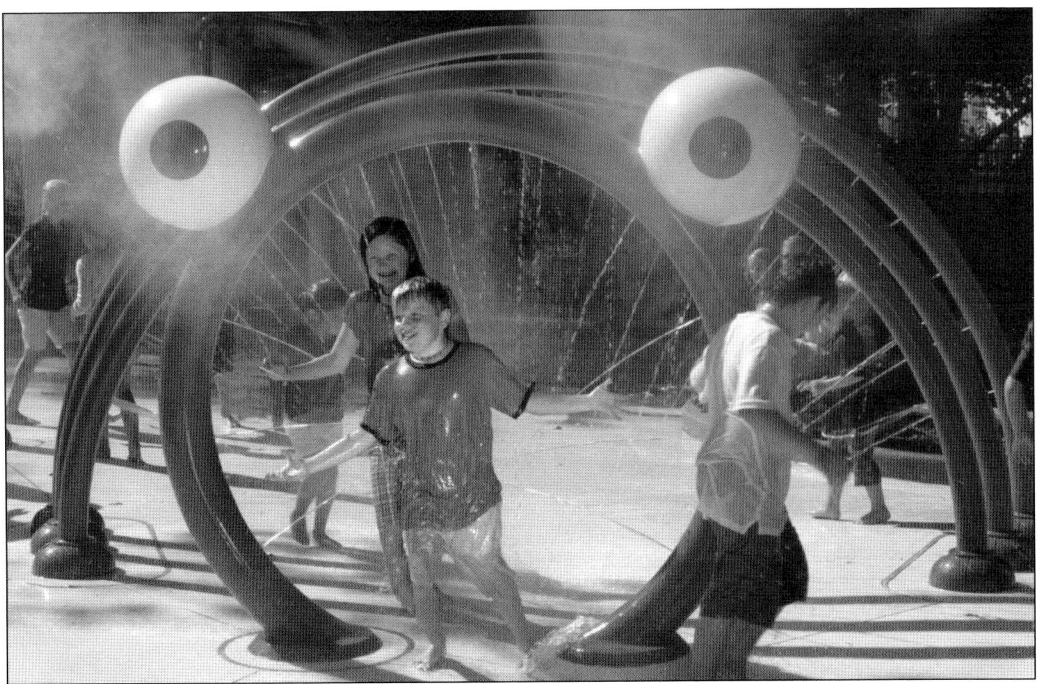

In 2009, the Chill Down Kid Town made its debut as a delightful children's splash pad area, designed to offer endless fun and refreshing play. This attraction served as a precursor to the SOAKya Water Park, which opened in 2013, setting the stage for even more aquatic adventures.

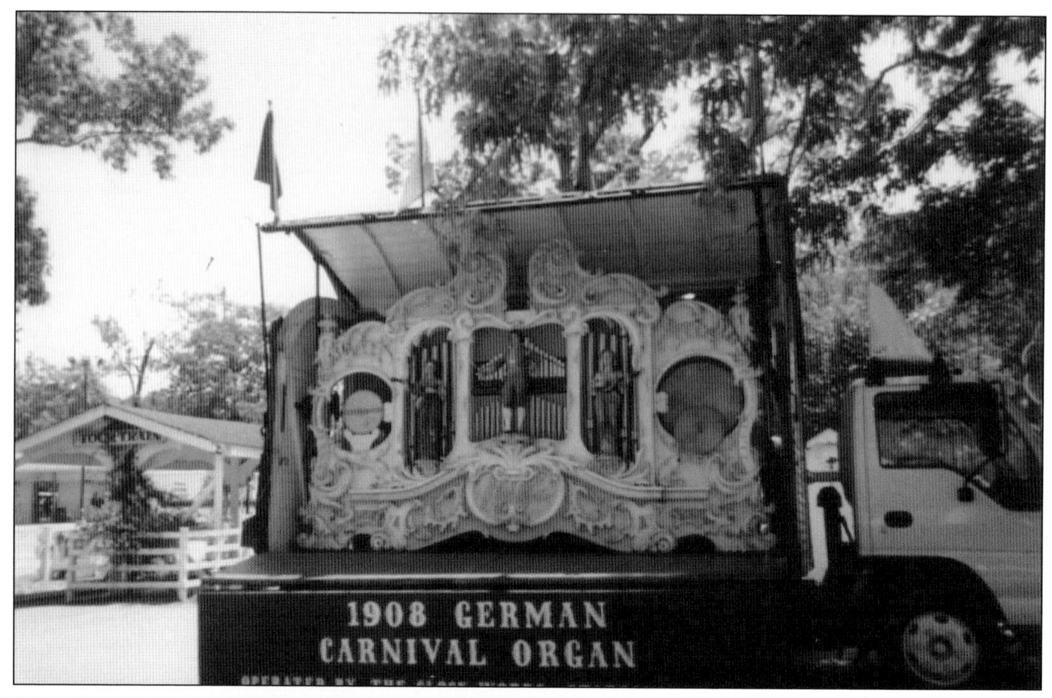

Lake Winnie welcomed the Carousel Organ Association of America (COAA) to the park on Memorial Day weekends. Members of the COAA brought their stunning antique organs of all sizes and played delightful tunes throughout the park, creating a nostalgic atmosphere for all the guests to enjoy. The special event was called the "Good Old Days" and was looked forward to annually by the guests and organ enthusiasts.

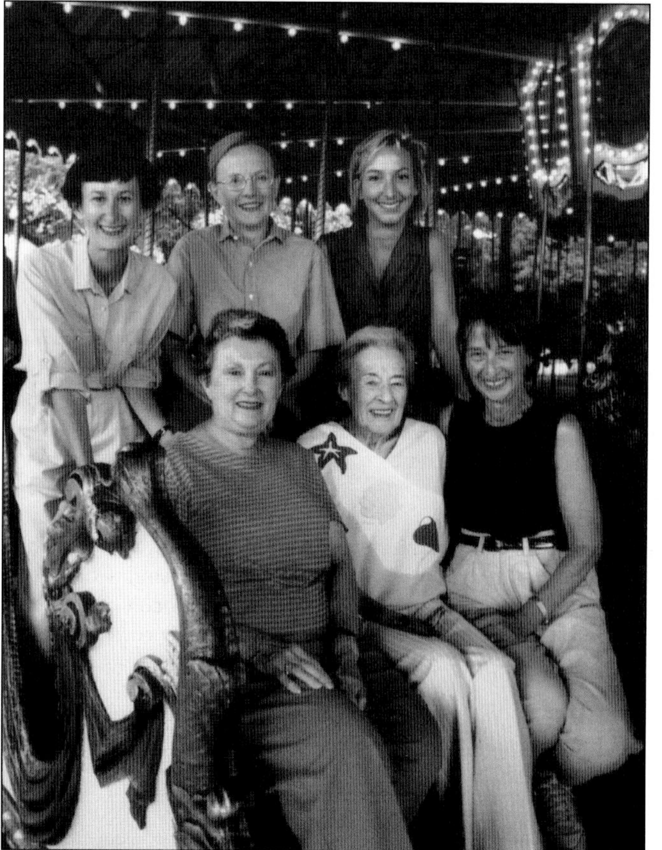

Evelyn White is surrounded by family members who returned to work in the park. Pictured on the carousel chariot are, from left to right, (seated) Adrienne, Evelyn, and Tootsie; (standing) Talley, Tennyson, and Evelyn.

Eight

The 2010s–2025

Making a Splash in the Past, Present, and Future

The period from 2010 forward brought additions, reflection, and time for celebrations. New rides such as the Sea Warrior, Fireball, and Twister were added. More importantly, a new tradition, Lake WinnepeSPOOKah, a Halloween festival held during October evenings, started. The goal was to provide spooky, but not frightening, Halloween fun to families. Alan Ledford led the creative efforts, and the talent of the Choo Choo Kids was again called upon to lead parades and enhance the festive spirit. Funnel cakes became "monster brains," picnic pavilions were transformed into scare houses, and employees donned costumes for the fun-filled evenings while the PA system celebrated Halloween-themed tunes. In 2012, the largest expansion to date was announced—transforming the "back" parking lot into a water park called SOAKya. The park staff researched and visited over a dozen other parks and gathered information on what they most wanted to offer. Construction began in January and continued over the rainiest winter in decades. Despite several obstacles, both known and unknown, it opened Memorial Day 2013 as planned. In 2014, a water playground was added, as were cabanas. Later, a mat racer ride, the Winnie 500, became part of the landscape. Lake Winnie, like others, suffered mightily during and after the COVID years. Restricted from opening until June was challenging but the fact customers were quarantined at home was a larger issue. Sales were at a historic low. Rejected repeatedly for PPP funds, the factor contributing to a successful application proved to be that the company was women-owned. Recovery came in 2021, yet a COVID resurgence shortened the season and canceled WinnepeSPOOKah. Adrienne Rhodes was unable to work due to health reasons, thus Tennyson and Talley took the reins, committed to the age-old task of putting smiles on faces. Smaller additions such as additional cabanas and ride revitalizations were the focus, along with the perennial interest in employee training. The 2024 season opened with a new ride, Catch N' Air, which is based on a skateboard theme. Soon after, Talley passed away, leaving a palpable hole in the hearts of employees and customers alike. Yet the park staff looks forward—forward for more ways to improve the current selection of rides and attractions, to improve staff training, to better customer service, to the future, and to put more smiles on more faces at "the Happy Place to Be."

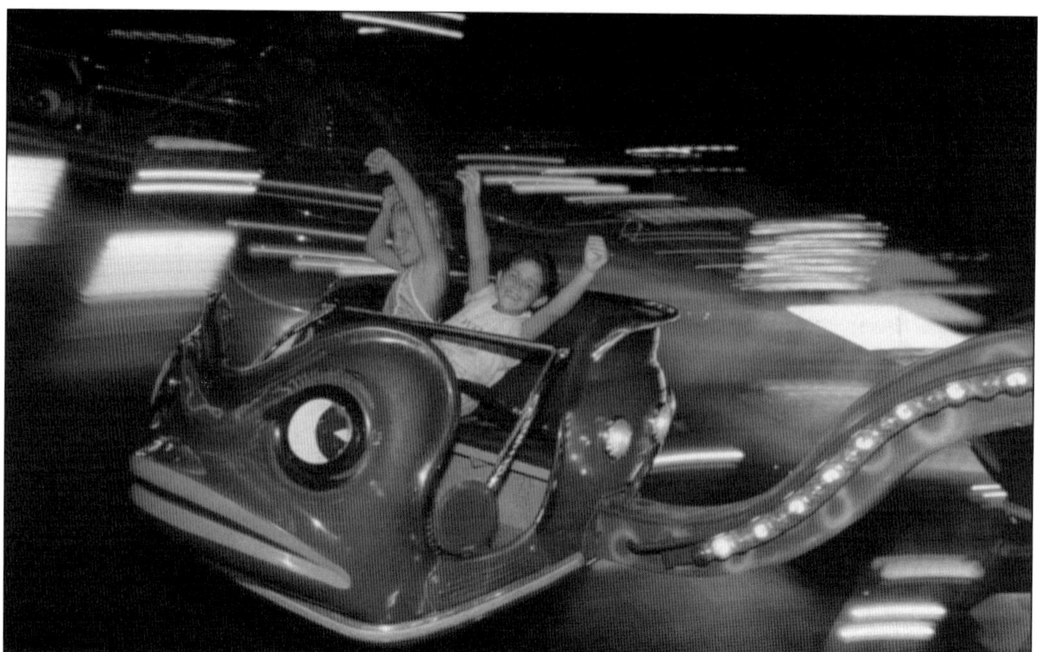

In 2000, Lake Winnepesaukah added the Sea Warrior ride, a throwback to the 1960s Spider ride. It was manufactured by Klaus and was a staple of fun at the park entrance until it was sold in 2020. It propels the rider through majestic sweeps while dynamically shifting speeds and directions.

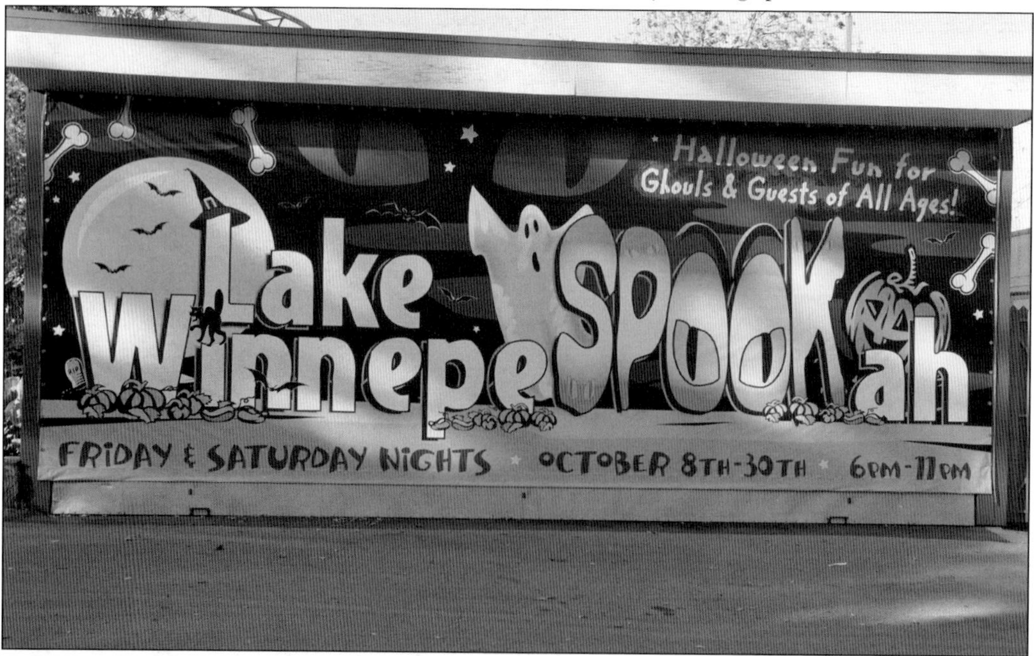

WinnepeSPOOKah debuted for the 2010 season, bringing hair-raising Halloween fun for boys and ghouls of all ages. Under the creative direction of Alan Ledford, this October evening event celebrates Halloween fun in a family-friendly way. Lake WinnepeSPOOKah serves up a bewitching array of creepy delights and frightening fun, featuring the exciting Monster Parade, a haunted train ride, haunted houses, and captivating hourly magic shows.

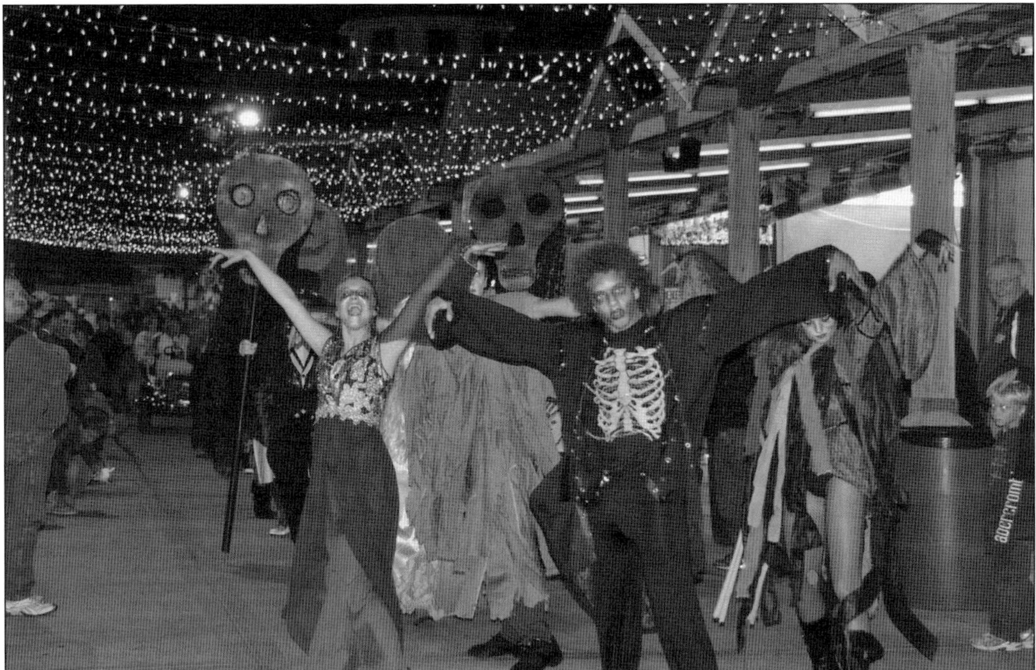

WinnepeSPOOKah required auditions for actors, dancers, makeup artists, and wardrobe personnel. Props, sets, magic, and special effects were all required to achieve the goal of a scary, but never terrifying, fun multigenerational Halloween event. Even the concessions get in the "spirit" of the season, with funnel cakes colored green, decorated with gummy worms, and tagged and sold as "monster brains."

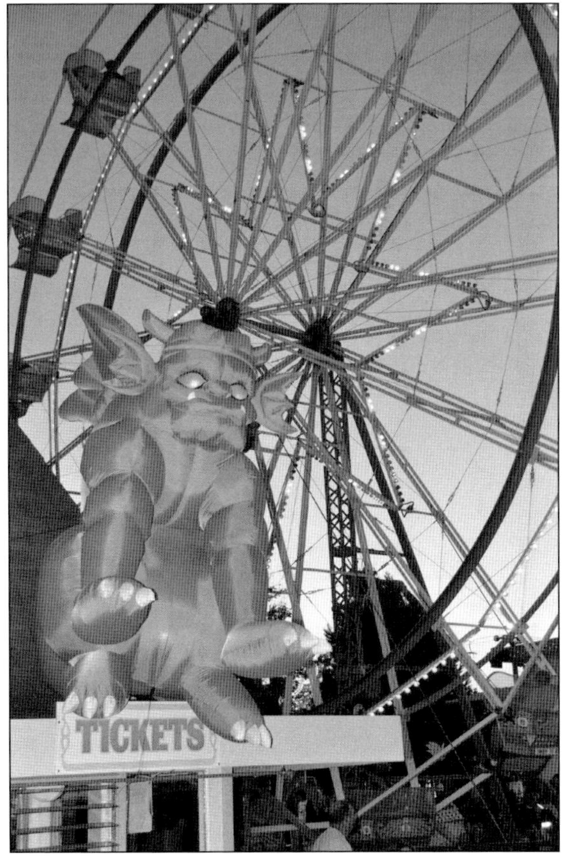

The goal of creating WinnepeSPOOKah was to entertain guests with a park transformed into a family-friendly Halloween experience. Haunted houses are built, decorations abound, and employees also are costumed. The music is turned up for this nighttime event, and it is not unusual to see customers of all ages dancing en route to the next attraction.

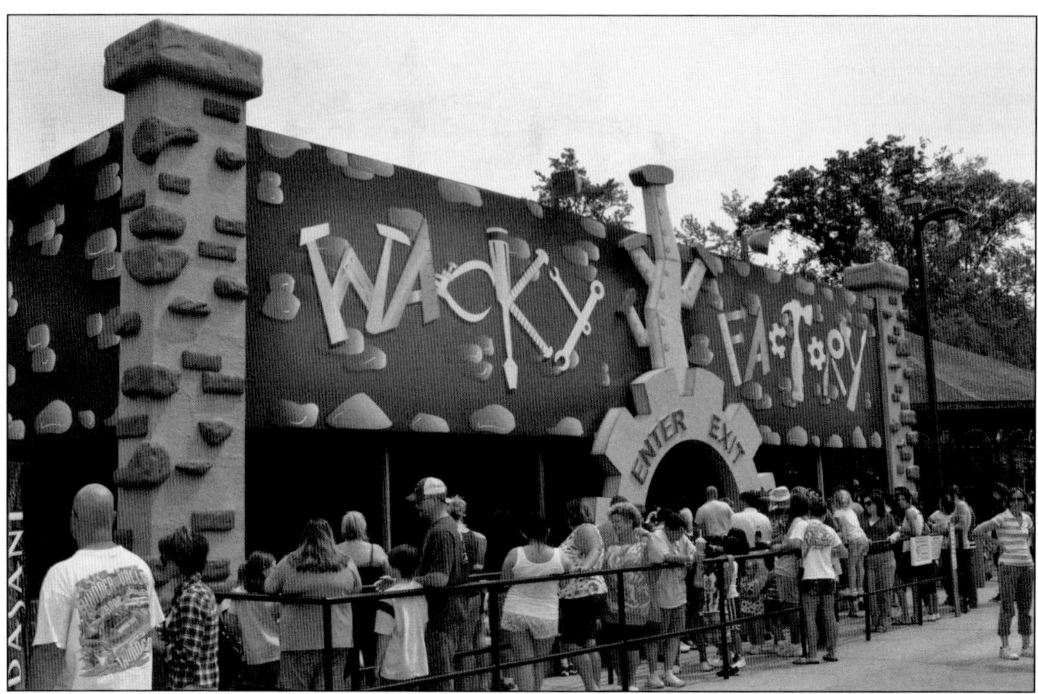

In 2011, the Castle was redesigned and became the Wacky Factory. The second floor had been out of use, as construction did not allow for a second sprinkler system to be installed. The space was transformed with tubes, conduits, hoses, blacklight paint, mirrors, and more to represent a truly "wacky" factory setting. Surprise elements awaited around every twist and turn.

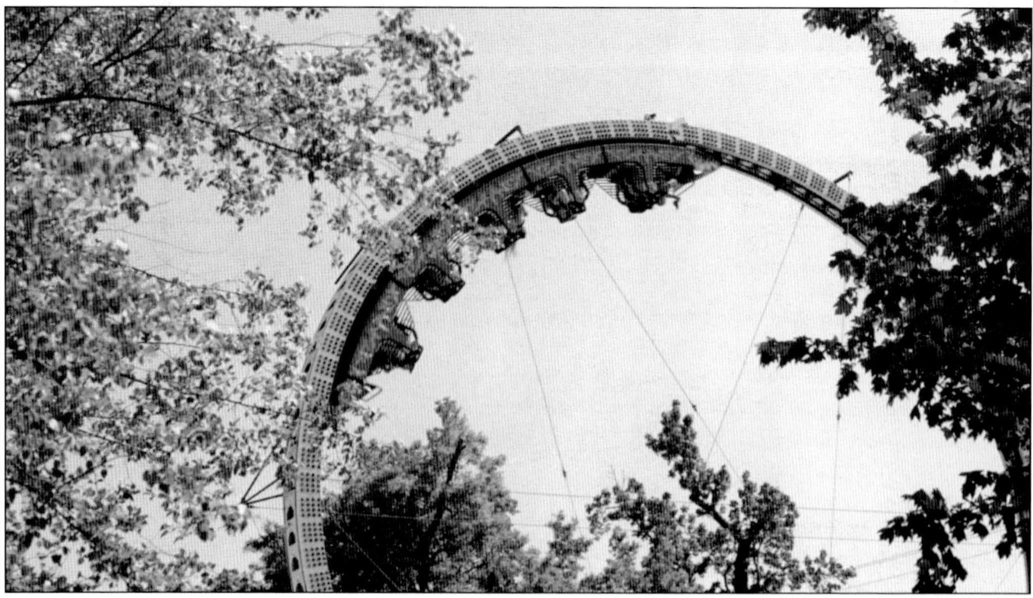

New for the 2012 season was the Fireball, manufactured by Larsen International. The ride consists of a looping coaster with a 20-passenger train that rocks back and forth gaining momentum until the ride reaches the top of the loop. Riders experience three full inversions in one direction, stalling inverted at the top of the loop only to change direction and complete three revolutions in the opposite direction.

It was a challenge to break ground on January 9 and build a six-acre water park in four months, but Adrienne Rhodes proved she was up to the challenge when she climbed in the backhoe to start the process. She felt strongly that making this expansion would benefit the park, as the public was ready to cool off in the hot summer months. The Aquatic Development Group was chosen as the builder, with Chris Jones as the architect.

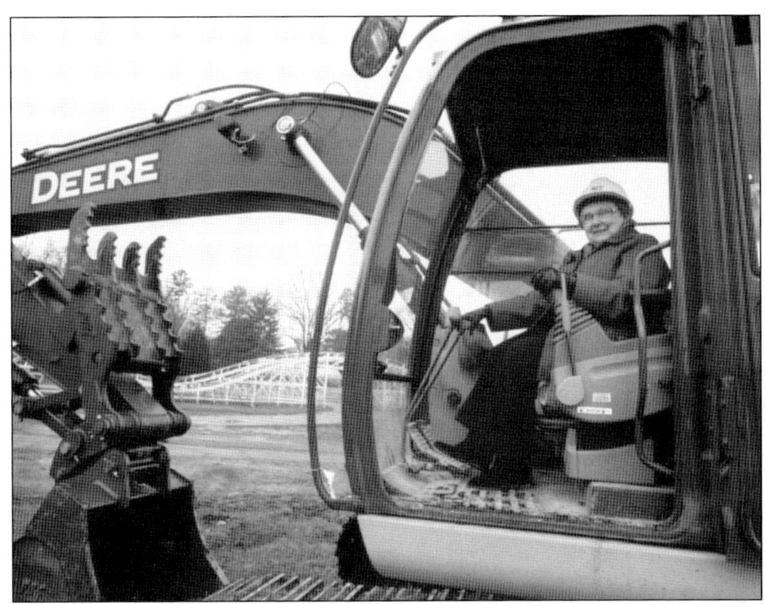

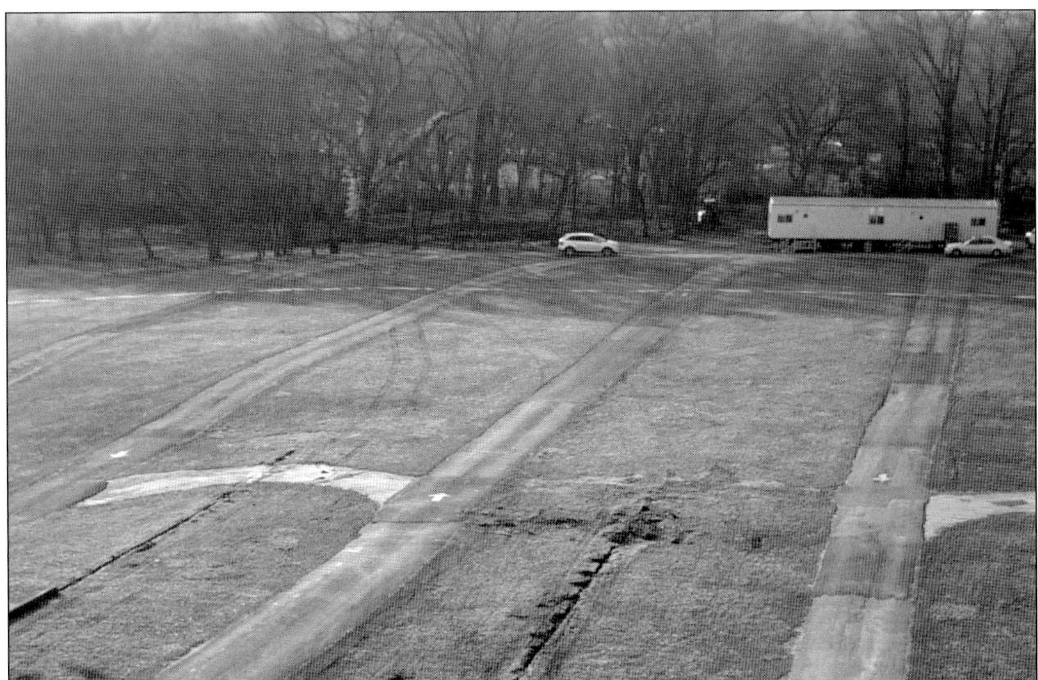

The view shows what had been the parking lot for decades. While engineers and architects worked six months prior to the announcement, Tennyson and Adrienne were busily visiting other water parks to evaluate features and add to the planning process. The trailer in the background was "construction central" for five months. The name "SOAKya" seemed a perfect derivative of Winnepesaukah.

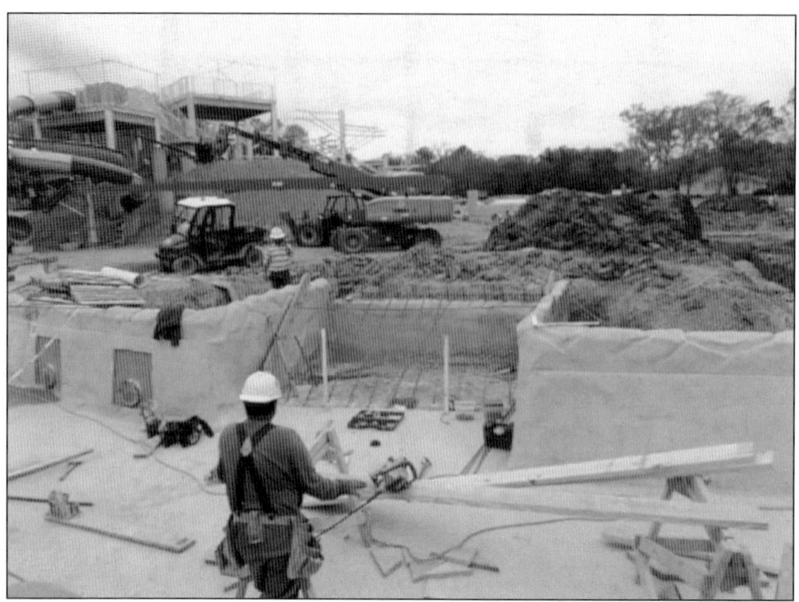

Crews worked through rain and weekends to make the dream come to life. There were some surprises along the way, such as natural springs being found where the service road was to be located. There were changes made in the field, many long nights of decisions reconsidered, and layouts and drafts referenced hundreds of times daily.

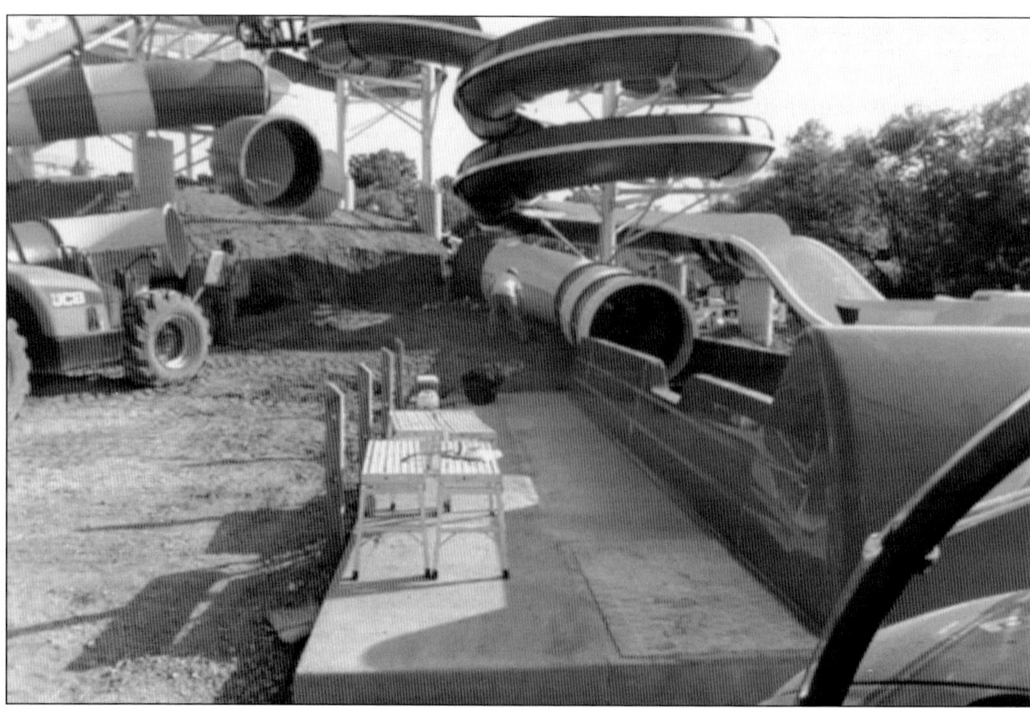

The goal was to seamlessly integrate the water park with the 90-year-old amusement park. It was decided the train would stop at SOAKya station both as an ease for customers and to create a transition. It was also a mission that the water park would not be a second ticketing opportunity, again for the convenience of customers. Also important was to have a walk-in entry to the Crazy River for accessibility. All this and countless more decisions played into the design and construction.

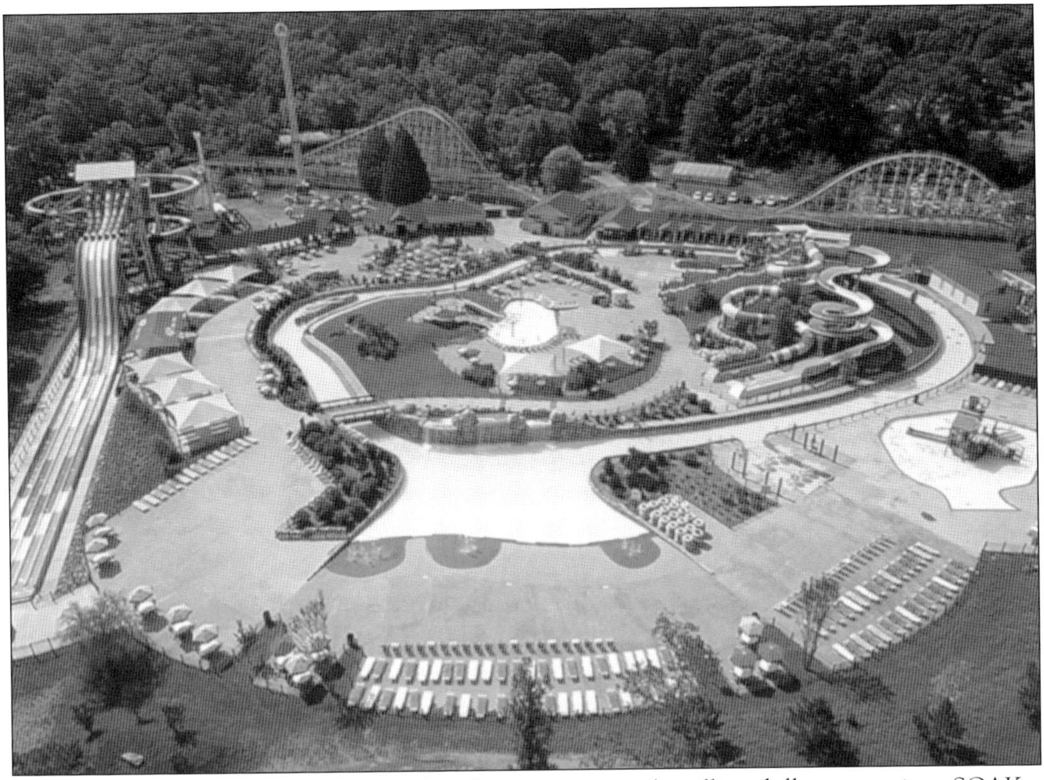

In 2013, Lake Winnie proudly introduced a stunning multimillion-dollar expansion: SOAKya Water Park, an exciting six-acre paradise of water rides and activities. Guests can enjoy the thrilling Crazy River, relax in the beach lagoon, and experience the adrenaline rush of flume body slides, tube slides, and an exhilarating 800-foot mat racer. It was immediately known there would be a lazy river, but a special feature of wave action was added, creating even more fun. A testimony to her heritage, when Adrienne Rhodes was told there would be a lazy river, her immediate reaction was "You can't be lazy and work at Lake Winnie!" It then became Crazy River, and unexpected water features were added along its path.

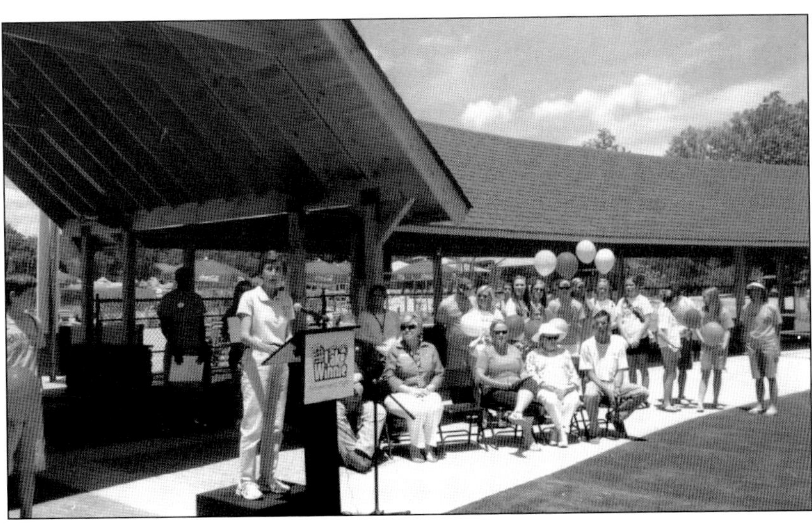

The water park opened on time on Memorial Day 2013, despite the rainiest winter and spring in decades. Local and state notables were present along with thousands of customers to test the waters.

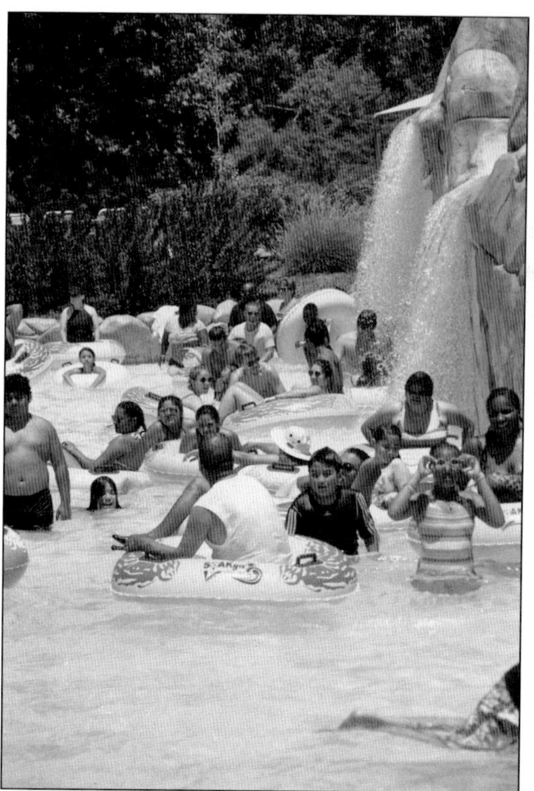

Whether one chooses to glide along in one of the provided rafts or swim at their own pace, on the Crazy River guests encounter rolling waves, playful geysers, and delightful surprises around every bend. Visitors are encouraged to see if they can find the sections where some of Evelyn's shells were embedded in the concrete during construction.

The Soak-N-Slide children's play area is a "splash-tastic" adventure, featuring four thrilling water slides, a zero-depth entry activity pool, and a variety of interactive elements that spray water. It is the perfect spot for endless fun and laughter for toddlers.

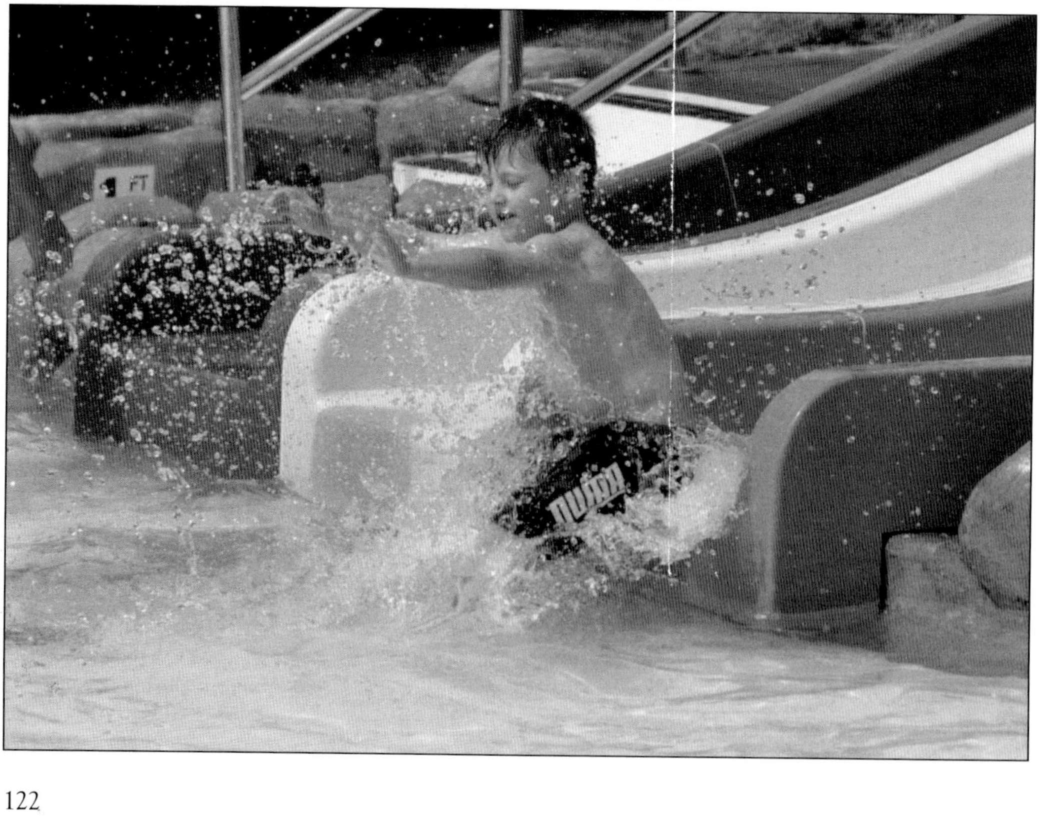

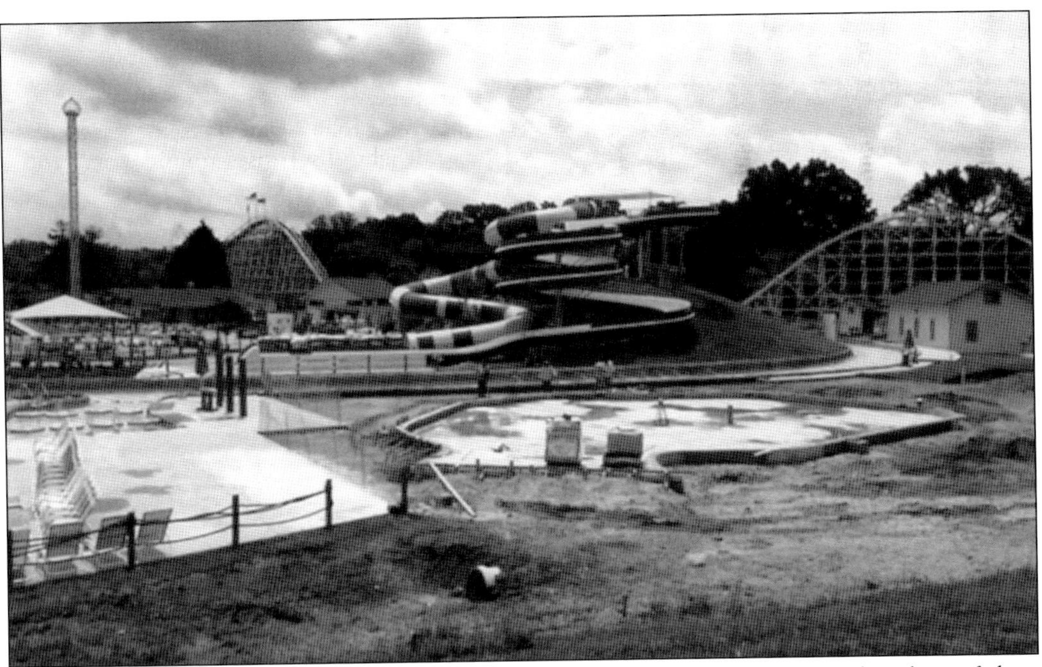

While the adults were busy in the Crazy River, the youngsters seemed to need a place of their own. In 2015, Water Works, an interactive water play structure, was designed and manufactured by Whitewater. Dirt was cleared, and more pipes and concrete were added. The park insisted on a wall around the kiddie pool for attentive parents to watch and cool off.

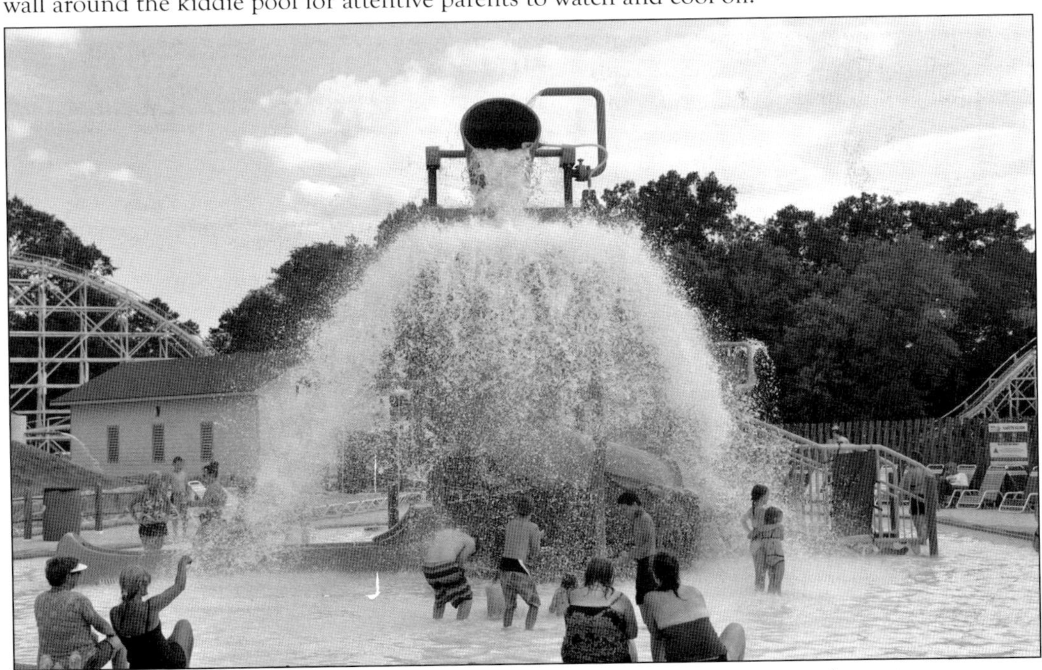

Towering over 20 feet, Water Works is packed with surprises, fountains, and exciting new water slides. The highlight of this vibrant play area is a massive bucket that dramatically tips over every few minutes, drenching guests in refreshing fun. Manufactured by Whitewater, this feature proved to be an immediate hit.

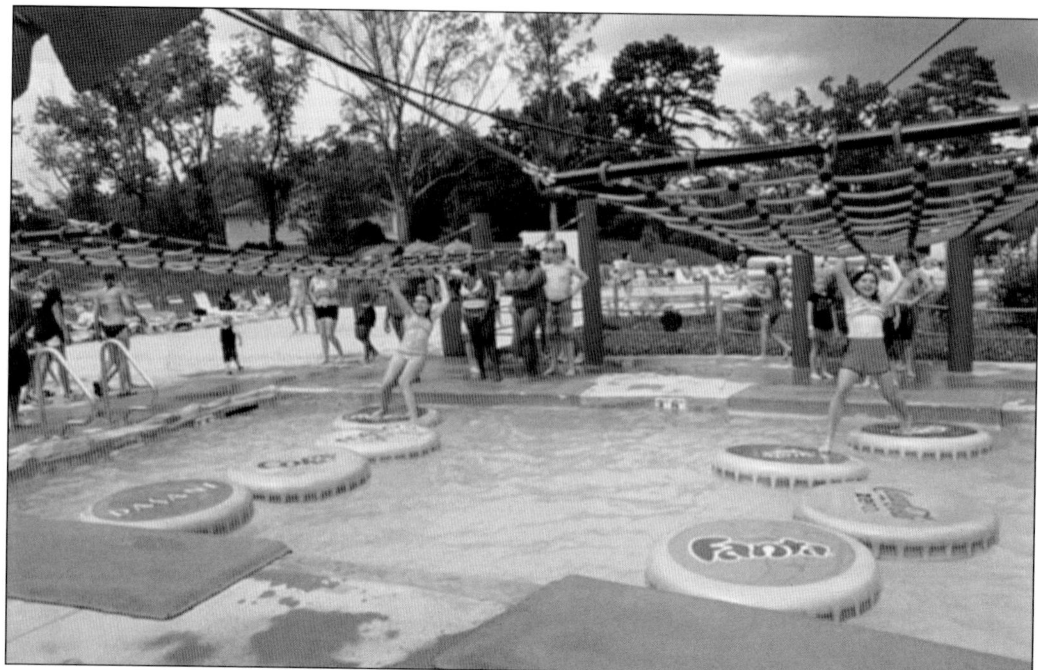

When the time came to address the theme of the crossing activity pool, many options such as sea and river life were presented, but they just were not the "fit." One night, Tennyson came up with "Coke Float" and presented it to Coca-Cola for their thoughts. The company immediately loved the idea. The brand bottlecaps offered width and safety as well as a colorful touch. Coca-Cola had been a long-standing supporter and supplier of Lake Winnepesaukah Amusement Park. The Coke Float attraction was soon featured on the cover of *Fizz Biz*, a beverage industry publication.

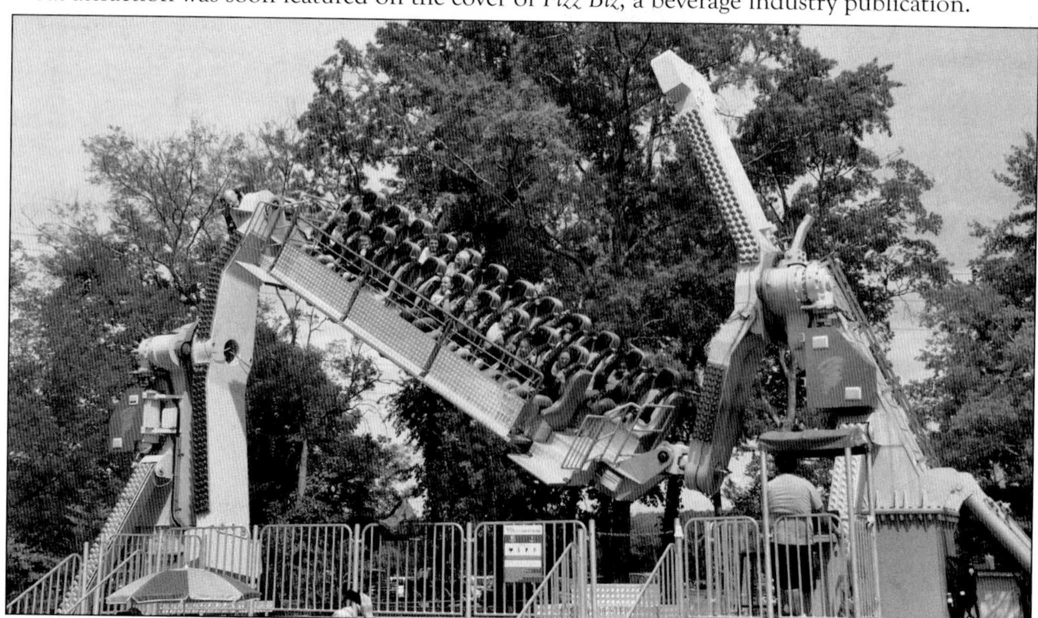

The year 2016 brought the addition of the Twister ride, manufactured by Moser Rides. The ride whisks guests into the wicked world of upside-down turns and twists as they are somersaulted into the sky.

The construction of the Winnie 500 posed some unique obstacles, as the train tracks to the left could not be bothered, nor could the Conestoga ride and the train station to the right. In addition, the ride was designed to fit snugly at the back of the shade pavilions, so accuracy in placement was paramount. Imagine workers coming in the morning and seeing fiberglass tubes with no run-out dangling in the air.

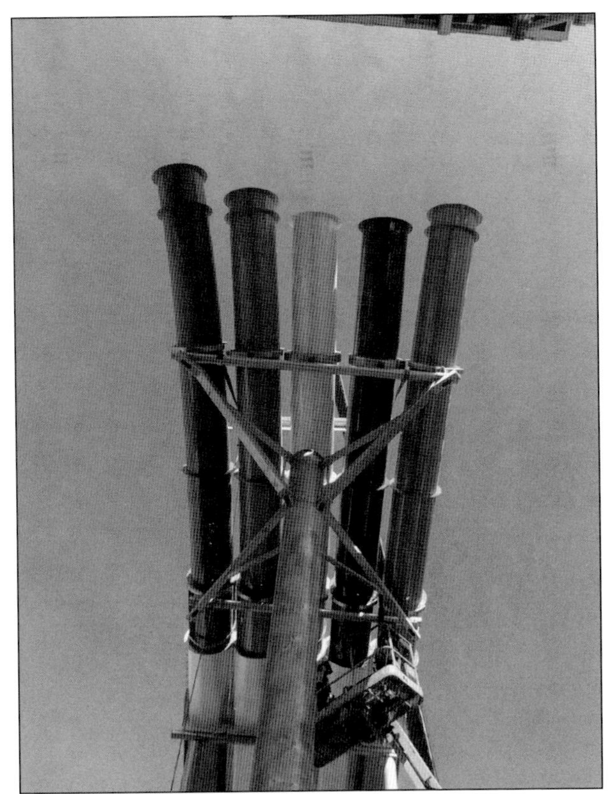

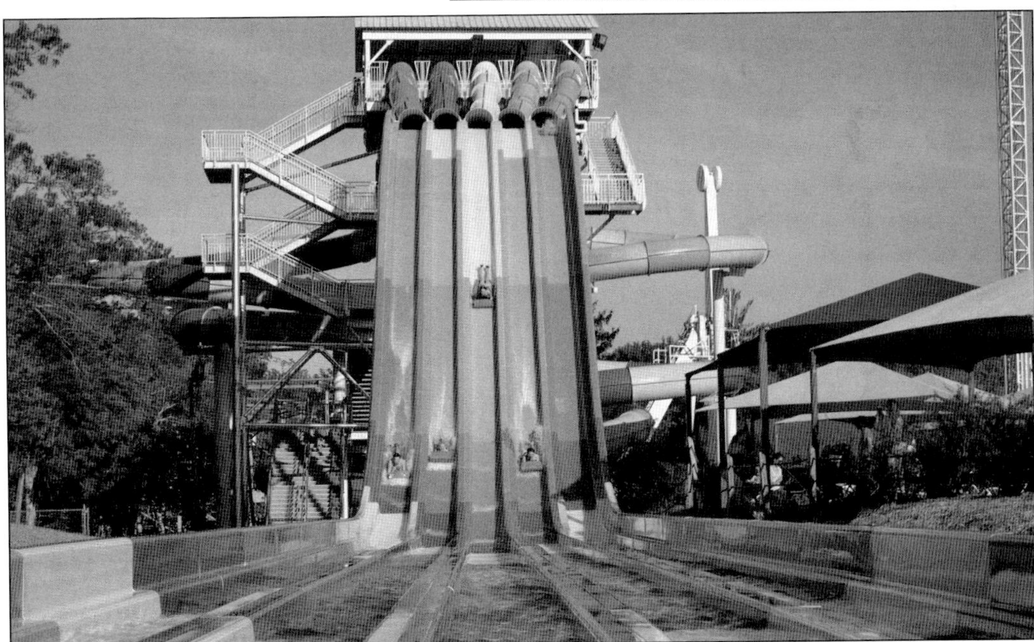

The Winnie 500 racing slides were named as a homage to the racetrack that was nearby in the 1930s. Guests glide nearly 300 feet headfirst, racing friends and family from 50 feet in the air, culminating in a spectacular splash as they chase the checkered flag. Manufactured by Whitewater, the mat racer was added in 2017 and shares the tower with the Zoom Flume.

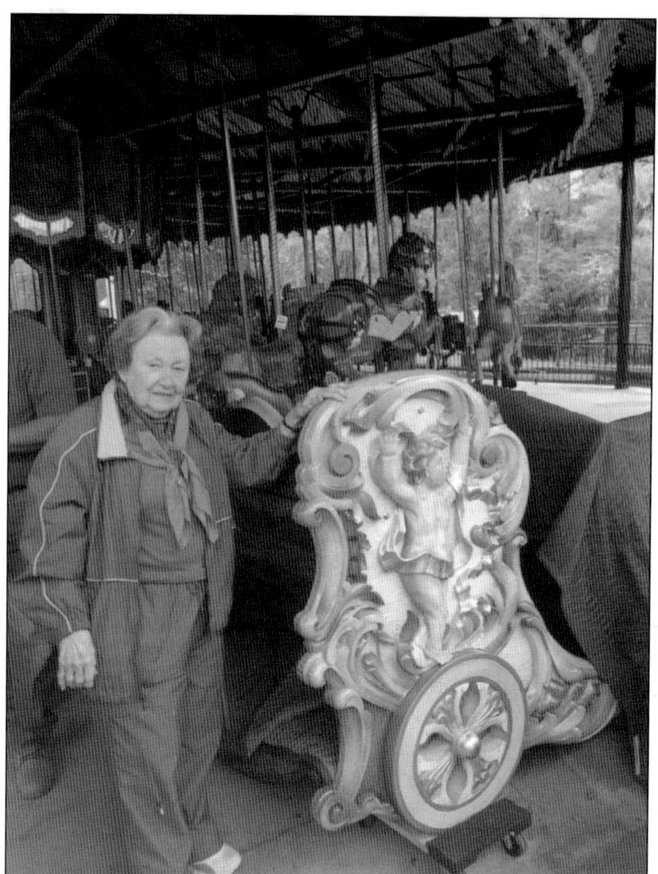

In 2019, a nationwide search began to start restoring the beloved carousel horses. Their coats had worn, and the love they had been given by countless children of all ages for over a century had shown. It was learned there were few true restorers remaining in the United States who understood the artistry and joining of the horses. A restorer was located in Plainville, Connecticut. A few horses were sent first, and after admiring the results, the two chariots were sent. The day they returned in April was better than Christmas for Adrienne Rhodes.

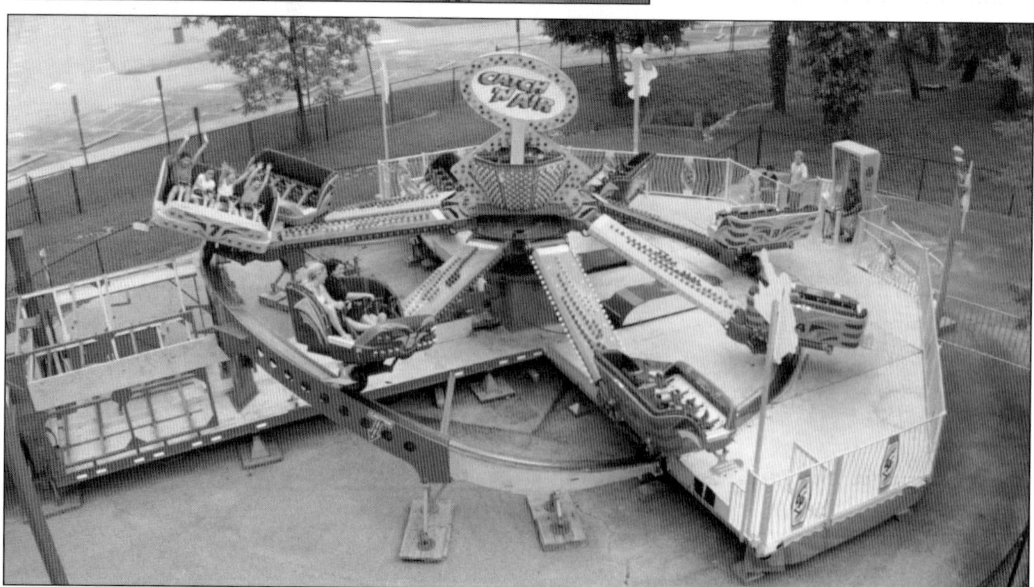

In 2024, a new addition, the Catch N' Air ride, was added and placed at the entrance gate. Manufactured by Majestic, this ride takes guests forward, backward, up, and down at varying speeds, simulating the thrill of skateboarding.

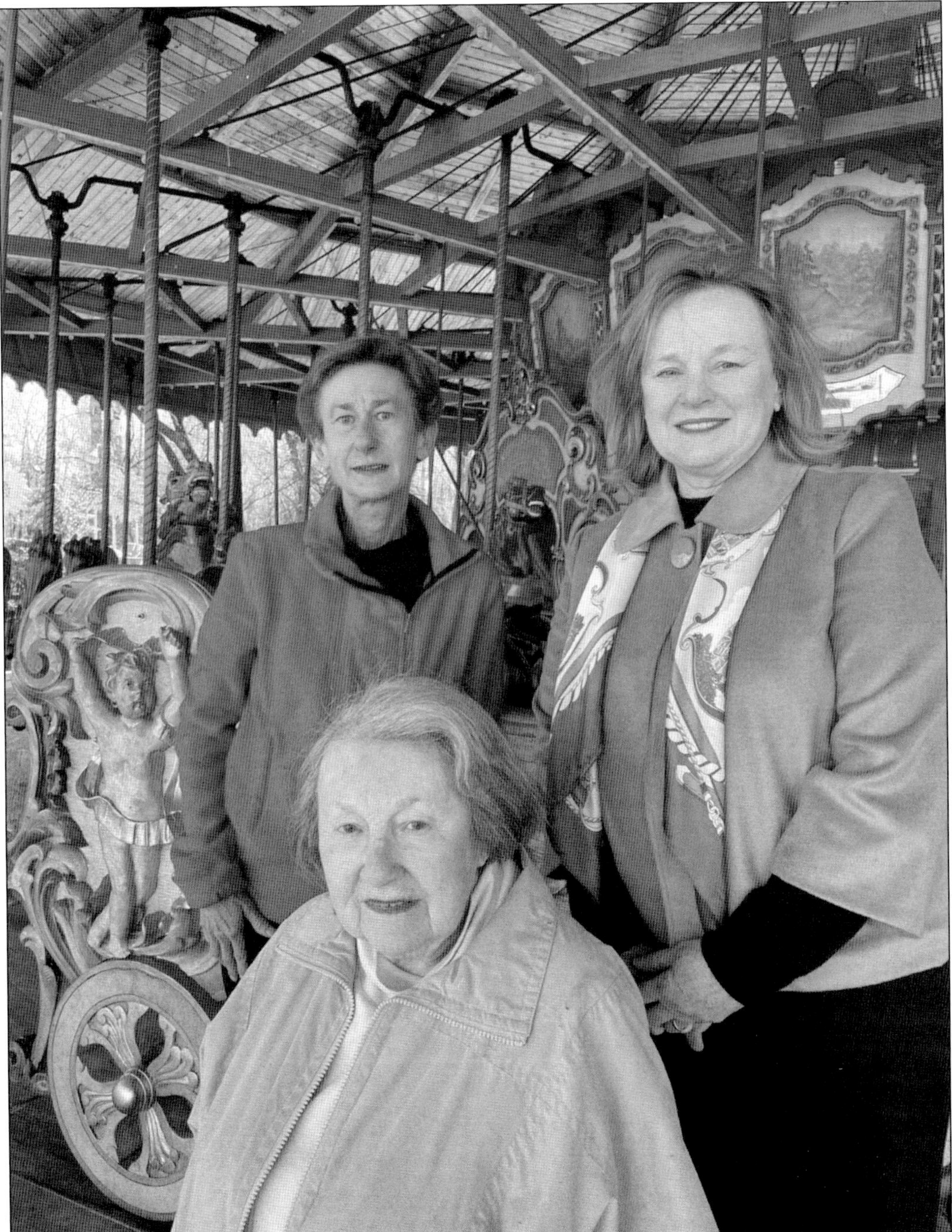

Whenever a photograph was needed, it was immediately known by Adrienne (seated), Talley (standing left), and Tennyson (standing right) that it would be on the carousel, for they all felt it was the most beloved ride in the park. This picture was taken in the winter of 2021 and proved to be their last picture together in the park.

Consistent with our mission to preserve history on a local level, this book was printed in South Carolina on American-made paper and manufactured entirely in the United States. Products carrying the accredited Forest Stewardship Council (FSC) label are printed on 100 percent FSC-certified paper.

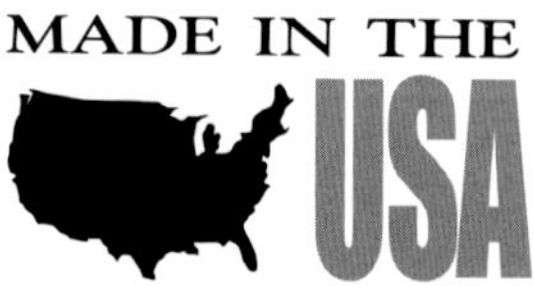